C000272661

CARP
The Quest for the Queen

CARP

The Quest for the Queen
Revised Edition

JOHN BAILEY
AND
MARTYN PAGE

The Crowood Press

First published in 1986 by
THE CROWOOD PRESS
Ramsbury, Marlborough
Wiltshire SN8 2HE

Reprinted 1988
Revised edition 1990

© John Bailey and Martyn Page 1986 and 1990

All rights reserved. No part of this publication may be
reproduced or transmitted in any form or by any means,
electronic or mechanical, including photocopy, recording or
any information storage and retrieval system without
permission in writing from the publishers.

British Library Cataloguing in Publication Data

Carp: the quest for the queen. — Rev. ed.
1. Carp. Angling. Manuals
I. Bailey, John   II. Page, Martyn
799.1'752

ISBN 1 85223 408 3

Dedicated to the departed greats:
Walker, Eric the fish,
and, in beginning, the monks themselves.

Typeset by Alacrity Phototypesetters, Banwell Castle,
Weston-super-Mare
Printed and bound in Great Britain by
Butler & Tanner Ltd, Frome and London

Contents

Acknowledgements

We wish to thank all contributors, especially Archie Braddock for his help at extremely short notice, our artist Chris Turnbull, Heidi Ahsmann for her translation of Nico de Boer's contribution, and Dennis Watkins-Pitchford (B.B.) for permission to use quotations. Thanks also to Pat for her help with typing, and also to Lynne and Sharon for their typing and assistance.

In addition, we are most grateful to *Angling Times* (and Greg Meenehan) for permission to use the photograph on page 179, and to all the following people for use of the photographs indicated:

Richard Bendall: pages 228, 230

Nico de Boer: pages 164, 165, 166, 167, 168; colour plate 22

Bruno Broughton: page 143; colour plates 46, 48, 50

Len Bunn: pages 91, 92, 105

Kevin Clifford: pages 109, 110, 112; colour plate 4

Graham Cowderoy: page 169; colour plates 34, 36, 39, 41, 47, 51

Chris Currie: pages 128, 134

Shaun Harrison: page 145; colour plate 49

Duncan Kay: pages 73, 86, 99, 190, 195, 196; colour plates 19, 20

Ritchie MacDonald: pages 198, 201; colour plates 17, 28, 29, 30, 31

Greg Meenehan: page 207

Stuart Moir: page 213

Gerry Morris: colour plate 6

Kevin Nash: page 205; colour plate 27

John Nunn: colour plate 25

Tim Paisley: colour plates 32, 33, 37, 38

Dave Plummer: page 10; colour plates 14, 15, 16, 18, 21

Phil Smith: pages 172, 176, 177, 178; colour plates 19, 20

Phil Thompson: page 170

Steve Tytherley: pages 216, 220; colour plate 35

John Watson: pages 161, 162

John Wilson: colour plate 12

Chris Yates: page 232; colour plate 13

Preface

For months we have talked, written and thought carp. Carp have taken over our lives as never before, and even though we have nearly forty years of carping experience behind us, we have never known anything like this.

Most of the conversations have been technical for, of course, good carp anglers must have sound methods and knowledge, but at times, something dream-like has emerged. Nearly every carp angler is streaked with romance; he has to be to keep him at the waterside through wind and rain and cold nights. There has to be a love in him, a passion for something greater than he has yet experienced. There has to be an ultimate adventure for us all.

Speaking to person after person, the scene is drawn: the water will be peaceful and unspoilt; it will have an intimacy, so will be either a small water, or the arm or bay of a large one. There will be beauty all around, in the sweeping jade cascades of the willow trees, or in the still, clear water that reflects the blue-skyed summers.

The fish will be legendary – old, wise and uncaught for years. She will hover over a bait, but leave it with the dignity of a precious creature. Often she will be seen, so that her life and the angler's will begin to become as one. She will be large, but, more than that, will be a carp of beauty and grace. She will be the final challenge and purpose in a carp fisher's life.

The moment will come at dusk or dawn, or some special time – perhaps after a summer storm when the water is smoking in the freshly revealed sun. The bait will be simple – a lobworm perhaps – and the drama will be watched through waters of glass. She will see the bait and, after years, come towards it. Her lips will extend and the bait will shift, stir from the silt and be drawn towards that cavernous mouth.

The quest for the queen will have begun.

Our Stories

Martyn Page's story

If I were to describe myself, it would be as a specialist angler who pursues carp of all sizes using certain chosen and aesthetically pleasing means. As a result my carp fishing consists almost entirely of visible methods: stalking and ambushing carp which can be seen. This suits my time limitations and is sufficiently rewarding to satisfy my angling addictions. I would be the last to knock the fashionable styles of long-range boilie and bivvy angling, as the efficiency of such methods on most waters cannot be denied. However, I prefer the adrenalin-causing and heart-stopping results of close-range visual fishing.

To understand why I prefer such methods, even at times at the cost of less fish, it is necessary to look back at my early angling days when as a lad I served my apprenticeship wandering the banks of the River Wensum in pursuit of grey shadows. My early cumbersome attempts resulted in few of those ghosts being hooked, until I discovered the floating crust. Soon I had scores of fat chub under my belt and no longer were they phantoms. With that experience came confidence and in turn the water craft and ability necessary to stalk the chub, to creep up to their lairs and watch them swimming unaware in their chosen sanctuaries.

Time passed and chub lost much of their attraction. Indeed, I have never truly recaptured the excitement of those early experiences in my chub fishing, which is a shame as I owe them so much. I progressed to tench and pike, and then later came one of my best experiences with carp on a small water with only average fish. Quite naturally, and knowing no other way, I adopted a chub-style approach towards them. All the excitement returned and more – these big fat 'chub' fought like demons once hooked!

I have progressed over the years to new waters and larger carp but throughout have retained a love for the excitement generated from this visual style of carp fishing. Also, being a realist, I have tried all the well-documented methods and found them successful, but still cannot help having itchy feet. Today I find it difficult to stay behind motionless monkey climbers, waiting hour upon hour without any sign of fish. Instead I prefer to pick up a soft action rod and go searching.

This, then, is my preference. For me, surface fishing has remained the most satisfying method of catching carp. It has also proved consistently successful on my local waters and for years I have been able to wander from water to water, fishing a method hardly used by the carp anglers in Norfolk, catching large numbers of good fish, whilst others compete over which flavour, particle or ingredient to use.

A few years ago I came to the decision that it was time to land a really big Norfolk carp. This was prompted by the fact that the regulars of my nearest carp water were just beginning to realise the potential of surface baits, so I decided it was time to

Martyn Page still takes his carp on floaters, as this recent twenty-pounder testifies.

move on to new pastures. With the very best of intentions I decided on a campaign after the Taverham Carp Lake fish, knowing that I was in with a chance of catching carp up to around thirty pounds. Even today a thirty-pound Norfolk fish is quite a monster and there is only a limited choice of waters from which this or even a twenty-pound fish can be taken. Perhaps life would have been a little easier at Waveney Valley Lakes, but I have a distinct preference for competing against the fish only and not against winds too! Taverham, therefore, was my obvious choice.

For the next few weeks, I talked with far more experienced carp anglers who had tackled the water, and attempted to obtain a picture of fish movement, feeding areas and a recommended approach. In the end a particle bait was chosen and a patrol route gravel bar elected as the target area. Leaving behind much of my past experience, I ventured totally into the realms of pure 'carp style' and began with a 'bivvy and bolt' campaign.

With only weekends and evenings at my disposal, and having decided that these wary beasts would require many hours of bait soaking to obtain success, I made the mistake of eliminating the evening sessions. Fishing was forty-eight hours non-stop from Friday evening to Sunday evening. In retrospect, the success of such a campaign probably rested on being at the water as many evenings as possible. Had I done this, I would have been able to piece the movement pattern together and would not have fished each weekend blind as I did.

The first weekend passed without event and the second found Dave Humphries and myself once more blanking in adjacent swims along the ambush bar. We were executing the perfect textbook approach. We were stereotyped, no doubt like 101 anglers before us, because our bolt rigged particle baits landed amongst the patch of free offerings at the point on the bar. It had to be the point, as the overhanging branches restricted casting to any other spot. We were doing everything right, or so we thought, and settled down to another uneventful evening, night and unfolding weekend.

By the third weekend confidence was definitely on the decline, but we started once more, going through the same motions with the same result. Friday evening and night passed totally uneventfully except for the odd crash elsewhere on the lake as some giant leapt unseen. As the sun rose the next morning the reassuring hiss of Dave's stove woke me from dreams of

Dave Plummer was more successful at Taverham Carp Lake, as this 23lb fish proves.

battles and monsters of the deep. I stretched off the 'bed-chair blues', stumbled over to Dave, mug in hand, and realised that there was absolutely no way I deserved to or would ever land a carp from that water by merely going through these unthinking motions. Why was I abandoning all my past experience in favour of a tactic which was failing for all the other, more experienced carp anglers on the lake at the time? It was time to get up, search for and find those fish. Reactivated, my mind started working logically once more. The mug steamed in the cold air. I looked anew at the lake, scanning, analysing, applying that necessary but previously missing ingredient. I was finding my water craft again!

One obvious fact soon became apparent – we were fishing the 'cold morning side' of the lake. Let me explain. I have noticed, especially when tench fishing, that the fish movement pattern on many waters coincides with the setting and rising of the sun. Fish may be on one side of the water in the morning and on the opposite side by evening. I have found, when tenching, that the first side of the lake to receive the sun will often result in a very early spate of bites, but as the sun rises the tench will drift from the bright sunlight and the 'cold morning side' will receive the activity for the rest of the morning. In contrast, I have found that the carp in my local waters show a preference for sunlight and are prone to move with the sun, drifting slowly to the other side during the day, allowing them to bask for longer. This is, of course, a generalisation and these basking carp are not usually feeding on bottom baits, but merely enjoying the warmth of the sun. Such carp however usually fall easily to floaters!

The swim we were on was totally shaded, at least until midday. I now became convinced that these large carp were not frequenting my swim during the morning hours and that this was an evening swim – and I had just wasted three weekends of fishing. I decided that during the greater part of the night there were no fish near my bait. I believed that they had drifted off earlier in the night, slowly moving on their night-time feeding route to the other side of the lake, ready for the early morning sun and the opportunity to bask in its heat.

Right or wrong, I was now thinking again. I took one rod, retackled with weighted float and greased line, some munchies and a landing net, and went on the prowl. By this time the sun had gained sufficient strength to heat the surface layers. I headed straight to the opposite sunlit side of the lake and made for a small bay. I approached quietly, chub-style, totally sure that the fish had to be in the area. Nevertheless, when I saw those five large submarines my surprise and excitement could hardly be controlled. I was on home territory now; this was a situation I had encountered hundreds of times before. There was one major difference however: the fish were much larger now and I had to steady my trembling hands before I catapulted the first batch of floaters towards them.

I aimed for the bait to land well upwind so it would drift slowly over their heads. This procedure had become so familiar that it was carried out with precise efficiency. Five 'pults' full of bait at spaced intervals would be sufficient. My idea was to create a steady trail of bait floating over the carps' heads, followed by my hook and bait a few minutes later when the fish were priming and searching for more. I knew these fish were accustomed to surface feeding as I had recalled that Len Bunn had caught fish many years before from this lake on floating crust. Even though I had heard of no one using particle floaters at that time, I was sure, almost to the point of arrogance, that I would not fail to get a take from one of the fish before me then.

Almost on cue, I watched fins energise as these near-dormant monsters sensed the juicy morsels drifting overhead. A small fish succumbed to the temptation, then another and another. Soon the five large, more wary sisters (or more appropriately mothers) joined the feeding spree. As they fed avidly with mouths slurping and backs humping, the fish lost all care and with gay abandon mopped up this new delight.

Despite my excitement, the cast was perfect, well upwind and out of the way of the unsuspecting, uncaring fish. Slowly my floating bait entered the feeding zone. I bided my time, there was no hurry now; I

The exciting sight of a surface feeding mirror.

felt that things would be easy. The float came to rest on the edge of the weed bed, the edge of the hit area, and was perfectly positioned for one of the big fish which was humping its way through the weed on a collision course with my bait. As the grey fish neared I clearly saw and identified her. She was a known and much-loved fish which free-wheeled in excess of twenty-eight pounds. This was my moment. I hardly dared breathe as I mentally conditioned myself, muttering over and over in my head the key words of 'hold back, hold back'. With floater fishing, the hard test comes at the crucial time. Anglers so often strike a false take or simply strike too soon. The rule is to wait; leave it until the line makes off and there can be no doubt.

The big carp sensed another particle. It sank from sight. I held my breath tighter, my heart was in my mouth and suddenly a great hole appeared beneath the bait. Line hissed from the reel. My time had come. The creature had made her mistake and in

an eruption of water the carp was on.

Epic tales of struggles with great fish have a tendency towards exaggeration. Here, it is sufficient to say that the fish ploughed off in carp style across the lake. There, well out, it cruised happily, allowing me the time to plan, compose and prepare. How much it would weigh was all I could think of and as the pressure told I gained yard upon yard of line.

Life, however, is never that easy. Complacency is a waiting trap and I had underestimated this quarry. Suddenly the carp surged towards me and before I could react was embedded deep within the weed bed from where she had been hooked. I was no longer the master, I had made the mistake and now stalemate set in. I would gain some line only to concede it again almost at once. I was angry, not at the fish, but at myself, when suddenly the weed broke loose and the line moved purposefully off towards open water. I sighed, no sobbed, with relief: the fish was mine after all. I relaxed and eased back very slightly on the pressure. At that instant the hook hold gave! My great carp rolled once, then sank from sight and bubbled away to sulk in some sanctuary.

Dave could offer me no words of commiseration. The loss of a big fish is a personal suffering which cannot be shared. I needed time to be left alone to recover and relieve the bitter frustration I felt. Healing time has let me reflect on two lessons. I have only myself to blame for the loss of that carp. I efficiently executed the trap and then I was lazy. But, if there is a very real lesson to be learnt from my story, it is that you can only expect to succeed if your full effort is put into the task and all your past experience, knowledge and water craft is used to the very fullest.

John Bailey's Story

I wandered, quite dazed, around the small lake. It was a fine day and jays screeched in the wood. My trousers were wet, my pullover was damp and there was fish slime on my forearms. My boots lay upturned to dry in the streaming sunshine. I had been carp fishing for just twenty years. I had had doubles and twenties and had always longed for a thirty – and now I have done it. I had just put back a thirty-four pounder! I could not contain myself. I sang. I ran. The sun beamed down just for me.

Yet, in many ways, the capture of this my biggest fish had been straightforward. I had formed a plan and followed it and everything worked out exactly. Perhaps that was luck. Perhaps though, if you fish as often as I do, things just have to go right sometime. Perhaps the number of times a great fish is missed by the length of one of its whiskers is either unknown or is forgotten over the years.

I sat on the upturned boat. I looked out over the acre of blanket weed, arrow head and lily to the tiny hole from which the huge fish had just come. I had only seen the water a few weeks before and now this extraordinary Norfolk carp had been mine. I mused on the story of the last few days.

My sessions had been short, a few hours each day split before and after work. June is the busiest time for teachers but I knew I had to use it before the rest of the syndicate members descended on the water. I had seen the fish on my second trip. I did not fish then, but watched him for some hours work around the largest of the pool's lily beds. His beat was between five and ten yards from me and I could see him well in the clear water, quite well enough to appreciate his length, his barrelled sides, and to know I was dealing with a super fish.

He was obviously very aware of surface foods in the shallow clear water. He bubbled at leaves, sucked at the waxed green lily-pads and eventually ate samples of the floating biscuits I threw in his path. Carefully, I climbed down the tree as the sun sank that day. The way forward seemed clear. The third day I fished floaters away from the lily bed after other smaller carp. I had not tackled such thick weed for several years and I wanted a trial or two to relearn the old tricks before setting to the big one. That day three fish took my biscuits and three fish broke me in the endless weed beds.

I could not forgive this. My guilt knew no bounds. On the fourth session I stepped up all the tackle strength, using a more powerful rod, heavier line and a stronger hook. The carp now were more wary of the bait, but late in the day one took. That eighteen pounder was never allowed to have even an inch of line. His head never got below the surface before he hit the net.

I realised that to play the big one in any other way would be a disaster. I had to hit, hold and pressure him out. If the battle were to last more than a minute, it would be a fight I would lose. It was a hard choice to make. No one wants a parrot lipped carp. Worse though, is a fish carrying the hook and line and which has been cut by hard weed roots.

The fifth session took me back to the lily bed for the big one. His patrol route was identical, clockwise around the lily-pads, high in the water, great rolling eyes scanning the surface film. Again he ate biscuits, but always on the far side of the pads. He might look at my free offerings on the bank side of the lilies, but refused

them invariably. He would take a bait. I knew I could put a hook into him, but I could not consider dragging him through those lilies. Not only could I do him damage, but I knew also that he would never consent to be towed through that jungle of roots. Somewhere on that journey, he would stick, get his head down, drive his pectorals and that would be the end of my quest. There would have to be another way.

On the nearside of the lilies there was, that month, a pocket of clear water. It was, I suppose, four feet deep and very clear over a slightly sandy bottom. The fish passed through it every hour or so, depending on the speed of his patrol. The clarity of this pocket of water made him less confident, and he seemed to sink lower in the water these two clear yards, before rising up once more as the weeds recommenced and hid him largely from my view.

It was, I think, the sixth session when all my attention began to focus on that tiny aquarium of clear water. Into that I knew I would have to introduce a bottom bait that he would recognise, enjoy and be willing to go down for. I had brought with me some peanuts. I was aware of their controversial reputation, but I was never going to use them in the quantities that were said to make them potentially dangerous. Rather, my plan was to sprinkle a very few nuts into the clearing each time he approached. Carp do love nuts, this one had not seen them before to my knowledge and I was hopeful that his interest would be aroused.

It was during my eighth session, at dawn, that the next step was completed. The big fish came into the clear hole, tipped up and head walked over the nuts. Glorious bubbles blew behind him as he

John Bailey's 34lb plus mirror lies beaten at last.

fed. The whole ambush was now coming together.

The climax was to come later that same day, my ninth session on the water. Sharon, my wife, was with me, and we both sensed that the trap could now spring. The weather was warm and the big fellow was up top, bulldozing the weed, breaking surface now and again at the far side of the lilies. From his speed, I knew I had half an hour before he passed the hole. Two nuts on a hair/bolt rig were lobbed seven feet out. About six more nuts were sprinkled tight around the hook bait. Sharon and I sat hidden by the alder tree to wait.

The fish reached the last few weeds before the hole and cruised slowly through the water. His back had that enormous breadth to it. He was a submarine of carp fishers' legend, but he did not look down. His slow patrol of the lily-pads began again.

An hour, slightly more, passed. I grew tense, but again he passed me over, nose literally in the air, his dorsal half erect, draped in leather-like folds.

The sun grew hotter and drew out the diamond-eyed horse flies that bit me, tortured me as I dared not move to brush them away. Sharon offered me the beer can. I refused for fear that the light reflecting on it might scare the fish. This was me and him. High noon at two paces.

For the third time he began to approach the hole and, as he was about to break into it, I dropped two peanuts a yard in front of his nose in the clear water. There was no doubting he saw these. They stopped him in his slow tracks. I could see his every reaction. I willed him to tip up and begin to eat. Now my hand trembled as it lay on the rod. Three minutes he hung there. He was like a Zeppelin becalmed in the summer heat. Three minutes and my face was drenched in sweat. Three minutes and I realised that the quest for carp is what life is about.

Then, gloriously, he tipped and went down. I caught sight of his flank deep as a tub and as golden brown too, as he turned and drifted from sight. I bit my lip until it hurt. I eased off my chair and hovered at the rests until numbness crept into my ankles and feet. The fish was doing nothing in a hurry this hot day.

Then the bubbles rose, the line twitched and with a magnificent certainty, like the breaking of a storm, the bobbin clattered to the rod butt. An eruption! I glued my hand to the reel spool. I strained backwards at the bank. The rod twisted like a python and out of the water on the fringe of the lilies in a volcano of foam lifted clear the hippopotamus head of the fish. I could not stop now. Winding and winding, I scrambled away from the water, heaving the fish down that precious clear channel towards me.

Sharon was already in position, the net ready to haul him in. He hit its folds. Only forty-five seconds before he had been eating, and now he was a furious captive. The old cane net handle cracked and splintered under the pressure. But it was too late for him now. We were not letting him go, not by a long way, not until he lay on the wet carpet of netting. The sun played on his heaving flanks. Sharon and I embraced. We had done it! The plan had worked, for once in life, without a flaw.

Techniques and Baits

Rigs and Presentation

TIM PAISLEY

John Bailey's first carp came from the Roman Lakes, Marple, Cheshire, and, by fishing there in the 1960s, he knows how hard a water it can be. Sitting, as it does, on the fringe of Greater Manchester, the water receives as much pressure as any other carp venue in the country.

Tim Paisley's observation on carp behaviour and fishermen's rig developments, based on his experiences at the Roman Lakes, are therefore straight from a crucible, from a hotbed of the carp scene. This is a difficult piece, but essential reading, we think, for it shows why rigs work, and how carp build up their defences. The Roman Lakes fish are analysed here for the benefit of all of us, wherever we might fish.

Presentation of the Rigs

I think that for someone to really understand what he is trying to do in terms of presentation, it is necessary to consider what has gone before. Modern presentations have evolved in the same way that baits did, to fulfil the need to overcome the increasing wariness of the carp. Each stage has come about through the inventiveness of those carp men who wouldn't take no for an answer. These thinkers were not willing to accept that because everyone else was doing it one way, that necessarily made it the right way.

I've always been fascinated by the whys and wherefores of paste baits, so most of my fishing has been done with specials, protein and nutritional baits, and it is with these baits that the difficulties of presentation have always been exaggerated.

Ten years ago, paste baits were carried to the water in a lovely big ball, the actual bait being moulded round the hook when you cast out. Standard presentation was either freelining or link leger, distance casting being best achieved with a three- or four-inch link and a hook length of about a foot.

My thinking at that time was based on what I was able to read and what I could see others doing. My earliest experiences of 'pressured' carp were at Roman Lakes in Cheshire, where the fish weren't 'hard' fish, but were wise in the ways of anglers. It took me some time to catch at Roman, and I had to adjust my thinking to do so. The few carp I saw caught there fell to luncheon meat and fixed paternoster rigs with long hook arms. That made me think. Why should carp that had learnt to avoid capture on 'standard' link leger set-ups fall to luncheon meat on long hook lengths? I didn't switch to luncheon meat because my baits were catching elsewhere and I thought they were good enough, but I did switch to long hook lengths. I couldn't rationalise fixed paternoster rigs initially and to start with I was using four-foot hook lengths, eighteen-inch links and fishing open bail arm.

My results improved immediately and I can still recall the excitement of a cool July evening in 1976 when I had four good carp, the biggest a fish that is now very familiar and which then weighed 19lb 4oz. I was still getting a lot of twitches though and I started experimenting with a fixed paternoster set up on one rod, in the hope that I could hit some of the twitches. Baits were still firm paste baits moulded round the hook and, because the fishing was all long-range heavy bombs, 2–2½oz were standard equipment. I never did manage to hit twitchers at that water. Even on the fixed paternoster rigs, which I hovered over like a match man so I could strike early, takes were suddenly rod-shaking reel churners. That did not make sense. No carp in its right senses would run off with a heavy bomb. It went against all the carp fishing teachings. I was still getting periodical twitches and lifts of the line and, occasionally when I wound in to see if the bait had gone, it would have been whittled down to a very small piece on the bend and shank of the hook. Were the fish sucking at the bait until they exposed the hook, then running off when they pricked themselves? Was that why luncheon meat was so successful – because it was firm enough to withstand the small fish, but soft enough for the hook to be pulled through it, allowing an element of self-hooking against the heavy leads? I rejected the idea. The books said that the hook had to be buried, so buried it would be. As it happened on other waters I was still able to get reasonable results by not sleeping for a week and hitting lifts of the indicator, but I should have followed through with the thoughts I had on the bank at Roman.

I was not in touch with the mainstream of carp fishing in the late 1970s, so I missed out on one stage of the rig development saga – the hook out presentation. I think it is fair to say that hook out methods have been used for many years as a necessity rather than a principle. Hard as we tried, it wasn't really possible to cover the hook completely with some of the particles so we had to use an exposed hook to some extent, but as soon as we went back to pastes it was right back in the middle of the bait. Lenny Middleton started using baits he couldn't strike the hook out of and mounting the bait on the back, or the eye of a big, wide gape hook to get round the difficulty (although I understand the method was in use well before Lenny arrived at it quite independently). The result was screaming runs on waters where the carp had been giving twitches for years. The big fish started to become more catchable because the long session men could start sleeping on the rods at the difficult waters. Twitching fish ruin your health because you hardly dare sleep, but fish that run until you climb out of your sleeping bag to attend to them are a different proposition altogether.

Like any other presentation, hook out was a principle rather than a rig. Hook lengths varied from three-foot confidence rigs to three-inch bolt rigs. The bait could be mounted at the eye of the bigger hooks or on the bend of a small hook – top hooking as Hutchie termed it. The link, which had previously been considered a necessity, was scrapped. A number of carp men in different areas worked on their own versions of the hook out or bolt rigs, but I think the first man to use them successfully was Rod Hutchinson in his particle and seed fishing experiments of the early 1970s. By the late 1970s they were in common usage throughout the south of

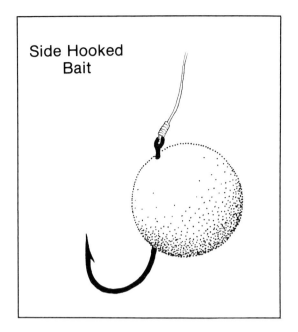

Side Hooked Bait

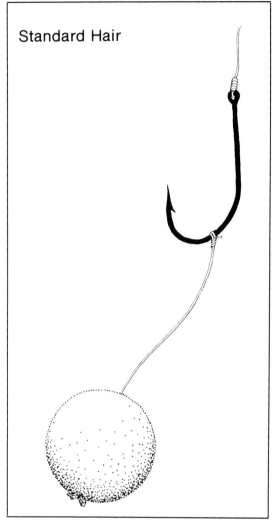

Standard Hair

England, both with particle and boiled paste baits.

The more people who use an effective method, the sooner its effectiveness will start to decline, and two or three years of the hook out set-ups again reduced runs to twitches. Carp soon learn, but just what they learn isn't always evident. Kev Maddocks, Keith Gillings and Lenny Middleton went back to the tank tests in an effort to find a way round these twitchers and again Lenny came up with the answer – the hair. Tying the bait to a smallish hook with fine line proved an even more effective method than hook out. Knowledge of the hair was a closely guarded secret for a surprisingly long time, but its use gradually spread through the south and was publicised by Lenny Middleton in *Coarse Angler*, and in the pages of Kev Maddocks' *Carp Fever*.

To my mind the method was undoubtedly most successful with educated fish which had been caught previously. Initially the bait was fished one and a half

to two inches off the hook, which meant that the best results were achieved on waters where the fish were sucking at the bait to assess its safeness. We first tried the method on Roman Lakes in late 1981 and early 1982 with excellent results; this was no reflection on our angling ability but an endorsement of the effectiveness of the method on a water well suited to its use. Comparisons can be meaningless, but my best day at Roman prior to fishing the hair was seven fish. I wish now that I'd

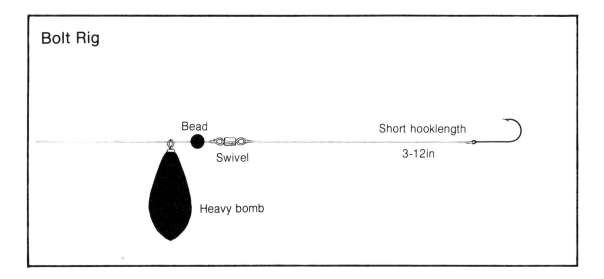

Bolt Rig

Bead

Swivel

Short hooklength

3-12in

Heavy bomb

fished the hook out method there to continue the comparison, but I didn't go to the water for a couple of years and when I did go back it was with the hair.

Initially with the bare hook method, using size 6 Lion d'Ors and a fine line hair of 1–1½in, there was no such thing as a twitch. Every indication was a screaming run and every strike a fish on the bank. Given a good smell and the ability to cast to the fish, results bore no relationship to anything I'd seen before. At times it didn't even seem like carp fishing, but while the purist in me had mild reservations, the carp angler was uppermost and couldn't get enough of it. It felt too good to be anything but temporary, but compared to the days of thirty nervous cigarettes and one run at dusk while you were trying to pack up, the periodical screamings of the Optonic were a joy. The initial set-up at Roman was a heavy bomb, which was needed to reach the fish anyway, foot hook lengths of six-pound mono and tightly clipped lines.

I went to Waveney for the first time in the summer of 1982 and my first two runs there stopped before I could strike. 'Foam it', said the local lads. 'You've got to keep

the pressure on the hook or the carp manages to get rid of it.' The bare hook rigs had been in use at Waverney for three to four years and were losing their effectiveness to some extent. I started heavily foaming the butt ring and took the method back to Roman Lakes with me. My mind wasn't clear about what was happening and I hate fishing in a state of confusion. But in fact, some of the Roman fish were coming to terms with the bare hooks fairly quickly, although that wasn't apparent until I started foaming and fishing the bomb on the end of the line.

The problems were exaggerated in winter. When you are foam tight the Optonic doesn't sound until you are away, so when I had a single beep on a winter's day when nothing was happening I picked the rod up and struck. There was a carp on, hooked in the bottom lip. I had a good winter on the water and takes were divided equally between screaming runs and single beeps. During the winter I changed from mono hook lengths and the hair to the braided rig, but the take pattern didn't change. When they felt the prick of the hook or the pull of the bomb some fish

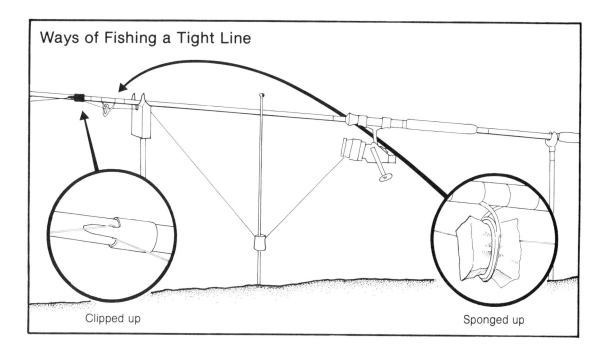

Ways of Fishing a Tight Line

Clipped up

Sponged up

ran, some didn't. The problem would get worse not better, and would be exaggerated on the pressured waters of the south, so what *was* the problem?

That brings us to a rationalisation of why the bare hook rigs work, because if you have no clear conception of why they work in the first place, you can't adjust your thinking when they stop working.

I think that the principal reason any bare hook rig works is because the hook is bare. Twitches on hook covered paste baits became screaming runs on the bare hook presentations. But what were twitches on paste baits? I got them when I was fishing four-foot hook lengths, which I never straightened out after the cast. In other words, a four-inch twitch didn't represent a four-inch movement of the bait but a full straightening out of the hook length and then some further movement. The carp were suspicious of the bait but they weren't totally spooked by the stiffness of the line or the weight of the hook in the

bait. The only way the carp could finally determine that the hook bait wasn't safe was to feel for the pull of the line against the buzzer, or the drag of the indicator. What happened when they did this testing against a bare hook, heavy bomb and clipped-up line? They were partly hooked and spooked into a run.

I think, therefore, that on some waters the 'natural' movement of the bait afforded by the fine line hair was important. I think that this movement can be achieved by the use of some braided lines, which is important when the distance of the bait from the hook becomes material. I also think that there was some element of an anti-eject rig in the long haired rigs and the braided rigs where the hook was fished well clear of the bait, but only an element. Anti-eject rigs are a desperation measure, to be used when the bait or the presentation can't be improved, and the fish just *won't* move when it feels the prick of the hook or the pull of the bomb. The vast majority of fish caught on the bare hook rigs run against the pull of the bomb, which is confirmed by the position of the hook in their mouths. Most of the fish I've caught on both the hair and the braided rig have been hooked in the bottom lip. On the very few occasions that I've used an anti-eject rig, the fish have been hooked in the side of the mouth, usually two or three inches inside the lips.

Bare hook rigs, confidence rigs, bolt rigs: it will all be a foreign language to some of you so I'll try and rationalise the situations that develop with pressured carp and how each presentation can be best used to overcome their increasing caution.

The Carp Trap

Because the hair was so effective, too many carp men gave too little thought to its use, or the full significance of it. A 'rig' became a relationship between a hook and a bait, and still is in the minds of many. Two-inch hairs, half-inch hairs, the hair tied to the eye of the hook; going on to suspended baits, or double baits, or one and a half baits. The hair was born of a carp angling situation which existed on certain waters and owed its original effectiveness to the state of mind of the carp on those waters. Haired baits passed the initial inspection and the bare hooks then pricked the carp into running when they cautiously felt for a dangerous resistance. I've seen it written that the hair stopped working on some waters. Well, perhaps it did in terms of the basic concept of bolt rigs, clipped up lines and hundred-yard-plus runs, but when you say the hair has stopped working you are either saying that the carp have stopped committing *hara-kiri* on the set-up, or that the fish have stopped picking up baits altogether.

Carp twitched at paste baits, then at side-hooked boiled baits, and became increasingly difficult to catch on each set-up. When they twitched at baits attached to a bare hook they were spooked into runs and put on the bank. In terms of self-preservation, carp do seem to be able to indulge in an instinctive thought process, and on those waters where the hair was most effective that thought process resulted in the staggering early results slowing down. The bare hook principle was made increasingly efficient to combat the carp's wiles by the various measures of braided hook lengths, back stops, fixed leads, better baits, better smells, anti-eject rigs and chemically sharpened hooks. In other words, the original basic rig was honed to perfection, but to a large extent the basic concept of a hook a foot to fifteen inches from a heavy bomb with the main line clipped up tight remained unaltered.

This is where the state of mind of the carp when it enters your swim becomes important. All the early hair fish were caught because the fish had got casual about testing baits. As long as they exercised reasonable caution they could get away with some movement of the bait. The longer a state of affairs exists, the harder it is to adjust to a new set of circumstances. The comparatively inefficient presentations we had used for carp fishing, freelining and link legers, had been around so long that the carp took some time to start to adjust to the new set-ups. They had to adjust otherwise they didn't eat or spent more time on the bank than in the water. They had to rethink the way in which they ascertained whether or not the bait they were inspecting was a free offering or a source of danger.

Leaving aside baiting situations and the relative strengths of baits, how does a carp

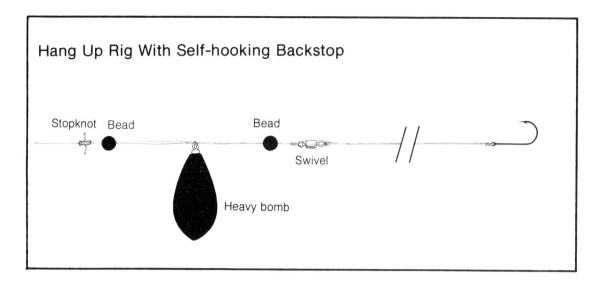

Hang Up Rig With Self-hooking Backstop

Stopknot Bead

Bead

Swivel

Heavy bomb

approach a bait of which it is suspicious? It can only do it within the confines of its own simple thought process, and those thought processes can only function in terms of situations it has already encountered. The majority of carp men will slavishly follow a fashion once it is set – and I mean slavishly. In the first flush of innocence, carp waters were turned over on set-ups of (about) twelve-inch mono hook lengths, size 6 hook, half- to one-inch hair. That was the rig and if it wasn't catching carp, then it was because the carp weren't having any of it. The hook length couldn't be more than a foot, because if it was any longer it wouldn't cast as far. It had to be mono because braided hook lengths of twelve inches tangled. The bomb had to be on the line because that was the way the rig was fished and the line had to be clipped up tight to help set the point of the hook. All of which made it reasonably easy for the carp to start to think its way round the bare hook rigs – because of their predictability. They knew that some baits represented a source of danger and that the danger was having a hook stuck in them within a few inches of

moving off with the bait, or while they were feeling for resistance. So they spent more time inspecting each bait and when they did pick up one they moved off very slowly with it so that when they felt the point of the hook they could stop and shake it out. The first time I got a dropped run on a bare hook set-up I couldn't believe it and dismissed it as a line bite, but the second time I knew there was a problem and started to try and think it out.

You can assess a carp's reaction to potentially suspicious baits in three ways: by observation, by guesswork and through logic, but you have to make some sort of assessment. If you don't you are relying on the thinking of others for each change in presentation you need to make, which means that you will miss out on a great deal because every secret isn't made public, or even discussed privately, and the angling situation on each water needs an on-the-bank assessment anyway.

Observation can be subdivided even further into what you yourself have seen or experienced and the observations and experiences of others. I'll pass on a number of random thoughts that have stuck in my mind and you can add them to what you yourself know about the problem. I've watched carp feeding on boiled baits. Carp in a water do *not* all act the same way when they wish to pick up a bait. Some quite clearly suck and blow from a distance, on occasions ejecting the bait quite forcibly immediately after picking it up, on others swimming a few feet chewing at it before ejecting it. At the same time other fish in the swim stand on their heads like tench apparently picking each individual item up off the bottom.

When I saw this latter occurrence I couldn't be sure what the fish were actually doing but I guessed that they were picking the bait up in their lips. Now I'm not so sure, although at that water my most consistent results came through fishing the bait tight to the hook. However, the water was very silty and it could just be that the carp's instinctive feeding method was to up end, stick its head in the silt – and then suck. The lesson that all carp don't use the same method to pick up the bait was an obvious but valuable one. Waters tend to be fished by a method by the majority of anglers, and we all know of lakes where some carp don't show up for long periods while others are coming out regularly. A method is often designed to catch a vaguely categorised 'they', the members of which are assumed to think, act and feed in a regimented fashion. In fact, it could be that the carp in a water act more individually than some of the carp anglers fishing it.

It makes sense to me that sucking and blowing becomes a defence mechanism in a carp's armoury for ascertaining the safety of a bait, but that is theoretical. All right, if a carp sucks from a foot away, a bait on a hook length of twelve inches or less won't reach its mouth, but can a carp

see that happening? I don't know. Undoubtedly some carp do suck at baits and then eject them; this happens repeatedly on some waters, but I don't know what the carp is feeling for. Having said this, I always opt for the softer feel of braided or Kryston and the greater natural movement of the bait that those materials allow, and I usually fish long enough hook lengths for the carp to be able to move the bait around as much as it wants in its effort to convince itself that the bait can be taken.

On many waters 1½- and 2-inch hairs become unfishable fairly quickly because there were too many takes when the carp moved off with the bait without getting the hook. On two very different waters I had aborted takes on double baits which appeared to be the result of the fish moving off with the bottom bait of the two between its lips. Activity of that type where the fish avoided the hook suggested that the carp were swimming off with the bait in their lips as opposed to well into the mouth. Observation and logic indicate that the fish were either picking these baits up in their lips or sucking them in gently, then repositioning them in such a way that they were held in the lips with the hook outside. A number of anglers I have spoken to have watched carp take the hook bait into their mouths and just not move off with it, although they gave the appearance of being agitated. Others have watched a carp spend some time shaking the hook out when it was apparently well hooked. One freed itself of the hook, then carried on feeding! I think this was the equivalent of the single beeps of the Optonic I was getting at Roman Lakes.

I am making these points to emphasise that there is no black and white as far as presentation goes. Getting the most out of

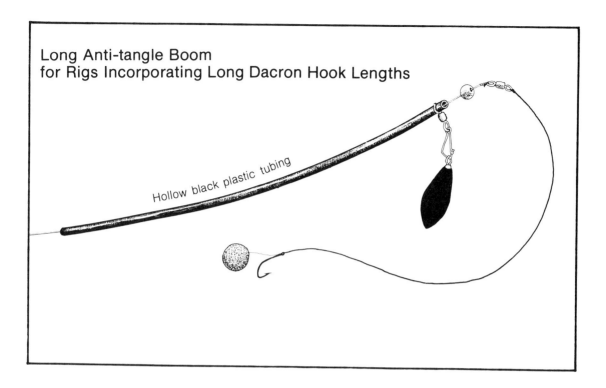

Long Anti-tangle Boom
for Rigs Incorporating Long Dacron Hook Lengths

Hollow black plastic tubing

bare hook rigs requires just as much thought as is involved in fishing any other type of presentation. The fact that the line is no longer springing out of the clip and the indicator yo-yoing up and down the needle doesn't mean that the carp aren't having it, it means that their instinctive thought process has enabled them to find a way of coping with the more predictable bare hook presentation.

PRESENTATION PROBLEMS

The angler has to be aware of all the possibilities and do all he can to make a hook bait appear to be just another free offering. Some suspicious carp will make a mistake while they are testing the bait and possibly be spooked into a run, but most carp will only run when their minds have been lulled beyond the point of no return, when a bait which they thought to be safe

turns out not to be so and they pull the hook into themselves. There is an important principle there and it emphasises the very fine line between success and failure at times. A carp which pricks itself before it has passed the point of no return may well be in control of itself and will stop to get rid of the hook. Once beyond that critical point where all its thinking is focused on assessing the safety of a bait, it may be forced into a panic when its carefully induced confidence turns out to be suddenly and traumatically misplaced. When you are fishing unclipped, how many of your takes have started out as steady lifts of the indicator which have suddenly transformed themselves into gut-churning flat-out howlers? For the most part a running carp is a spooked carp.

Given that the carp in front of you are still feeding on the bait you are offering them, what means have they got of ascertaining whether a bait is safe or not? You may think I'm labouring this, but knowing what the carp is likely to be doing in any given situation is the only way you have of thinking your way round his defences. If you don't know what the problem is you may not be able to find an answer to it. Again I'll make the point that what has gone before on a water will, to a large extent, dictate the carp's approach to the bait.

A carp can examine a bait in the following ways:

1. Move the bait around.
2. Pick it up to test it for an unnatural feel.
3. Suck at it or suck it in.

Concealment is essential if an angler is to observe carp from close quarters. Binoculars are a useful aid.

4. Blow it out.
5. Move off slowly with it.
6. Get rid of the hook once it is in.
7. Get out of the sack.

I mention the last one because it happens to you once and you don't make the same mistake again. The rest of the list isn't quite as easy to think your way round. That list is the basis of how rigs work, so I'm going to consider each point individually to make sense of the presentations which are the most effective weapons against each defence.

MOVING THE BAIT AROUND

The fish can do this in a number of ways, but the obvious ones are fanning the baits with their fins, nudging them along the bottom with their noses, sucking and blowing at them and picking them up and moving off cautiously with them. The lengths they will go to in making this examination will depend on the desirability of the bait, the pressure the carp have experienced and the various other factors that contribute to or detract from the carp's confidence in its feeding.

Obviously when a carp moves a bait around it is going to be suspicious of any unnatural movement, so the angler's defence is to try to make the hook bait act like a free offering. Braided line acts more naturally than mono: a light hook allows more natural movement than a heavy one, and a long hook length is less restrictive than a short one. Can you imagine how obviously restrictive a nine-inch hook length will be if a carp can normally blow a free offering twelve or fifteen inches?

PICKING A BAIT UP

Picking a bait up to test for an unnatural feel sounds a bit vague but I think it happens. It is naïve to suggest that some carps' mouths are more sensitive than others? I think not. Some fish avoid capture for long periods, even on the hardest fished waters, while others are caught regularly. When carp are able to determine the dangers of the hook bait without moving off with it, the baiting situation is inadequate. You can achieve a greater degree of preoccupation with very small baits in an attempt to get round the inspection of each bait. On most waters you won't even be aware of this particular problem unless all the fish in the water are well known and some obviously aren't being caught, or you can observe them avoiding the hook bait.

SUCKING AT A BAIT

In theory, a carp sucks a bait in to blow it out when it is testing, but I'm not sure that this is so in practice. Watching carp stand on their heads to test a bait suggests that this may be a very cautious test for movement which will even detect the danger of a bait on a long hook length. If the carp's open mouth is pressed down against the bottom round the bait while it is in this position and then the fish sucks, what happens? The movement of the bait is severely restricted because the carp's open mouth is pressed down on the line. If that is the reason for the up-ending it is a very good defence mechanism. The most obvious ways around this defence are bolt rigs with about three inches of hook length folded back and PVA'd.

BLOWING THE BAIT OUT

For the most part I think that baits are sucked in so that their action can be observed when they are blown out. Carp can blow baits a fair distance and I think it is commonly accepted that the lightning-fast twitches we used to get before the bare hook rig days were from ejections. You have to know your carp well before you can specifically fish for ejectors. Carp on all waters don't suck and blow and I don't think that all carp on any particular water

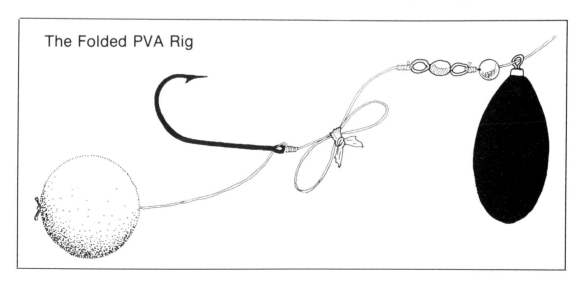

The Folded PVA Rig

do so either, but where most presentations are failing to produce results it is well worth fishing an anti-eject rig. Used in the wrong circumstances these rigs can work against you, so assess the situation carefully before committing yourself to the use of such a set-up.

The application of an anti-eject rig requires some thought. The idea behind them is that the bait carries the hook and line into the carp's mouth, but that the bait and hook separate when the bait is blown out, leaving the hook inside the carp's mouth. The carp bolts either as it blows the hook into the inside of its mouth or when it finds the bait hanging some distance outside its mouth, making it more difficult to shake the hook out.

The most widely known, and to my mind fairest, anti-eject rigs are those designed by Roger Smith, Rod Hutchinson and Albert Romp. In order, these are the 'D' rig, the sliding hair and the sliding rig. Hutchie's sliding hair rig is illustrated in *The Carp Strikes Back* and while Rod doesn't actually describe it as an anti-eject device I think it can successfully be used as one. I've drawn a sliding hair rig in a version I've used and which I'd stumbled on before I know it was in use elsewhere. On all these rigs the bait must be PVA'd in position next to the hook before casting and as a rule these presentations are used in conjunction with PVA stringers.

MOVING OFF WITH THE BAIT

If a carp fails to convince itself that a bait is unsafe by the various means of testing that it has at its disposal, it has two choices – it can either leave the bait or move off with it. But the fact that it moves off with it doesn't necessarily mean that you will catch it. I've already touched on this when

Anti-ejection
Hair

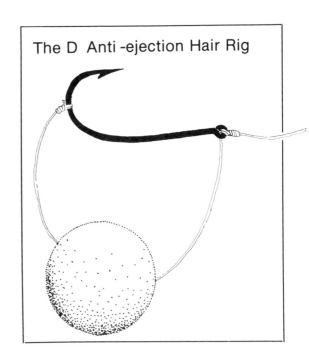

The D Anti-ejection Hair Rig

I was talking about the point of no return so I won't labour it.

If the carp pricks itself in the first few inches of moving off with the bait its defence mechanism will still be operating and it may well be able to stop and get rid of the hook.

The further it moves without being aware that the bait is a dangerous one, the more likely it is to bolt when it feels the prick of the hook or pull of the bomb. The more nervous the carp are, the longer the hook length may have to be. The vast majority of my carp have come on medium to long braided hook lengths, and some of these fish have been from very hard fished waters that have 'seen everything'. Give a carp enough line and it will hang itself up.

Confidence rigs, long hook lengths, aren't the answer to all carp fishing problems by any means, but they can be the answer to many of them. Long hook lengths can cause casting difficulties and where distance and a confidence rig is required, an extending hook length can be used to give you the best of both worlds.

Where you are using an extending rig it is essential that it doesn't tangle on the cast, so always use it with some form of anti-tangle device. Tubing behind the bomb is currently favourite but stick to whatever system you are happiest with.

GETTING RID OF THE HOOK ONCE IN

When you get a single beep of the Optonic and there is some movement of the line, or the rod tip is wagging about, there is a hooked carp on the other end of the line intent on going nowhere until it has got rid of the hook. They don't always manage it, in which case they will eventually belt off, but more often than not they do. The problem is a vexing one, particularly when you get a minute movement of the indicator at night and the baited hook is a long way away under a branch three inches from an island. To strike or not to strike? On waters where the fish are not all bolting when the hook goes in, the current trend is to use heavy indicators and not clip up tight (or to leave a drop on the indicator and clip at the butt). This still gives the angler the vexed question of whether or not to strike, and only experience can answer the question.

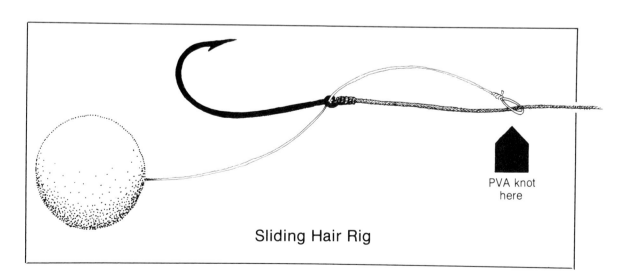

PVA knot here

Sliding Hair Rig

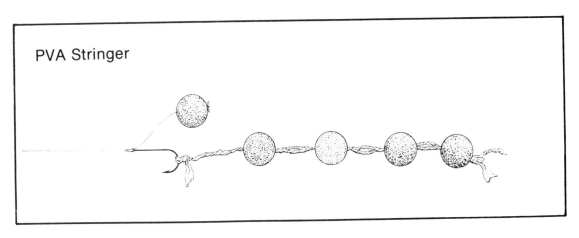

PVA Stringer

Make it as hard as possible for the carp to get rid of your hooks, which should always be needle sharp. Again, confidence rigs can help because the further the fish has travelled before the hook goes in, the further it is likely to be pulled in. Flatten the barb as much as fishing conditions allow, or fish a barbless hook. Ultra-cautious carp aren't likely to pull a hook in beyond the barb, so a barbless hook might make more sense than first thoughts may suggest. If it weren't for the problem of drop back bites, which make Optonics doubly valuable, I would be inclined to suggest that the old-fashioned antenna buzzers would be a useful defence against the carp that don't move when the hook is in. A single beep from an Optonic may register as a long buzz on an antenna buzzer because the tightened, unmoving line will give a continuous indication. You may not have encountered the problem yet on your water but it is all part of the evolutionary process of carp reacting against the bare hook rigs so you will come up against the problem sooner or later.

Conclusion

There comes a point where information tends to inhibit thinking rather than encourage it. I do know that some of the presentations are fished incorrectly, and therefore ineffectively, and that some of the rigs we've looked at here will be abused. A little knowledge is a dangerous thing and too much can be downright confusing. Any presentation is a basis for thought. I could write a chapter about each rig that I've mentioned and even then I wouldn't come anywhere near explaining it properly. The way in which the carp are feeding; the strength of the bait; the pressure the fish are under; the methods other anglers are likely to be using; hook size; type of hook; hook length; whether to use mono or braided or multistrand; single hook bait or double; stringer or isolated hook bait – all are parts of a never-ending problem.

Then, at the end of all that, someone will come up with the observation that location is more important than bait presentation. That always takes my breath away. Anyone who insists on fishing where there are no carp is beyond help.

A final observation: the more I write, the more I become convinced that carp anglers are born, not made. You need experience and you need knowledge. Books and articles can provide some of the knowledge, as I've tried to do here.

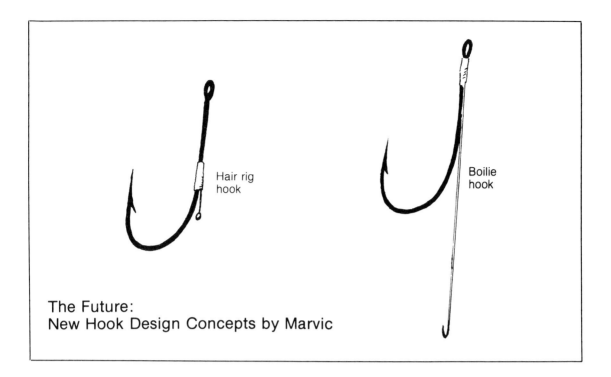

Hair rig
hook

Boilie
hook

The Future:
New Hook Design Concepts by Marvic

Experience comes from applying the knowledge and learning how to make it work on a variety of waters. You can teach someone to catch fish, but you can't teach them to be a carp angler. Some of you will read this as the key to success on any water. It is not. Many hundreds of carp anglers already know everything that I've written here, and many of them will be having a lousy season right now. Absorb everything that has been written, then keep applying it all to your own experiences; that way you may learn to think. All the consistently successful carp anglers have been great thinkers. They can analyse the problem and come up with the answer – eventually. Often it takes time and a few blanks to figure out how the carp are reacting to a feeding situation, a bait and a presentation. Try to think one day ahead of the carp, because yesterday is a very different day in terms of outwitting fish.

Float Fishing

CHRIS YATES

A few yards from a big lily bed a cluster of bubbles rose to the surface. A carp had obviously discovered the beans I had thrown out there an hour earlier, and by the cloud of silt that soon became visible, he obviously appreciated them. I allowed him about five minutes of undisturbed feeding, then baited a hook with a red kidney bean and cast. The fish was only twenty feet away so I needed no weight on the line and the bait landed noiselessly in the middle of the bubble-cloud.

Tense with anticipation, I waited for the line to tighten and draw off the reel. I waited and waited, but for half an hour there was no sign that the carp was the least interested in the hook bait. Once, after only two or three minutes, the line had quivered tantalisingly where it entered the water, but nothing further developed.

I tossed in some more free beans, a little to the right of the original offerings. Bubbles soon began to rise over them so it was obvious that the fish was still interested. I rebaited and recast. Again there was a slight trembling to the line a short while after the bait had settled. I presumed it was nothing more than the carp wafting the line with its pectorals. I certainly did not think it worth striking. Eventually the bubbling stopped, the carp drifted away and I was left wondering if that was going to be my only chance of the day. Should I

have tried a method other than freelining? Should I have put in less or more free offerings?

I went and fished elsewhere on the large and beautiful lake, but there was nothing else happening, carp-wise, and after an hour I returned to my original patch by the lilies. Out went a handful of beans and, sure enough, back came the carp, his appetite restored.

Remembering those vague tremors of the line and thinking that they must have signalled the fact that the fish had picked up the bait, mouthed and ejected it, I now attached a small quill float and cocked it with a knob of Plasticine about four inches from the hook. I deliberately over-cast, let the tackle settle, then drew it back into the feeding area. Within a minute, the red-topped quill rose up an inch, lay slant-wise and then slowly began to sink. I struck and sent a powerful carp ploughing into the lily-pads. He came out, after a stop-start, line-chiming tussle, and I was soon gazing down at a gloriously coloured fifteen pound mirror carp.

Without the float, I feel sure I would not have caught that fish. I would have seen another tremble running along the line, or the line may even have tightened momentarily, but the movement would not have been positive enough to give me the confidence to strike. With the float, there was no question about it. The bite was slow but deliberate, and no one would have missed sensing the right moment to hit it. In fact, I am sure an experienced float fisher would have struck the bite as the float *lifted* and not waited for it to submerge.

I use this incident to illustrate the classic conditions for float fishing for carp. Many similar experiences have convinced me of the deadliness of the technique. By the time I first fished Redmire, I had every faith in the float and I know I was the only angler to catch carp regularly there using standard float methods. Float fishing is not very effective when fished at anything over, say, twenty or thirty yards, but as virtually every carp I have ever caught has been taken at close range I am not worried about distance fishing. (I like to feel the excitement that only comes from being in the presence of a big carp: when the fish is far off and remote, not a presence at all but a mere ripple or shadow, I feel as if I am looking at a distant star.)

At a small lake, or pond, I would probably always float fish before trying any other method – except, of course, if it was obvious that the carp could be taken on a surface bait. Even when using large sized hook baits, float fishing can be more effective than any other technique. As long as the breeze is not too strong, you can shot the float right down and strike the moment the carp closes its lips over the bait. Using any other method, you always wait for the line to at least tighten properly. Fishing around snags or weed beds, it is especially important to get a fish's head round before it builds up tackle-smashing momentum. You cannot do that with the bolt rig, but you can if you use a float. I will not compare its effectiveness with the hair rig, for I have never been desperate enough to use the hair (nor will I ever be).

The biggest carp I ever caught while float fishing weighed 38 lb. The circumstances of its capture were almost exactly the same as described earlier, when I took that carp by the lily bed – a cloud of bubbles indicated a feeding fish, a freelined bait produced merely a twitch of a bite, but a float fished bait brought instant success. The quill slid sideways perhaps three inches, not enough to move the line at the rod tip, but enough to give me ample notice of a bite – and ample time to strike.

The nicest thing about float fishing is not so much its effectiveness as its attractiveness. There is no more pleasant way of catching fish than by watching for that sudden, exciting and mysterious vanishing act of a painted float tip. H. T. Sheringham, writing about carp fishing in 1911, described it perfectly: a 'float tip is pleasing in its appearance and even more pleasing in its disappearance'. Most carp anglers miss out on this pleasure though, for they do not even have a float in their tackle bags.

Float Fishing for Carp

JOHN BAILEY

What is important about Chris's piece is that if the record carp holder can and does often float fish then it must serve as an inspiration to others to follow. A common lament in the carp world of today is the lack of individuality amongst anglers who in their thousands fall into that mould stereotyped by boilies, by rigs, by bivvies and by the usual big fish trappings that can deny brain power and skill. Use of the float gives variety, brings back beauty, invites invention and catches carp!

Float fishing for carp is a wonderful thing in that there are no rules but your own feelings and impulses. All the writer can offer are guide-lines, hints and possible suggestions but in the end, on the bank, a float is to be used as the conditions, the fish, the swim, the bait and the angler all demand. A float in the hands of a master carper is an infinitely flexible tool and this is why, I believe, Chris Yates kept his article lean on technique but strong on inspiration. Chris knows there is no set way to use a float but adjusts it to fit the occasion and even perhaps the mood. This is what you yourself must remember as you follow these faltering steps in usage of the float for the carp. Whatever is said is to be adjusted and developed by you the angler, on the swim, in the twilight as the carp come on the feed . . .

No more traditional way of float fishing for carp exists than laying on. The diagram, I believe, explains a method better than a thousand words and all I would add is that the line from the rod tip must be kept as tight as conditions allow. A good man laying on for carp will be utterly alert. The rod will always be in his hands, even though perhaps also on a rest, for, as the float can be up and flat in a split second, striking must be immediate. Laying on comes into its own in many situations. Perhaps the swim to be fished is so close to the bank that the entry of the lead and the angle of the line are undesirable. Perhaps the swim is very close to snags and the carp must be struck at once to be kept from them. Perhaps the baits to be used are particles and the expected bite must be hit quickly before they are rejected or swallowed. Perhaps the water has been heavily fished with the usual methods, and the angler, searching for novelty, actually goes into anglings past for the solution . . . indeed, the past, just now and again, should not be scorned entirely. The following story might reveal what I mean.

In winter 1987 I fished a very hard, small pit for its carp. My target was an uncaught mid-20lb fish but any of the other carp I knew I would be pleased with. I fished at first with methods typical of the summer – boilies, hairs, bolt rigs and the like – and failed utterly. Only late one afternoon did I see some carp activity tucked in tight to low sweeping alders. I crept round to

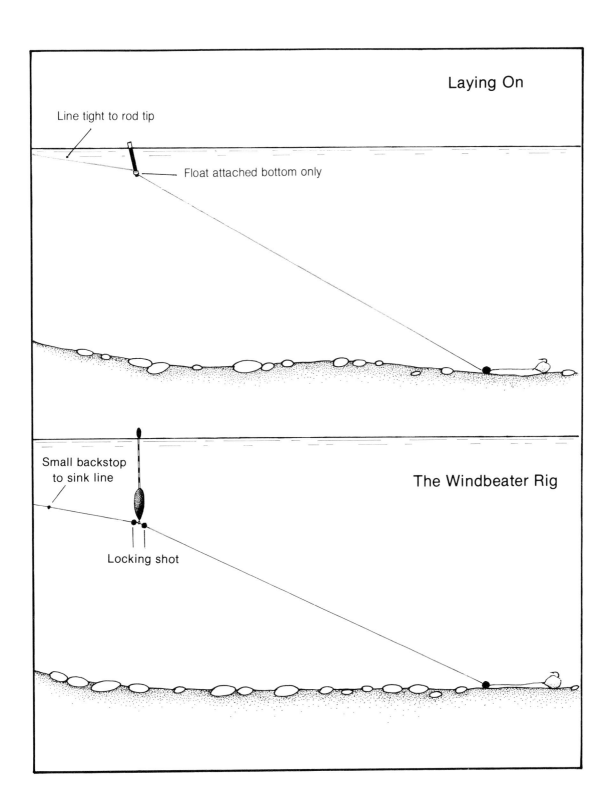

Laying On

Line tight to rod tip

Float attached bottom only

Small backstop to sink line

The Windbeater Rig

Locking shot

Wet and windy, and the carp still feed close in.

them: the water was opaque, the light was dim but I could just make out the slow moving bodies of some five or six fish – mostly commons with perhaps two mirrors amongst them. The next afternoon obviously I was back ... with perhaps the most unusual of carp baits used that year – a bucket of bread, mashed and flavoured with maple!

For two hours I sat in the alders baiting an area a rod length before me. The roach went crazy, splashing, rolling, gorging on the stuff. This was my intention: to stimulate a feeding frenzy that would transmit to the carp. After an hour a carp did appear on the scene and then two more. The roach grew scarce, pushed from the area by the bigger fish. A common head

and shouldered. Bubbles appeared in patches of fizz. The time had come. Bait was flavoured flake on a size 6, two inches beneath an SSG shot and a quill float. The rod was hand held, the float cocked on a tight line. Five minutes, ten minutes, my left hand constantly feeding in dribbles of bread and then, at once, quick as an eye's blink, there was the float flat, the rod hooped and the water in angry foam. It was not the 20lb fish but a good one just the same. As the week progressed, several more carp were taken from the same swim on the same bait using the same technique.

I believe that most of the really good carp men, whenever the water is quiet enough, pick up a prepared rod and go stalking. They know that not all the carp will be in a pre-baited swim and that opportunism is amply rewarded over the course of a season. On any long session my third rod always leans ready-made against a tree. Invariably a float is on the line for I do genuinely believe one to be the stalker's most valuable aid. As a general rule – if there is one in carp float fishing – the float would be a windbeater shotted roughly according to the diagram. I choose this because the lakes I fish are generally open with some ripple and a drifting bait is suicide. Note the tiny backstop a foot up the line from the float to sink the line and make stability even more rock solid. The windbeater can be dotted right to the water surface and the bite, however slight, is immediately seen and hit.

The advantage of the float is in its precision. A low-20lb fish always sticks in my memory. I found him grazing the flats early one July morning, travelling very, very slowly, zig-zagging, meandering all the while and feeding heavily as he went. Small silt clouds ballooned after him, patches of bubbles blew up close by. Had a

Stalking is an important strategy for any carp man.

lead dropped on him he would have bolted. A lead cast ahead of him could have been yards off course, its position lost to my eye and, buried in the silt, impossible to reposition anyway without disturbing the fish. The float, though, landed three yards ahead of him silently enough to have been a twig from the oak tree. I waited until he was close and simply manoeuvred it to within a foot of the fish's head. In twenty seconds the carp was over the bait, under the float, and the tip of red was gone – neat, effective simplicity and the only carp of the session.

For the stalker the traditional float can be married to the modern shock rig with devastating results. The 28¾lb fish from summer 1987 was a spectacular victim. I had found the carp in a secluded corner of the pool, hemmed in by branches and long fallen trees. There was no bank-side swim to attack the area from so I was forced to

fish from the tree I had climbed to spot the fish earlier. Fishing presented all manner of problems. The water was deep – around seven feet – and wind was piling up into the swim blowing debris and masking the clarity. The swim was a nightmare of snags, and the carp, if it were to take, would have to be hooked and held on the spot. I had an advantage: the small table-top of clean swept sand set amidst the general backdrop of silt and mud had to be the carp's main feeding area. A bait placed there would have to be seen at least, eventually. I had to hold the rod – rests were out – and the float was the obvious indicator. Equally, though, I needed the fish to hook itself, as a strike in those trees was difficult to impossible. Five inches from the hook, I placed the bomb, and the whole rig was swung underarm onto the sand. The use of the float in this way also allowed me to know that the bait was positioned with absolute accuracy.

The big carp was still in the area and, though spotting was a hit and miss affair,

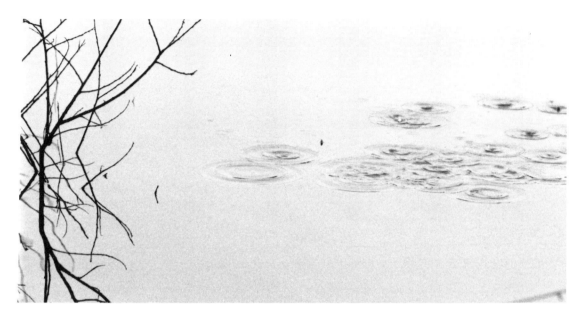

A float fished tight in to the branches as the free offerings drop around.

A carp taken on the drop in the full heat of the day.

every few minutes a gleam, a heavy flat on surface, or a patch of bubbles betrayed his presence. An hour on, the bubbles became a constant stream over and around my sand bar. A gleam beneath the float. I tensed and, just as I had hoped, the float dived, the rod bucked and I was in, playing the fish immediately from the elevated position in the pine tree. From above, I kept a tight rein on the carp and hammered him from the encompassing snags. Within minutes he was wallowing, in the net, and a pretty little plan had, for once, succeeded.

There are many, many times in the carper's season when the fish is catchable, not obviously so perhaps, but its defences are down and for an instant it is vulnerable. A man glued to his rods so long that a change of swim is tantamount to a holiday, will miss out badly on these moments. A float man, though, will capitalise. There are many instances ...

Take, for example, a typical summer morning when the sun is up, the heat is growing and the carp are drifting off their food and beginning to move around the lake. There is still some feeding urge but it is on the wane and the fish are looking for sanctuary or for areas of warm sunlight. Still, there is a carp here and one over there, both moving slowly in mid-water. Over there a couple of dark shapes show below the surface in the margin, their backs actually coming clear. You have all seen this type of behaviour before and know what I mean. A bottom bait is three, five, ten, even fifteen feet below the fish and will be ignored. Yet the fish are not really on the surface and a top bait will not be nearly as acceptable as one on their nose level. The ideal is a bait slowly sinking near them as they travel and to present this a float is almost a necessity.

A self-cocking float is excellent for shorter ranges and at longer distances a bubble float is still a very useful tool. One filled with water goes out like a missile and does not disturb carp – on the contrary, they will frequently mouth the bubble itself! The length between float and hook depends to an extent on the depth of the water and the levels the carp are cruising at. What is important is that the line above the hook should be greased slightly so that the bait sinks as slowly as possible. The bait itself can be air injected or inserted with polystyrene to slow the sinking process even further. Experimentation with different baits to get the combination correct for a single cast is all the day may permit and it needs therefore to be absolutely correct.

Once a cruising carp is sighted, cast the float ahead and beyond his path and draw it back into line so he is not disturbed. Of course, not a carp in five, perhaps even in ten, will see the bait. Perhaps the eleventh

A lovely fish taken from a gap in the lilies behind.

will follow it down. It could be the twelfth that will take it on or above the bottom and a bonus carp indeed takes the float away.

Everybody knows that in the heat of the day, carp tend to bask in the sunlight. However, if this heat becomes too oppressive they may move under branches or beneath lily pads. Lily carp proved difficult to me over and over again. A floating bait was rarely accepted and a freelined bait simply sank and tangled with the bottom roots. A partial answer – certainly one that has caught me fish most years – is to suspend the bait, even a boily, under a float in a gap between the pads. I set the float at between six and twelve inches so that the bait is literally on the carp's passing nose and, believe me, it is often taken. I feel strong gear *must* be used for this ploy. Get

A beautifully scaled mirror.

on top of the fish as soon as the float dips and hustle it clear of the lilies before it can even think of reaching their roots. To lose a fish in snags without considering and preparing for the difficulties is, I think, unforgivable. It not only hurts a fish but if sanctuary is invaded for no good purpose, it unsettles them to the point of neurosis.

The same goes for reed-bed fishing. Carp really do scrape reed stems for the life that clings there and they can be picked up in the beds in the most unpromising hours of the day. Again, the bait is suspended one to three feet below the surface, right in close to the reed fringe. A quill float cannot be bettered for the job but in my experience it really should be fixed on the line by top and bottom rubbers. If it is

A pleasant double taken on the float from a rush bed.

put on the line by a bottom rubber only there is the ever present risk of it catching and snagging between the stems when a fish runs. Fastened top and bottom, the float hugs the line and follows it through the reeds in a more streamlined, less dangerous fashion.

A float can also be used to change the position of the line in the water. A good example of this occurred in my years-long struggle with Eric, the notorious Norfolk small-water carp. Long observation showed he fed well on the small gravel hump only three feet deep and surrounded by water between six and eight feet deep. If a normal ledgered bait were put on the bar, however, he always came across the line in mid-water or slightly below because he always swam around the hump twice before rising to browse on the gravel. I do not know if he did this to test for line but certainly he seemed capable of feeling it and avoiding the hump whenever I used to ledger there. Eventually I tackled the job with a float. This had the advantage of keeping the greased line on the surface so that Eric could circle the hump without suspicion. On two occasions he made to take the bait before veering away at the last moment. Still, without the float, I would not have got even so far with this astonishing fish.

Crucian Fishing

BERNI NEAVE

Introduction

I seem to have gained something of a reputation on the Norfolk angling scene as a crucian specialist. This is probably down to 'novelty' value as much as it is to my success or otherwise with the species. Certainly, I appear to be one of the few anglers prepared to put in as much time and effort in pursuit of these 'lesser' carp as others devote towards its larger (and dare I say, more fashionable) brethren.

If that last statement conjures up visions of my spending long sessions bivvied-up behind matching carbons and Optonics in pursuit of crucian carp, then nothing could be further from the truth. Crucian fishing to me is light years removed from the general carp 'scene' – probably one of the reasons it appeals to me so much.

This isn't to say that the many other facets of carp fishing do not, at times, hold my attention, but crucian fishing requires a completely different approach, one which might appear somewhat alien to many modern carp specialists. In fact, some of the techniques I have developed for crucian fishing might seem more akin to a match fisherman's approach to catching fish.

There are many reasons why crucian fishing appeals to me so much. Perhaps most importantly, it takes me to delightful, wood-fringed pools, usually small gravel workings, clay or marl pits and farm ponds, which seem to suit the species so well. Not for me acres of wind-swept water with the baits up to 100 yards distant and the nearest carp probably as far away again from the angler. I like to fish close enough to see the merest tremble on the float, the tiniest pin-prick bubbles arising round it and, hopefully, the golden-bronze flank of a big crucian rolling just a couple of feet beyond the rod tip. It is this close approach to the quarry which can make crucian fishing so intimate and yet, at times, intensely exciting.

You will probably gather from this that there is no place here for what I disdainfully call the 3 'Bs' of present-day carping, namely buzzers, boilies and bolt rigs. In fact, it is probably true to say that 95 per cent of all my carp – mirrors, leathers, commons and genuine wildies, as well as crucians – have fallen to float tackle, but that's not for discussion here.

Then there are the fish themselves, so hump-backed and deep in the body as to be almost round, dark bronze on the back and upper flanks, shading through gold to butter-yellow undersides – chunky fish that seem to be made of solid muscle. If a fish is capable of wearing an expression, then that of a crucian is almost comical.

The fight of a crucian, even a sizeable one, could never be described as spectacular, even on the delicate tackle needed to

The delightful wood-fringed ponds the crucians adore.

catch them consistently, but striking into one at close range is like hitting an immovable object. This is followed by a steady, jagging pull with an occasional power-dive for the bottom, often resulting in a burst of bubbles and bits of rotting debris hitting the surface as the crucian seeks sanctuary in the bottom silt. However, crucians seem to know exactly when they have had enough and will suddenly roll over on their sides and obligingly allow themselves to be drawn slowly over the waiting net. Quite often, the only movement from the fish at this point is the ineffective waggling of their pectoral fins as they slide into the net, looking for all the world like a gesture of surrender, as if to say 'All right, enough's enough, let's get it over with'!

Early Days

I caught my first crucians at a popular day-ticket water near Hevingham, in Norfolk, this in fact being the only water I knew of at that time that held them in any numbers. Although the water had produced an enormous crucian of 4lb 12oz, I soon realised that the water swarmed with fish of 4oz to 6oz, with a fish topping the pound mark being exceptional. However, having never caught any crucians before, I became enchanted with these miniature golden-brown 'nuggets', although I was already experiencing the frustration of missing countless bites. This was to become so typical of my crucian fishing.

Bait in those early days was small pinches of bread flake and in that respect I had made a good start. I have yet to find a more effective bait for crucians.

Although I had bags of crucians containing up to thirty individual fish, the biggest I had only just made the pound mark and I started to look to other waters for bigger fish. Just how big the next fish would be I could not have imagined in my wildest dreams!

One water I had fished for many years was one of the numerous gravel pits at Lenwade in the Wensum Valley. It was one of the smaller pits, less than an acre in area and known to the locals as 'Kidney' pit, due to its characteristic shape.

In the summer of 1976, when we experienced the infamous drought throughout England, the water levels on many of these pits fell to abnormally low levels. My favourite swim on Kidney was only six feet deep instead of its usual nine feet, and the gravel bar that ran along the right-hand side of the swim was within two feet of the surface.

I was tackling up, intending to fish for

rudd, one hot sultry evening, when I noticed a fish basking motionless in the weed on top of the bar. The bronze-scaled flank was clearly visible and I had no doubt it was one of the water's small population of common and mirror carp. Although these were not of any size, the fact that it appeared to be one of the scarcer commons tempted me to put a bait to it, especially as there seemed little prospect of any rudd moving until later in the evening.

A piece of freelined bread flake was cast beyond the fish and drawn slowly back to rest on top of the weed, only inches from the nose of the carp. I was fully expecting the fish to bolt out of the swim as soon as it saw the bait, but in fact there was no visible reaction at all. I lay the rod in the rests and sat back in my chair to await events. The incongruous sound of an open-air disco drifted across on the warm evening air from a nearby hotel and soon I was half-dozing, only checking every now and then that the fish was still there.

After about thirty minutes and with no previous movement whatsoever, the fish slowly edged forward, brushed past the bread flake and sank from view into the deeper part of the swim. That's that, I thought and was about to retrieve the tackle when the carp reappeared in exactly the same place as before. As I began to wonder if the bait was still attached to the hook, the fish repeated its slow move away from the bar into deeper water, exactly as before. The only difference this time was that the flake had disappeared with the fish and my slack line was rapidly drawing tight to the rod tip! Usually, on seeing a fish actually take the bait, I would strike much too soon and of course botch the opportunity. However, on this occasion all went well, probably because I was only half awake and my reactions were some-

what slowed! As the hook went home, I braced myself for the expected charge across the lake by the carp, but to my surprise it just plunged down deep in front of me and proceeded to swim strongly round in tight circles within the confines of the swim. With snags and weed beds on either side this did not seem right to me, but I cautiously started to pump the fish up towards the surface. There was still no violent reaction from the fish and, sensing that perhaps I wasn't the only one half asleep, I was able to draw the fish over the landing-net as soon as it hit the surface. As soon as it felt the mesh of the deep net it went berserk and started thrashing wildly, but of course to no avail.

I was feeling pleased enough to have caught a 'bonus' common carp. Imagine my reaction and surprise then, for on removing the fish from the folds of the net I saw no common, but a magnificent, gold-bronze crucian carp, its deep, round body almost seeming to fill the frame of my 18-inch diameter landing-net. Suddenly, my personal best crucian had gone from 1lb 1oz to 3lb 1oz!

The scales of the crucian reflected the glow of the setting sun and the sight of that fish was indelibly imprinted in my mind for ever. My love affair with crucians was confirmed!

This episode could well be described as a fluke capture and certainly not typical of normal crucian tactics, but I felt it worth recounting in detail, not only because it resulted in the capture of a crucian that I may never better, but also because from that moment on my interest in the species was well and truly established. Never before had I caught a fish of such joyous beauty. It was a gem and one that I wanted to see again!

A postscript to this story, albeit a purely

coincidental one, was that I was later that week to read of the capture of a British record crucian carp, at a weight of 5lb 10oz. This was caught on exactly the same day as mine! However, trying to picture a crucian virtually twice the size of mine I found quite impossible!

Frustrations and Breakthroughs

It wasn't until I moved to East Dereham from Norwich in the mid-1980s that I really renewed my acquaintance with big crucians. I had managed a few nice fish to around 1¼lb from two or three waters in the north Norfolk area, but nothing even

approaching 2lb, let alone the size of my Lenwade fish. However, I was now living within a five-minute drive of reputedly one of the best crucian waters in Norfolk. Enquiries at the Hall secured my season permit and so the scene was set for the best and most intriguing crucian fishing that I had yet experienced.

There were two lakes at the Hall, both around 1.5 acres in area and both with steep, high banks all round and a profusion of dense, overhanging trees and bushes, which in some cases grew right over and into the water. I was later to learn that these were favourite holding areas for the crucians. The lakes were usually well coloured, with an almost total lack of sub-surface weed growth. Depths varied

A lake at the Hall.

dramatically from four feet to fourteen feet in one lake, the other having a more consistent eight to ten feet all over. This deeper lake also had a much more irregular shape, comprising three main 'arms' of water separated by long, densely wooded peninsulas and joining together in a wider area of water at the 'dam' end. It was this lake which had given the venue its reputation, holding a relatively small head of crucians of very high average size, most fish coming out at between 1½lb to just over 2lb, with small crucians almost unheard of. The other lake also contained crucians, a much larger head of them, but varying in size from a few ounces through numerous ¾lb to 1¼lb fish up to an occasional 'biggie' at 2lb plus. Both lakes also contained a fair head of roach and perch, with just a handful of mirror carp and tench as well.

Because of the numerous smaller fish in the heavily stocked lake, I decided to concentrate my efforts on the bigger fish in the other one, with a 2lb-plus crucian as my ultimate target. You must appreciate that, although my best crucian stood at over 3lb, I had yet to catch a fish between 2lb and 3lb (imagine catching a 3lb roach before you've even had a '2'!) and in fact I had only had a handful of fish over 1lb. In my book, a 2lb crucian is a real specimen and fish of over 3lb exceptional.

All of my early season sessions on the lake were in the late afternoon and evenings, fishing usually until dark. Night fishing was not allowed, but this would not have appealed to me anyway. After the encouragement of a 1lb 11oz crucian on my very first session, I experienced something like a dozen consecutive blanks, save for the occasional roach, despite trying various likely looking swims. At this stage, I was fishing bread flake or sweetcorn on a size

10 hook beneath a standard 'onion' antenna float. I was becoming increasingly puzzled by tiny knocks and movements on the float which never developed into 'hittable' bites. I had put these down to small roach attacking the bread without managing to engulf it properly, but was later to learn the true significance of what was causing them!

Having seen very little evidence of crucian activity, only the occasional splashy crucian rise and a total lack of bubbling in any of the swims I had tried, I decided to have a few sessions on the other lake. This, I thought, with its large head of crucians of all sizes, should at least provide me with some fish to boost my confidence and still with the outside chance of a '2'. Well, that was the theory! Several evening sessions again produced only roach and just a couple of 6oz crucians and still with a distinct lack of visible signs of feeding fish.

The season was now into August and I was feeling somewhat discouraged, to say the least. I had never expected the crucians to be easy, but not as unresponsive as this. I was not even getting the encouragement of visible signs of crucians feeding or just being present in the swims I was fishing. What had happened to those characteristic, splashy crucian surface-rolls and trails of bubbles over the ground bait I had read about?

There was a distinct lack of angling literature to refer to and I had come to the conclusion that no one in the specimen hunting world wrote about the humble crucian carp. Then I came across an article in an old back issue of *Coarse Fisherman* magazine, written by John Bailey, on the species so dear to my heart. Now I knew that the rumour circulating Norfolk had to be true and that he really did possess a float – how else could he fish for crucians?!

One statement above all others registered in my mind after reading and inwardly digesting the much sought-after information – that far and away the best time of day for observing crucian feeding and activity was the dawn period. The author went on to describe his total frustration at getting crucians bubbling and rolling in his swim for hours, unable to get a positive bite from the fish other than tiny knocks and movements on the float which were virtually unhittable. If a fish was hooked, the chances were it would be very lightly hooked in the extremities of the lips or even just on the outside of the mouth.

Of course, I immediately recalled the finicky bites I too had found impossible but had put down to small roach activity. Could I have been getting crucians actually mouthing the bait without my even realising they were present in the swim? Above all this, how could I have reached this stage of the campaign without trying even one early morning session on my crucian lakes?

It should perhaps be pointed out at this stage that this was my first year of married life (my reason for moving to Dereham in the first place). Now, I have never been brilliant at rising at 4 a.m. in the morning (or at any other time of day, according to my wife!), even though it can be such a glorious time to be by the water. Somehow, the warmth and comfort of the nuptial bed made this task even more difficult! However, after reading John's piece, I knew I just had to be at the crucian lake by first light the next morning, a Saturday as luck would have it.

I set the alarm for 5 a.m., knowing that with only a short drive to the water, I could be set up and fishing by 5.30 a.m. The morning was clear and with quite a chill in the air and as I drove up the track to the lake, I could see a thick mist was hanging over the water. I had decided to fish the more heavily populated crucian lake, as a crucian of any size would have been welcome at this stage. I walked round the lake to a swim I fancied and put my gear quietly down. The mist was so thick the far side of the narrow lake was indiscernible.

Even as I started tackling up, I heard a heavy splash just down the lake from where I was standing. As I peered into the murk, another fish rolled not five yards out immediately in front of me. At that moment, I instinctively knew that this was it, this was the breakthrough I was after. After all those fruitless, uninspiring evening sessions, I had cracked it. The lake was transformed from its normally dead appearance of the evenings. Heavy fish were rolling all over the lake, unseen in the mist. The atmosphere was incredible and with excitement and anticipation mounting, it took me all of fifteen minutes to set up a rod. I cursed myself for not setting the alarm a bit earlier.

I had thrown two slices of mashed bread and a handful of sweetcorn into the swim about two rod-lengths out. By the time the float was being lobbed into the swim, patches of bubbles were appearing over the ground bait. The peacock quill cocked and settled as a single BB shot carried the sweetcorn-baited hook to the bottom. With hardly a pause, the float lifted slightly and slid slowly away, gathering speed as it went. After all those blank evening sessions, I could hardly believe this was happening. I struck, much too enthusiastically of course, and only succeeded in depositing the tackle in the bushes behind me. A big surge of bubbles appeared at the surface where the float had been.

Somehow, my now useless, shaking hands managed to extricate the tackle and

The tranquility of a crucian water – and how they love the shade of the lily pads.

rebait the hook and soon the float was settling again amidst the now frenzied bubbling activity. I was still trying desperately to calm my nerves when the float slid under with no preliminary indication. I counted slowly to five and attempted to strike with a bit more restraint this time, bearing in mind the float was only about twelve feet beyond the rod tip! Yes, I missed it again and the hook came back minus one grain of sweetcorn.

At this point in the proceedings, I didn't know whether to laugh, cry or deposit all my gear in the surrounding bushes! As I baited up for the third time, another big, golden crucian rolled not a rod length from where I was sitting. This time the float remained motionless for at least two minutes, just long enough to pour a cup of

coffee which I hoped might help to restore calm to my shattered countenance. This was duly deposited scalding hot into my lap in time-honoured fashion as the float slid away again. Well, it was worth it, as this time the hook thumped home and the rod bent to a really solid resistance. The warm glow of satisfaction that registered on my face was matched only by the even warmer glow as the hot coffee bathed my loins! As the fish bored deeply under the rod, I knew it was a crucian and a big one at that. A minute later and a gorgeous, golden slab wallowed obligingly into the waiting net.

I'd 'scored' at last and all was right with the world! Even the prospect of possible damage to my wedding tackle could not diminish my elation at that moment and J.B.'s name was God! The scales were zeroed for the weighing sling and the fish lifted clear of the ground. The pointer hovered a fraction past the 2lb mark and I settled for a weight of 2lb 0oz. I think I felt more ecstatic than when I'd had the 3 pounder some years previously.

I slipped the fish into the keepnet and sat back to check the time. It was still only 6 a.m. and I had been fishing for only fifteen minutes. Yet I seemed to have had more action in those fifteen minutes than in fifteen previous evening sessions. The sun was starting to break through and disperse the mist now and the water smoked in a soft golden light. The wood pigeons were in full voice in the copse nearby, their soothing calls a perfect complement to the peaceful scene that lay before me. I could have been in heaven.

Suffice it to say that, having finished that memorable morning with another big crucian of 2lb 3oz and with the hectic crucian activity continuing until the sun really got on the water at about 8 a.m., I knew that dawn sessions had to be the answer. What did surprise me was the size of the fish I had taken, from the lake known more for the quantity of crucians it contained rather than their individual size. Perhaps I had misjudged that too, but at least I was learning and at last tangible progress was being made.

That summer saw a few more dawn visits to the same swim but, although I had several more big crucians from 1lb 10oz up to a best fish of 2lb 5oz, plus a few smaller fish, nothing quite matched that first early morning session. As September arrived, sport declined noticeably and I turned my attention to other species. The other lake would have to wait until next summer!

The start of the following season saw me foresake my usual tench fishing on opening morning, as I couldn't wait to try a dawn session on the 'difficult' crucian lake. I decided that a much more sensitive float rig was required in the hope of converting some of the tentative bites I was experiencing on standard float rigs into something more positive and therefore more 'hittable'. I had come to the conclusion that crucians are very dainty feeders, preferring very small portions of food and that even these were often sucked into the mouth and then blown out again without the fish moving off. This I felt could be responsible for the tiny float movements I had been getting.

My rig now utilised the smallest Drennan mini-windbeater float, with the bottom shot, a BB, positioned only 4 inches from the hook. The depth of the swim had to be very accurately plumbed so that this bottom shot was suspended just clear of the bottom but with the bait lying just on the bottom. In other words, I had to have the depth set to an accuracy of within plus or minus 2 inches in a swim ten to twelve feet deep! This task was made even more difficult by the fact that the swim I favoured shelved steeply from right to left and also away from me, the depth varying by as much as 6 inches in a horizontal distance of 1 foot in any direction. Thus, extremely accurate plumbing of the depth and precise positioning of the float in the swim was vital. Low overhanging tree branches did nothing to help in this respect, although, as I mentioned earlier, the cover and shade these afforded seemed attractive to the crucians. The bottom shot was enough to sink the fine antenna of the float so that only the top quarter inch of the sight-bob remained above surface. This shot was to act as the 'tell-tale' and I reasoned that a fish picking up the bait and sucking it in without actually moving off would still lift the bottom shot, giving a 1-inch lift of the sight-bob. This, I felt, should be clearly visible at the close range I would be fishing, even with my eyesight!

I arrived at 3.30 a.m. on opening morning and was dismayed to find many swims already occupied, despite the ban on night fishing. I couldn't believe my luck when I saw that the swim I wanted was the only one still vacant! It was a clear, cold morning, almost with a hint of frost on the grass – this in the middle of June! Consequently, sport was very slow all round and by 8 a.m. many anglers were packing up and leaving. I had only had a couple of roach, with no signs at all of crucian activity. I was fishing small pieces of bread flake on a size 12 chemically sharpened hook to 3lb BS line. Ground bait was a small amount of mashed bread fed periodically into the swim in tiny balls.

The sun was starting to warm the still air now and, despite the lack of action, it felt good to be fishing again on such a glorious morning. Then, unexpectedly, at about 8.30 a.m., a big crucian rolled about a foot from the float, actually rocking the sensitive antenna in its wake. My concentration returned and about ten minutes later the float lifted about one inch and moved a couple of inches sideways at the same time. I needed no further encouragement and struck at a bite I knew would hardly have registered on my old float rig. The rod bent into a satisfying solid resistence and I knew instantly what was on the other end. A typical crucian fight ensued, although I had a few anxious moments when the fish dived for the bottom and snagged itself on an unseen rotting branch close to the bank. Fortunately, the fish came clear and in characteristic manner then allowed itself to be drawn easily over the waiting net, with a piece of rotting twig still attached to the line.

That fish went 2lb 1oz on the scales and,

J.B. with a 2lb crucian.

despite the sun getting warmer by the minute, two more fish of 1lb 11oz and 1lb 15oz followed in the next thirty minutes. Then, just as suddenly as it began, the swim was dead again and I knew there would be no more action that morning. To have caught three superb crucians at that late stage of the morning, well past the time when I would normally have given up hope, made this a most satisfying opening to a new season. Perhaps more significantly though, the new float rig was working like a dream and I felt that had I fished with standard float tactics that morning I could well have blanked and seen no bites at all.

That swim produced several good early morning sessions for me over the next few weeks, with a best catch of five crucians between 1lb 10oz and 2lb 2oz in a three-hour session. Invariably, bites were tiny lifts or dips of the float but I became very confident of hitting the lift bites; in fact, some of these resulted in crucians with the hook well back towards the throat. This convinced me that crucians often suck in a bait confidently but remain in the same position in the swim, thus giving little or no indication on a normal float rig. As the season progressed and the fish became more wary, I had to reduce the bottom shot to a no. 6 and position this within 2 inches of the hook. Even so, my catch rate was dwindling and I turned my attention to the other lake again, as I had heard that some bags of crucians of good average size were being taken.

Latest Discoveries and Developments

It was at this time that I made what I felt was another major breakthrough in my crucian tactics, concerning attracting and holding the fish in a swim. Up until this point, I had fished almost exclusively with either of two baits, bread flake or sweetcorn. Logically enough, free offerings consisted of sparing amounts of mashed bread, mixed into an almost liquid slop to give a quick break-up and 'cloud' effect in the swim, together with the occasional handful of sweetcorn. I had already come to the conclusion that it was easy to overfeed a swim where crucians are concerned, especially if not many fish are present.

Anyway, one wet August Saturday, I drove into Norwich to attend a fishing tackle show being held in the majestic surroundings of St Andrew's Hall. Former world match angling champion, Ian Heaps,

was on hand to give talks and practical demonstrations on ground-baiting techniques, as well as promoting a range of ground-baiting products for the manufacturer he represented. Although these were primarily aimed at the match angler, I still found a lot to interest me, especially regarding two particular products. One of these was a continental ground-bait mix from France, now being made available in this country, called Katch. It was a coarse brown mix consisting primarily of ground hemp and other 'secret' herbs and attractors. Ian Heaps demonstrated, with the aid of a mixing bowl and a large tank of water, how, if correctly mixed to a very dry consistency with lots of entrained air in the mix, small compressed balls of this ground-bait would sink rapidly to the bottom and then virtually explode as water was absorbed, causing a rapid expansion and sending a column of minute particles and bubbles fizzing back up toward the surface. The idea was that this fine cloud of tiny particles ascending and descending on air bubbles in the swim, coupled with the undoubted drawing power of the aroma of hemp, would attract and hold fish in a swim for long periods, without actually overfeeding them, there being little actual bulk or edible substance in the mix – just what I wanted for crucian fishing!

The other product that intrigued me was a strong-smelling brown liquid which was claimed to be 100 per cent liquidised earthworm extract! This was reputed to have phenomenal attracting powers to most species of fish. Needless to say, I left the proceedings laden down with enough supplies of the two products to last the rest of the season! I felt the fickle-feeding crucians would be a good test of the claims made for their drawing and holding properties and certainly Ian Heaps had stimulated the thought process in my mind again after a period of relative stagnation.

I did not have to wait long to put things to the test. Following a day of continuous rain on the Saturday, Sunday dawned fine and clear, and 5.30 a.m. saw me tackling up at the crucian lake. Before commencing fishing, the ground bait was carefully mixed, using a 10 per cent solution of the worm extract instead of plain water. Two small, compressed balls were lobbed into the swim. There was so much air trapped in the mix, the stuff actually floated for a few seconds before descending to the bottom! Moments later, I was reassured to see tiny air bubbles breaking surface above the ground bait, confirming that the mix was breaking up and 'fizzing' in the prescribed manner.

For the first thirty minutes, I had no bites at all and began to wonder if I had 'killed' the swim with the new ground bait. Then bubbling activity started again; this time it wasn't just air being released from the mix. What followed over the next five hours was the most intensive crucian feeding activity that I had ever experienced. It would be no exaggeration to say that I had a bite, on average, every couple of minutes during the whole of that period. Bait was the usual bread flake or sweetcorn and many takes were occurring on the drop, which in my experience was unusual for crucians. Most of the bites were good positive 'unmissable' takes – again most uncrucian-like – the float never seemed to be still for more than a few seconds and it appeared the swim was literally boiling with crucians!

I said the bites were 'unmissable', but, of course, true to form, I was only connecting with about one in six, which was unbelievably frustrating considering how decisive they appeared to be. However, even at this dismal rate of return I was putting something like half a dozen good crucians on the bank per hour of fishing, giving a final tally of around thirty fish for five hours' fishing. They ranged in size from about 8oz up to a best fish of 1lb 10oz, with the majority being 'pound-plusers'. This gave me, at a conservative estimate, a 30lb bag of sizeable crucians, which was staggering compared to previous catches. You don't need an 'A' level in maths to calculate what the total catch could have been with a more successful striking rate!

In addition to this, I lost a huge crucian at the net which I put in the 2½–3lb category. I actually had its head on the rim of the net when the hook pulled out and the fish dived to freedom. Inevitably, the loss of that fish overshadowed the fact that I had just experienced my best crucian session ever, at least in terms of quantity of fish. I also felt physically and mentally shattered after such an intensive five hours' fishing and actually packed up while the fish were still feeding. Every time bites started to dwindle, a further ball of the 'magic mix' would have them back and feeding as hard as ever.

Analysing things in my mind later that day, I had little doubt that the new feeding technique had been largely responsible for such an outstanding catch. Obviously, you can't make a full judgement on just one session, but never had I experienced so many confident bites or caught so many crucians. The only conclusion I could come to was that the competition in the swim between so many fish for relatively few food items was causing fish to seize the bait and dash off with it away from the others, thus giving rise to the positive 'sail-away' bites which previously had been something of a rarity. I further deduced that so many of these were subsequently missed because the bait was only being held lightly between the lips as the fish made off with its prize, instead of being sucked back fully into the mouth.

I have to confess that, although the new feeding technique had improved my catch rate immeasurably, nothing since ever quite matched that first trial session. Perhaps it just happened to coincide with a morning when the crucians were well and truly 'on'. As with most branches of angling, I suppose, it is necessary to keep trying new baits and techniques as the fish soon wise up to a different approach. This is certainly true of crucians.

This season has seen me scaling down tackle even further and all my crucian fishing is now with 1.7lb BS hook lengths. With a stretchy 3lb BS main line, coupled to a very forgiving soft-actioned carbon float rod and lightly set clutch, I have been amazed at how few fish losses occur on what to me is ultra-fine tackle, even for fish the size of crucians. Bread remains the best bait for crucians as far as I am concerned; however, I have found wholemeal brown bread more effective than white, especially for sorting out the better specimens. I have also experimented with some of the many flavourings now available, mainly to improve the effectiveness of sweetcorn and also as ground-bait additives. I can report very good results with a sickly sweet dairy-cream fudge flavour, which incidentally seems to work very well with other species.

Efforts early in the season focused on another Wensum Valley gravel pit which contains just a few crucian carp of very high average size – indeed, I had heard rumours of fish to 3lb 12oz! These fish were present in amongst legions of small roach, bream and tench, which I felt would present the major problem. Would my small baits remain free of their attentions long enough for a big crucian to find them?

This water is another relatively small (one and a half acre) pool, so surrounded by dense woodland and high banks that the strongest of winds does not ripple its surface. As will be recalled from my earlier comments on choice of venues, this was my sort of water and I was happy to spend many hours in tranquil peace at this delightful place, miles from the sound of traffic and the hustle of town life. This was just as well, for the crucian fishing was decidedly slow, morning or evening.

After several sessions in the only lily-fringed swim on the water, and one which I really fancied for a big crucian, I was drawn to a swim on the opposite side of the lake under an overhanging tree, where I had often seen a solitary big crucian roll in the late evening period. My total catch to this point had been a few reasonable tench and just one fine crucian at 1lb 7oz, my first from this venue. Next session I decided to try this new swim. It was a warm evening with a hint of thunder in the distance. I had just two bites in the three hours I fished, both mere half-inch lifts on the float, so reminiscent of earlier times. The first was missed, the second, some two hours later, came within an inch of producing the second 3lb crucian of my angling career. This time it fell short by just a single ounce, but I couldn't possibly be disappointed with such a magnificent fish. As the setting sun filtered through the trees and illuminated the fish my mind went back to that first big crucian some twelve years previously – history had almost repeated itself. I wondered to myself just how many anglers see just one 3lb crucian grace their landing-net in a lifetime, let alone two, and knew that I was a lucky man. But then no one fishes for big crucians, do they?

Floater Fishing

MARTYN PAGE

Just as a cat toys with a mouse before the kill, the carp mouthed my floating crust. Then, suddenly, she froze – our presence had been sensed. Now the decision had to be made – to leave the remaining piece, just in case, or to take it and run. At last animal preoccupation for feeding dominated as she sucked it in with a great slurp and bolted out of the shallows, away from that sense of unease. John's camera clicked, my rod arched, the water heaved and the hook whistled past my ear.

It happens occasionally when floater fishing, that seemingly unmissable takes result in nothing but thin air. It was more annoying on this occasion as we had been attempting to obtain some action shots for this chapter – some pictures of carp rising to floaters, taking the bait and the action which follows. It would have made a perfect sequence but now all that was left were the dying ripples spreading across the lake. It was late autumn and we were making use of a mild spell in the weather to obtain the photographs. However, the fish were not responding at all well that morning so we resolved to return the next day. John left for lunch while I baited an area with some bottom baits so we could be sure of some action shots later. Whilst baiting I craftily slipped a rod out – why waste an opportunity?

Sure enough minutes later I was into a small carp, which heralded disaster number two. As there was no point in netting such a baby I brought it to the side in order to unhook it in the water. I was soon to discover that the banks at the lake are deadly if you have no grips on your shoes! Inevitably, I found myself at one with the carp's environment, trying to unhook a frantic little carp and pull myself back out of the lake and all whilst nursing a near broken arm!

Eventually, tranquillity returned and I sat dripping wet and swearing about the best laid plans of mice and men! As soon as I recovered some degree of composure, I bundled the tackle together and made for the car. At that stage an arrogant carp had the audacity to come to the surface and proceed to slurp ravenously on the top, at the edge of the lily-pads. I was not going to let it get away with that. Disregarding the possible broken arm and the soaking wet clothes, a piece of crust was gently flicked ahead of its apparent course. I never caught that fish, however, although I will not complain, for as soon as the bait settled, a much more weighty beast appeared from nowhere to deny it of its meal. Minutes later I returned a satisfying twenty-one pound mirror. The wet clothes and aching (but thankfully not broken) arm were forgotten. Such is the way with fishing!

The Challenge of Surface Fishing

You will have gathered from my story at the beginning of the book, that the majority of my carp fishing involves the use of floating baits. The reasons are simply that I find surface fishing aesthetically pleasing and also tremendously exciting. That breathtaking moment when a big fish sucks in your bait, perhaps less than a rod length out and in full view, can hardly be described in words. Yet despite this, floater fishing is sadly neglected by many carp anglers in favour of more conventional bottom methods and baits. Often it is dismissed as less effective. This it may be on some waters. However, on many waters it proves to be a style which can consistently produce fish for year upon year whilst other baits and methods come and go.

Andrew Hitchings plays a carp caught on surface-fished dog biscuit.

John Bailey kneels with the net.

An added advantage of surface fishing is that other anglers are likely to be competing with each other over baits, rigs and swims but will ignore the surface layers. I have often found that I have had to keep ahead of only the fish and not the anglers. The floater man may, therefore, be at a considerable advantage when he first arrives at a new water. Otherwise shy carp will often fall easily to his baits and with care he will be able to enjoy a long-lived success. Indeed, this was the fortunate position that Steve Harper and myself exploited on at least one of our local carp waters for years until, eventually, our secret was discovered.

To this day I wonder why we had it all our own way for so long; perhaps it was because we would arrive at a 'sociable' hour, having allowed the sun to rise well into the sky. This was a time when most of the regular but more conventional carp anglers were packing up. We would then catch a carp or two and would normally have left before the evening shift arrived. Those that did fish all through the day obviously slept because if they had been watching the water, the sudden appearance of carp bow-waving across the lake with mouths and backs exposed to the air would surely have made them realise what method we were using.

Having praised the style and hinted strongly at its potential, I will now try to explain some of my thoughts and conclusions, drawn from many years of catching carp on the top. I will not attempt to mislead anyone by pretending that this is a golden method without problems – it is not. Like any other style, when a new water is fished, or one which has not seen surface baits, the fishing can be very easy, but as the carp become wiser life can get tough and there are some unique problems associated with this style which need to be overcome.

It can also be a tiring method. The stalking so often necessary for this approach can lead to hour upon hour of standing or crouching behind some hidden bush, hardly daring to breath, and holding the rod whilst watching the frustrating antics of a wary fish as it keeps avoiding the bait and eating all the free offerings around. Even the lighter carbon rods available nowadays soon begin to feel extremely heavy when held, poised, in such circumstances.

Floater Waters

Floater fishing is not always successful on all waters. It may fool some of the carp all of the time, but not all of them all of the time. Of the lakes at which I have applied the method, I can only recall one which has not responded to the surface. That lake is known as Days Water. It is usually fairly coloured and has only a small head of carp. I managed only one take in about ten sessions using floaters, which I consider is a very poor response indeed for this method. I have not fished the water since 1981 so possibly the fish will by now have seen more surface baits and have become more accustomed to surface feeding. I firmly believe that on most waters, it is merely a question of educating the fish to surface feeding.

I would, at this stage, add one caveat concerning common carp which is discussed later. Fish in small shallow waters usually respond very quickly to top baits as do fish in medium-sized waters where stocks are good. I cannot speak from experience on large waters (twenty acres plus) but I suspect that just like small, less densely stocked waters they will respond if enough baits are introduced in the first place. A classic example of such a weaning process was mentioned when we interviewed Len Bunn for his contribution to this book. Len wished to catch carp from Taverham Carp Lake (many years ago) and literally filled in the water with bread crust, obtained from a local baker, week in and week out throughout the close season. Eventually, those fish responded to the baiting programme and Len's hard work was indirectly to lead to the occasion narrated in my story at the beginning of this book.

FEEDING TIMES

Throughout the summer and early autumn fish can be caught on floater baits at practically any time during the day. I am sure, however, the method was discovered for those textbook warm summer spells when the fish bask lazily on the surface just waiting for the odd 'munchy' or 'chum mixer' to drift overhead. I personally have never found the early morning to bring good surface results. The cool of the night tends to put the fish down and hence a mid-morning start usually suffices. As the sun warms the water, the fish will normally respond for the rest of the day, but on different lakes various times throughout the day will see changes from intense feeding activity to lethargy.

Obviously, feeding patterns vary from lake to lake but surface fishing is less affected by those doldrum hours when nothing seems to be happening. As the season develops, the best times may alter and on some waters the evening will go 'off the boil'. Mid-morning and late afternoon are, however, nearly always two of the best times to take fish from the top. This seems to coincide with the periods on either side of the most intense heat of the day when the fish are at their most lethargic.

Almost invariably, there will be a fairly active feeding period in the evening, often as darkness approaches, and this is usually highly productive as the declining light reduces one of the most frustrating problems of surface fishing – the visibility of the line.

Night fishing with surface baits can also prove productive. I have found some waters to be totally 'dead' to this style at night, whereas others may only respond during the first few hours of darkness and only few seem to respond throughout the night.

Basically, therefore, one should expect to catch fish on floaters at any time, but invariably it is necessary to obtain a knowledge of the behaviour of the fish in the particular lake as opposed to being guided by any so-called hard and fast rules. Indeed, I have even fed surface baits to carp in the depths of winter with ice around the margin. Hence I feel that surface fishing is worth considering at almost any time.

AN APPROACH TO A WATER

My local carp lake is an estate water of a few acres with a very good stock of fish to just under twenty pounds. On a typical day, a mid-morning arrival will usually see a couple of the members fishing the lily-pad swims, leaving the rest of the lake free. The best floater swim on the lake is one known as the Punt Swim, which controls the main central area of the lake. This swim offers a choice. For instance, a mid-range cast of forty yards puts a bait on the back edge of the pads, an obvious patrol route for feeding carp. In addition, being an estate spring fed lake, there is a deeper central channel along which the fish patrol. An alternative method is to draw the fish from the central channel and the pads to within feet of the near bank in order to enjoy the satisfaction of seeing the fish taking virtually under the rod tip.

I can well remember the day I used this drawing method to bring fish to the edge of some sleepers on which most people sit to fish, to the left of the Punt Swim. I was well back from the sleepers with the rod lying across them and had brought the fish to a point where they were slurping in free offerings flicked so that they bounced on the edge of the sleepers and dropped over to the waiting lips. Having hand fed the fish in this way for a few minutes, I then bounced a bait off the edge into the mouth of an unsuspecting seventeen-pound mirror carp. With less than twelve inches of line between the rod tip and bait and with the fish in only twelve inches of water you can imagine the resulting eruption on the strike.

This is the beauty of surface fishing. Fish can be moved from their usual feeding areas to where you want to catch them. This drawing of the fish is achieved by using a constant stream of floating particles drifting in the wind. My initial approach is to walk to the side of the lake from which the wind is blowing and to commence baiting, firstly with a fairly substantial number of floaters and then tapering to a constant stream. They then drift slowly across the lake enticing the carp up, causing them to follow the main body of the floaters to the swim from which I will eventually fish. Once the fish are active, it is possible to return to the swim and keep the fish within that area using a catapult as a means of replenishing the feed.

As an alternative, and one which I use frequently, it is possible to use a spare rod tackled with only a giant adapted swim feeder. One end of this feeder is left open and the other is weighted so that it enters the water first. Hence the bait immediately rises out of the feeder as it sinks below the surface. Substantial numbers of particle floaters can be put out quickly in this way. Upon arriving at the lake I

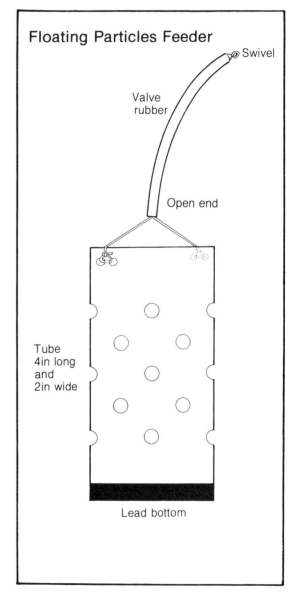

Floating Particles Feeder

Swivel

Valve rubber

Open end

Tube 4in long and 2in wide

Lead bottom

A near twenty mirror falls to floating bait.

usually cast this from my chosen swim, upwind, five or six times. The feeder is cast beyond any known holding or patrolling area so that several hundred particles will drift over the fish in order to draw them, unsuspecting to me. The method is, of course, dependent on there being some wind drift.

At this stage, with the fish feeding well only a few yards out, the baiting should be scaled down so that they have to search harder to find the few remaining offerings. If too many particles are in the swim the carp will develop a frustrating habit of 'random mopping', where they will just swim with open mouths hither and thither sucking in anything they can find. They then seem to lose all sense of purpose and direction and invariably seem to fail to locate the hook bait. Time and time again a carp will appear to be coming towards the

The prize is photographed before being returned.

bait, its mouth sucking at any and every-thing in its path, only for it to change direction not once but two, three or four times in as many feet. All this movement on the surface often causes the line to drift the bait away from the fish before it reaches it. The fish then changes direction once more and goes wandering off.

It is much better, once you have the fish in the feeding mood, to 'starve' them so that they search for any remaining bait and take it purposefully and far more regu-larly. Initially, when many baits are in the area, several carp may be frantically 'hoovering' the feed. At such times it is pot luck which fish will eventually take a bait. Once the amount of bait is cut down the fish tend to break out of the feeding area and individual fish can be selected. By using this means of selection I have man-aged to achieve many fifteen pound plus fish from the particular lake mentioned, even though the average size of fish caught in that lake is substantially less than that figure.

This drawing approach does not work on all waters or swims. For instance, there may be large weed beds which stand in the way or there may be no wind on a particular day. The lake may predomi-nantly contain common carp, which seem to have a peculiar habit of spending much of their time near or under cover around the water edges, under overhanging trees or in weed. As I hinted earlier, common carp are unusual in another way. They often prove the most difficult to tempt on floaters and the drawing style can prove difficult. Indeed, of the hundreds of carp which I have caught on the top, I have yet to catch a common carp off the surface in open water and can only count a handful which I have caught on floaters. True, the common carp is more rare in the lakes I

fish, but on many occasions I have watched their reaction to surface baits at close range and I am convinced that they do not respond anywhere near as favourably to floaters as do mirror and leather carp. I mentioned this to Ritchie MacDonald when we interviewed him and he agreed it was an interesting point, especially con-sidering that very few fish have been caught in the past on floaters at Redmire, and that lake abounds with common carp.

In circumstances where the fish cannot be drawn to the swim it is necessary to go and catch them from the environment of their choosing. They will be more at ease in their chosen location and hence should prove easier to catch, provided the ap-proach is made with caution so as not to spook them. For instance, catching carp amongst lily-pads is relatively easy (or at least hooking them is) for they feel safe in such a retreat. I am reluctant, however, to fish in the pads in view of the damage which can occur to their mouths in at-tempting to extract the fish from their chosen sanctuary. Also, of course, there is the risk of broken lines. If the fish insist on keeping within the pads I am content to take the odd fish from the edges until the autumn when, as the lilies die back, it is possible to fish amongst them for the first time without fear of lost or damaged fish as long as adequate tackle is used.

Tackle and some Tackle Problems

At this stage it is useful to consider my usual tackle for floater fishing. The majority of this fishing requires some form of float as a casting weight, although if I can eliminate this when margin fishing and dap for the fish with no float, or in some cases with no line on the water, then so

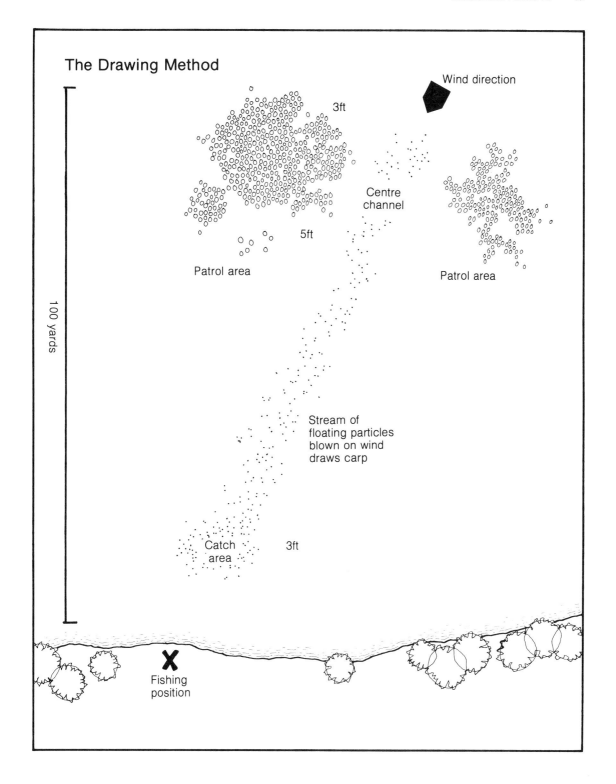

The Drawing Method

Wind direction

3ft

Centre
channel

5ft

Patrol area

Patrol area

Stream of
floating particles
blown on wind
draws carp

100 yards

Catch
area

3ft

Fishing
position

much the better.

The basic tackle involves the usual eleven to twelve foot rod (I have used shorter rods at times for fishing between gaps in the trees) and an all through action with around two pounds test curve is ideal as this adequately copes with the short range fishing involved and has the power to turn the fish from nearby snags. There is, therefore, plenty of choice on the market today.

Line is much more important and I do not believe in using lines so light that fish will often be lost. There is nothing sporting in leaving hooks in fish. In turn, this presents me with a problem as line is unquestionably the single greatest problem to overcome when floater fishing. The line on the surface stands out like a sore thumb and I believe it is magnified further by the grease needed to keep it floating. The grease can be eliminated but there is then a problem with sinking line catching on the fish's backs and they will spook at this. The answer is to use a line as fine as possible without running the risk of lost fish.

With the introduction of the modern 'super' fine lines it is possible to use a line with a 9 or 10lb BS which is as thin as 6lb. Certainly this assists in overcoming the problem of line-shy carp. However, these low-diameter lines must be used with care. A finer diameter will mean less safeguard against knocks and abrasions and less stretch. This can lead to disaster, particularly if snaggy swims are being fished. As always it is essential to balance tackle to the particular conditions – it's no good deceiving a shy carp into taking the bait if the tackle cannot cope with the resulting battle!

Developments in modern tackle leave one or two questions, however, for with finer lines one must look for finer hooks, which still have the present power and strength characteristics. Where will our incessant drive to be one step ahead of the fish eventually end?

There are other ways to overcome the line problem. For instance, as the light fades the carp either lose sight of the line or perhaps even lose their caution. Certainly fish which minutes before ignored a bait because of the line, will suddenly start taking confidently. Alternatively, fishing in areas of accumulated scum, which carp seem to like, can overcome this visibility problem as the line becomes hidden within the surface debris. In areas where weed reaches the surface the line can also be hidden amongst this so as not to spook an approaching carp. In open water though, where the problem is more acute, the method I usually adopt is to cast slightly short of the feeding carp. As they patrol around in search of the last remaining baits their feeding area enlarges and eventually a fish will approach the bait. In these circumstances, more often than not, the carp will be approaching the bait before it comes across the line and hence will not be scared by a visible line overhead.

Another trick which I have used to fool line-shy carp on a number of occasions is to use a specially adapted float which is shaped like a very thin twig and painted brown. The idea is for the float to represent a twig. The float is drilled through the centre, threaded on the hook length and stopped so that it rests against the hook. I usually use a float of about nine to twelve inches. The idea is that the carp will approach the bait and although it may have seen line further back, all it actually sees when viewing the bait is a small juicy offering resting against a dead twig. I have used this method very successfully on a number of occasions. The diagram more

1 Above   *The beauty of an estate lake in the summer.*

2 Right   *Coming up close on a small water.*

3 Above *Never neglect the margins even during the day.*

4 Left *A truly magnificent small water forty.*

5 Opposite (top) *Holding an estate lake carp away from the distant island.*

6 Opposite (bottom) *Gerry Morris's fabulous common.*

7   *A small water mirror taken on a floater.*

8   *An upper double for Martyn Page from a small Norfolk pool.*

9   Opposite   *Chris Turnbull cradles a low twenty from a one acre Norfolk lake.*

10 Above *Martyn Page holds a summer-caught upper double from an estate pool.*

11 Left *John Bailey leans into a small water common.*

12 Opposite *A jubilant Dan Leary deservedly nurses Eric at last.*

13 A lovely common caught in the last
light of dusk.

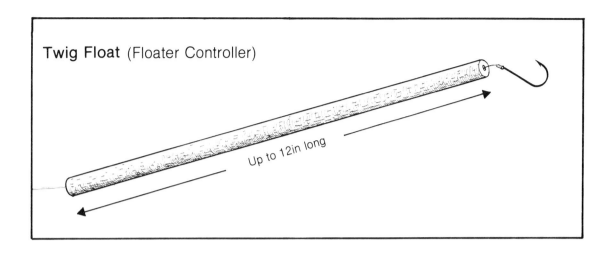

Twig Float (Floater Controller)

Up to 12in long

*John Bailey holds a big mirror that fell to
a hair rigged floater.*

accurately explains the presentation. An alternative is to use a cylinder of foam, such as the new Marvic boilie foam, threaded on the line just above the hook.

FLOATER FLOATS

This is an ideal point at which to discuss floater floats. These are important items in surface fishing for not only do they add casting weight to enable perfect distance to be achieved, but they can also be used to help counter the other problems caused by line, drift and drag in anything like a wind. If a bait behaves unnaturally then the carp will view it with suspicion. This will happen where a bow in the line forms and causes the bait to drift faster than any free offerings. A suitable float can be used to assist by enabling the line to be mended without affecting the bait itself.

I have already mentioned that in certain circumstances I prefer freelining or dapping, especially when margin fishing. Inevitably, however, most floater fishing requires a cast of at least a few yards, and

with small particle floaters some weight is needed to assist the casting. I have tried the floating substances, such as Evode putty, as alternatives, but have found the most convenient and best method is a weighted float.

One of the best floats I have ever used was a French bubble float shaped like a torpedo with lead in the bottom. It was made in clear plastic with a red tip. The float had holes in both ends, although passing the line through the top eye proved best. I enlarged this eye to assist the line moving through on a take and painted the tip a fire-coloured orange to aid visibility. These floats originally came in three sizes and the largest enabled a cast of up to forty yards, which proved an asset at times. Unfortunately, my supply ran out and I had to make my own for some years. They are now available again as part of the Gardner range.

Interestingly, the carp seemed to have an imaginative passion for the French floats – time and time again a fish would approach and suck the bottom, even runn-

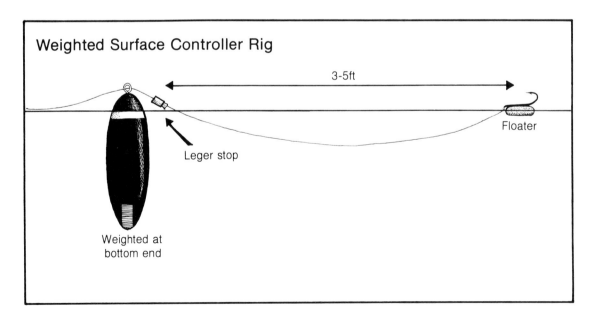

Weighted Surface Controller Rig

3-5ft

Leger stop

Floater

Weighted at bottom end

ing with the float in its mouth for a few yards. One day I decided to stop the float right on top of the hook and attach my hook bait right next to the float. Within minutes a carp approached the float and sucked in as usual, thereby taking the bait at the same time. The result – a fine double. However, I gave up this method out of a sense of ethics as I could not convince myself that the bait had mattered. I believe that a bar hook on the end of the float would have proved just as deadly. However, from that original concept I developed the twig float as a means of overcoming wary fish.

During the years without the French floats, I religiously made my own controllers, improving slightly on design. Ultimately, these prototypes were incorporated into the Middy/Marvic carp bomb which I consider to be the most versatile float controller on the market today – although, naturally, I'm biased.

The carp bomb has had swivels incorporated into both top and bottom to enable a bomb link to be incorporated quickly for static anchorage (particularly effective on windy days). Even though I am extremely satisfied with the end result, I have mutilated one or two of mine by matt finishing them. This is just an extra precaution for ultra-shy carp in order to eliminate any problems associated with sunlight flashing off the glossy body.

Nowadays, there are other floats available following experimentation with antenna-style floats (such as described by Tom Boulton later in this section) for long-range carp fishing, and 'flip'-style antenna (such as that available from Gardner Tackle) which are designed to keep that vital few inches of line off the surface. I have, however, found that shadows from these types of float can cause

problems at times; nevertheless, they are further useful weapons in the armoury. The flip-top floats use a heavily weighted self-cocking antennae so that when the carp takes, the sight bob keels over to lie flat on the surface. Although much experimentation has still to take place, similar ideas will continue to evolve and I fully expect to see other improved floater floats appearing within the next year or two. Having said that, the original French-style bubble float and the Middy carp bomb which I am now using are possibly the most convenient and, for me, have proved the most successful. They also have more uses than the other specialist floats I have tried.

HOOKS

The second biggest problem of floater fishing concerns the hook. Needless to say, its strength and sharpness are crucial to this style, as with any other. There is something even more important for, just as with the line, carp which are wary of floaters will sense danger if anything appears unnatural. The hook, weighing more than the actual bait, will have a tendency to lie under the bait in the water and also to pull the bait down slightly compared with the natural loose feed.

Let me explain further. Anyone who has fished surface baits will have encountered drift problems and baits that behave strangely because of the line drag and resistance. This requires constant line mending and, of course, is less problem with lighter lines. They will also have seen carp shy from a bait on countless occasions for no apparent reason. The fish will have appeared from the off side of the bait and hence not seen the line but still have realised something was wrong. The weight of the hook can do this as can sight of the hook if it is not masked by the bait. Effectively, therefore, it becomes an alarm beacon to the carp. A wary carp will be examining the bait very carefully before making a decision and when it does, it will usually be a grab and run if it is not fully satisfied that there is no threat or danger. If something is obviously wrong, no matter how small, the bait is likely to be ignored. With a large piece of floating crust or floating paste the bait can be used to hide the hook. Then there is only the line problem to overcome. If you are fishing surface particles, however, then the hook is bound to present a problem.

I have tried several methods to overcome this. Firstly, the hook can be hidden between several particles. After a while the carp will wise up to this but it is a very useful and fairly long-lived method on relatively unfished waters. Eventually, however, the carp will only be prepared to take one particle at a time and will ignore any bunch. Then it is necessary to disguise the hook in some way. The use of dyed polystyrene, balsa wood or the new Marvic boilie foam on the hook can be effective when fished in conjunction with a single particle. The aim is to attempt to simulate a small piece of bait and also to keep the hook in the surface layers making it more buoyant. Further use can be made of the twig float described earlier by balancing the hook in the end of the twig with the bait on a small short hair.

Indeed, anything which masks or balances the hook so that it floats is worth a try. For instance, one season I enjoyed excellent success with small, shaped pieces of brown bread crust fished in conjunction with Go Cat. My crust was shaped to look exactly like a piece of Go Cat, but the hook was buried within. This fooled the carp for quite a while whereas all the other trials with Go Cat on the hook were far less successful.

HAIR RIG

We move now to the hair rig. Later, I discuss baits and you will see that most of my surface fishing is with hard cat biscuits which need to be tied on to the hook. This being the case, a form of hair rig is used almost by necessity. However, I am not yet convinced that a hair in the true sense is advisable for most surface fishing. My conclusions over the years are that the hair, for surface fishing, only works well on 'smash and grab' carp and even then there is a tendency to miss fish or indeed even foul hook them.

As I cannot ethically justify to myself the use of a method which causes a high percentage of foul hooking, I do not nowadays use the hair for surface fishing. Instead my baits are tied tightly to the hook and I concentrate more on presenttation, so that the fish happily sucks in the bait unaware of any dangers and then either gently sinks from sight or ambles slowly along towards its next offering. In such circumstances the take may be so gentle that a hair rigged bait would result in the hook remaining outside the mouth.

In summary, both the line and hook are problem areas where constant thought, experimentation and adaptation are needed to ensure consistent results on the more hard fished waters. The float is also an important item as is experimentation with the hook length. Generally it will be found that long hook lengths will result in significant increases in catches. However, there are constraints, such as trying to fish a long hook length in a snaggy swim.

FLOAT LEGERING

English summers are not all glorious, hot, sunny, calm days. All too often the days are wet, the weather cold and far from ideal. Naturally, continuous heavy rain does deter fish from surface feeding. Windy weather, however, can be very productive despite the obvious problems of excessive wind drag and drift. In such conditions, I usually opt for a completely different, perhaps a lazier style. On these occasions, I will change the rig to a float legering method.

There are several forms of rig which can be used depending on the distance required. The method is also of use for long-range floater fishing where the ordinary weighted floats do not achieve the distance. Generally the float running on the paternoster length (*see* diagram) is excellent and on the windy days the takes normally result in a churning reel handle. The constraints of this method are the depth in which one is fishing and hence for deeper waters it is necessary to have the float running on the main hook line and fished with a back stop (as in the diagram).

Whichever method is used the bait will not behave naturally, in that loose feed will drift with the strong wind whereas your bait will remain anchored. However, in these windy conditions the carp do not seem to be adversely deterred by this. Possibly it is because the wind is chopping up the surface and making the line and hook problems less acute. Therefore, carp are less wary and more prepared to take the bait.

Additionally, even very wary carp seem to take bunch baits much more confidently on very windy days. I also prefer to keep my feed on a very tight path on such days so that the carp will move along a trail of

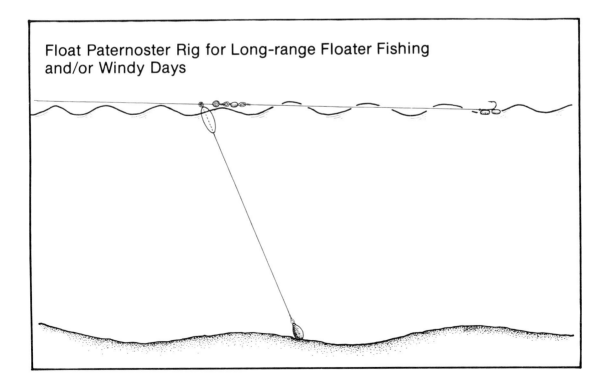

Float Paternoster Rig for Long-range Floater Fishing and/or Windy Days

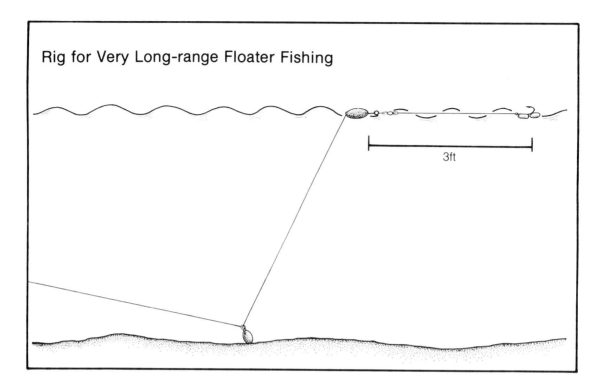

Rig for Very Long-range Floater Fishing

3ft

bait towards the hook offering. To achieve this, PVA strings can be used to good effect. As the PVA melts a steady stream of a dozen baits will drift down in a line attracting the carp to move along that path.

Float legering can, therefore, be a useful method of catching fish from the top. However, it is obviously less exciting than the stalking, closer range float fishing methods.

Baits

I have deliberately left baits until the end of this chapter. The reason is that anything which floats and is edible will catch carp. The traditional floating crust still has a place today in carp fishing although its life is relatively short-lived unless used in a more specific circumstance (such as the brown bread crust described earlier).

There are numerous recipes for floating boilie-type baits available. Basically the use of baking powder and the oven can make virtually anything float. In addition, floating boilies can be bought off the counter in numerous flavours and colours. Large round boilie-type floaters can work very well in areas of scum and dead leaves as they are more visible to the carp swimming underneath than lighter particle floaters. However, once again, my experience is that such floaters have a relatively short useful life.

For me, the temptation to move quickly on to particle floaters is bred from the success I have achieved with them. On a new water I will control this tendency while I explore the avenues of floating crust and one or two other larger floaters.

However, on a water which I know has been fished conventionally, I would immediately start using a particle. The beauty of particles is that you can work the carp into a feeding frenzy and, by fishing to the 'feed and starve' technique described earlier, the carp can become very easy indeed to catch.

My favourite floater was Go Cat until the shape was changed. Originally it was like a Polo mint and much easier to tie onto the hook than the later triangular shape. Go Cat was also unquestionably one of the best floating particles around. I even found that from lake to lake the carp would show preference for particular flavours although beef was the all-time favourite. With the change in the shape of Go Cat I moved on to Munchies. These star shaped baits are easy to present on the hook, either by tying a fine line around the shape and then nicking the hook under the line or by using a baiting needle to pass fine line (1lb BS) through the bait. Of course, there are many more varieties of cat and dog biscuits on the market and the carp seem to like them all.

The Takes

There is one last area which must be discussed. This concerns the actual takes from the fish. Often the fish will rise towards the bait only to turn off at the last second leaving a great boil. Sometimes they will actually pick up the bait between their lips, ejecting it as they surge away. Time and time again I have seen inexperienced floater anglers striking at these abortive takes. The only result is that the fish will quickly become spooked to surface particles and will become harder to catch as they increasingly treat every bait with more and more suspicion.

The golden rule I apply is never to strike until I see the 'whites of their eyes'! Abortive takes should be ignored, despite the temptation to strike, as the carp will frequently come round again and have another go unless it has been alarmed. Constant striking and recasting are not the answer if consistency of results is wanted. When the carp has taken, either the line will stream off or, if it is a gentle take, it will move off purposefully. When the carp has taken properly, it is very rare for it to eject the bait before you have the opportunity to strike.

The situation can become even more tense where the fish are at your feet. In these circumstances, you will actually see the lips engulf the bait. It is crucial not to strike at this stage. Just like a chub, the carp which gently takes in the bait from the surface will purse it between its lips for a few seconds before sucking deeper and then swimming either to the next piece of food or sinking to digest its meal. As the fish moves off, the strike can be made with confidence – not before!

Even having issued the warning concerning striking too soon and too often I appreciate the temptation, for it can be very difficult to restrain a strike. Continued false striking really does ruin floater fishing for all.

Floater Fishing the Layer Way

TOM BOULTON

There are times and places where angling goes, quite simply, crazy. Normal methods fly totally out of the window, the textbook is a mockery and all a man's experience counts for nothing. All he can do is sit back and marvel. Such was the case at Layer Pits, near Colchester.

Layer became a legend. It also became a most remarkable carp water. Many heard of the pit through the grapevine, but the rumours did not always put across the truth. Of course, the pit was carp fished conventionally and still produced very big fish. It was also very heavily match fished and it was from these Goliath 'carp' matches that the strangest stories emerged.

Essex County matchman and Norwich tackle dealer, Tom Boulton, heard that we were including a chapter on surface fishing in this book and suggested that there has never been carping off the top quite like those Layer matches. Hearing his account of surface fishing match style we tend to agree.

The History of Layer

Layer is something over twenty-five acres in extent and is actually fed by one of Colchester's reservoirs. The pit is enormously rich in daphnia, but vegetation is restricted, in part because of weed killer infiltrating from the reservoir. For this reason, in the 1970s spawning was restricted and a fisheries expert was called in to advise. His solution was to create an artificial spawning site. Trees, rush matting and branch cuttings were sunk into one of the shallower bars. This work coincided with the hot summer of 1976. Water temperatures rose and for possibly the first time the stock of old carp spawned successfully.

In 1977 the early season matches produced large bags of pole caught carp babies. Jimmy Randall, for example, took 140 fish for 20lb plus. Angling pressure led to increased food supplies and the growth of the fish was rapid. By September a bag of eighty fish weighed in at 50lb and the following June individuals were topping the 1½lb mark. These fish were becoming hard on the pole, stretching even elastic gear to the limit and the first stage of fishing was all but at an end.

The move from the pole was to the lead at longer range with heavy caster laced ground baiting. Tom himself caught 30lb in what was a no hope area by cashing in on the change early. But even small carp learn quickly and a progression to light lines and small hooks was soon necessary. Range had to be increased and sensitive quiver tips and swing tips were soon in use.

Fish were lost and lead and hook links were juggled with. Rigs close to the bolt were used and the bites became screamers. The churning reel handle was a new sight in match fishing circles and attracted the attention of all the big club outfits. Ivan Marks and Johnny Rolfe were fishing at adjacent pegs in this period. Rolfe lost his entire rod to a fish and, hearing the splash, Marks asked him if he had had a bite. There was a pause and Rolfe replied 'Might have had a knock a minute ago!'

In 1980 the carp were still growing. Some were topping seven pounds and five

A big carp rides high in the water excited by the floating food around him.

pounds was the norm. Though light lines were still standard, the fish were wary of the leads and beginning their move off the bottom. Now the match men began to pursue them on the drop. Legering still, they used twelve to thirteen foot rods with a ten to twelve foot hook length. The bait, therefore, was on a very long drop and bites were coming on the way down. To slow the drop even further, floating casters were used as the bait to counterbalance the weight of the hook.

Great care was taken with the ground bait. The intention was to produce a slow sinking curtain of bait from top to bottom which would have the carp milling at all levels looking for food. Feed was heavy and the bites were very bold. Winning bags were sixty to eighty pounds of

these fish, now edging towards doubles.

The next phase, 1980 to 1981, was taken by the club as much as by the fish themselves. A series of evening fixtures was arranged that would be float-only matches. This was a serious attempt to achieve more sensible fishing methods, but it backfired or rather it heralded the beginning of the big float era.

THE BIG FLOAT ERA

The carp would not pick up bottom baits or indeed baits within the standard float range. Match anglers being inventive, the solutions were soon forthcoming. Shot was taken off the line. Reel line of 2½lb was fixed to a 6lb shock leader and from the float ran a 10ft 1½lb length to a size 20 hook. Bait was floating caster or floating red maggot. When I say float, I do not mean any ordinary float, not any float either you or I have seen before, rather a two foot long float, especially made; able to carry well over an ounce of lead; able to be cast the range of a bomb; arrow-shaped and sliding, visible at eighty odd yards.

Ground bait was still very important, partly to attract the fish and get them up and partly to mask the presence of the line lying on the surface. A film of bait particles provided the back cloth against which the line merged in well. Ground baiting techniques varied and even included floating swim feeders.

Big weights were still taken, but now of big fish. Tom took three fish for 37lb and Bob Cheeseman landed an upper 20lb fish again on 1½lb bottom. This, of course, led to absurdities: in a five hour match, four and a half of those hours could be spent playing fish. Heavier tackle meant a rapid decline in bites. One attempt to overcome this was to move into more exotic ground

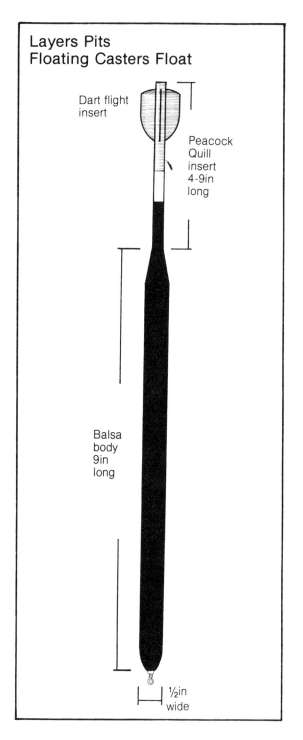

Layers Pits
Floating Casters Float

Dart flight insert

Peacock Quill insert 4-9in long

Balsa body 9in long

½in wide

A lovely common 'scaled like a Norman man-at-arms' taken on floater at sixty yards.

baits. Additives, essences and colourings were now used to even greater extent. Green ground bait, blue rice and odours that could drift yards down the bank became part of this bizarre match scene.

Applications

We believe that the Layer scene has some messages for the floater fisher. Remember that before going on to the top proper, the match men did well on the drop. This is a little used technique in standard carping circles.

John Bailey in particular has done well with dog biscuits, boiled just long enough to take in water. They expand and with the hook weight added, they sink very slowly and for a short while prove irresistible to carp wary of true top bait.

The big float itself is a very useful tool on larger waters. John Bailey has made some up himself and finds he can far outcast normal bubble float gear. This increased range has given him the edge on a Norfolk pit which is fished hard on the top. His results have outclassed those of others for this simple reason.

We feel that the complex floating ground bait does have a definite place. The sight, smell and sound of this going in does draw fish fast and does put them in an avid feeding mood. We include therefore a basic recipe to be used and then individualised as you wish. We do have doubts, however, about the use of 1½lb hook lengths. A water has obviously to be snag-free to even contemplate this type of tackle, but even then the strain of such long fights must show on the fish themselves.

FLOATING GROUND BAIT RECIPE
The essential ingredient is floating casters. These are mixed with floating breakfast cereals, for example, cornflakes, sugar puffs, rice crispies and so on.

A usual addition is Uncle Ben's long grain rice, sinking slowly, often dyed (blue is the current colour). Floating hempseed can be used in conjunction – baked first to become buoyant.

All these ingredients are mixed up in a normal cereal ground bait as a carrier. This can be dyed and flavoured.

Constant experimentation is necessary. These are only basic guidelines. For example, alga red and yellow (made by Sensas Groundbaits) are both being used as additives and as carriers.

Winter Carp Fishing

GRAHAM COWDEROY

The first days that make up the typical English summer seem to pass me by only too quickly nowadays, mainly because of work commitments. When I should be out behind the rods on those warm June nights, I find myself hard at work, bagging the bait up so that other people can be out there fishing. I am not complaining – far from it, I always used to like fishing from October onwards, even before becoming involved with the bait business. I have always found the fish to be in peak condition and at their highest weights at this time of year onwards.

Most people consider November as the start of their winter season. I personally do not go along with this, as some Novembers can be unusually mild. Therefore, I generally consider the first few heavy frosts of the year to herald the start of my winter season and these normally fall between the middle and the end of November.

Water Temperature

The first golden rule I learnt early on in my winter carp fishing exploits was to throw away my thermometer. I found that it knocked my confidence for six after turning up at the lake and finding that the water temperature had fallen below forty degrees Fahrenheit. For was not this the temperature when the carp stop feeding? Or at least this was what all the angling

books would have me believe. I now fish on, regardless of water temperatures, unless the lake has frozen over completely. I look back now and regret the time I have spent indoors whiling away the hours, when the only thing that was keeping me from fishing was the belief that water

'A bitter spell of weather when the lakes and the streams were frozen.'

temperature was the key factor to the fish feeding. Obviously it does play a part in the fish's behaviour, but I do not take it as a guide as to whether or not I should fish in the same way as I used to.

Back in the days of Dick Walker and the Carp Catchers Club, nearly everyone stopped fishing around the October time, in the belief that the carp were holed up almost in a state of hibernation, buried in the silt at the bottom of the lake. To a certain extent this belief is true and this does sometimes happen. Obviously the carp do not bury themselves, but they do lie up almost motionless on the bottom for long periods. Fish I have caught in the latter part of the season prove this, for when they were inspected, it was found that they had literally hundreds of tiny leeches attached to their bodies. These can only attach themselves if the fish has been lying up on the lake bed for some time.

I feel this so-called hibernation period in the colder months can be avoided, providing you can keep the fish interested in searching for food and generally moving about. A lot of people in the past have advocated fishing just stringers or very small amounts of free offerings. This is fine on hard fished waters where you have anglers on the banks seven days a week and can be sure that a regular amount of bait has been going in before you fish. To use a lot of bait in this case would be pointless for the fish are almost certainly active at times over the period of twenty-four hours, and you would be reducing the chances of the fish finding a hook bait. This is especially so as the amount of time they actually spend searching for food can be very short compared with summer months. On the waters that are not fished on a regular basis there is a great chance that the fish will lie up all winter unless you can keep a steady flow of baits going in to interest and occupy the fish. By this, I do not mean use as much as you would in the warmer months' pre-baiting schemes, but introducing a couple of bait mixes every week on a regular basis during the winter before actual fishing can certainly help to keep the fish active and generate a searching behaviour pattern. If the fish do stop moving about and feeding it will be almost impossible to regain their interest even with regular baiting, and fishing will be very hard until the water warms with the rise in temperatures in spring.

Classic examples of this are the two waters I am currently fishing, Darenth and Homersfield. On Darenth I can usually be sure of a couple of fish per session, mainly due to the number of people fishing and the fact that the lake in question is particularly barren of natural food. The fish's diet consists, therefore, mainly of anglers' bait and I can be sure a fair amount has gone into the lake prior to my own fishing.

At Homersfield it is a different situation. The water can sometimes go weeks with very few people actually fishing it and, therefore, there are no regular supplies of bait going in to keep the fish active. As the water is a fair distance away I cannot do any pre-baiting, so, because of all this, on the occasions I fish it I find it hard going. To make affairs worse, the water is also very rich in natural food. Therefore, once the fish's metabolism has slowed they show hardly any interest in anglers' baits, as they can obtain all they need to sustain themselves from small amounts of natural food which is abundant around them. The odd fish I have managed to catch there in the winter have all had signs of leeches on their bodies, which proves they have been dormant for a fair time.

Obviously they do occasionally feed when they are in this dormant state, but they travel no distance to do it and generally just eat what is within close proximity to them. Some of the fish I have caught at Homersfield back this theory, as when I have been lucky enough to get a take it has generally come within minutes of casting. Presumably I have placed a bait within inches of a fish who has sucked it in without having to move or use any energy to find it. As I believe this is a sound theory, I always work with three rods in winter where legally possible, casting each one regularly to different areas, leaving them there for half an hour or so before rebaiting and hoping that the next cast will land close to a fish.

Location

Location, as in summer, is extremely important, though finding the fish in the winter is obviously much harder as the fish very rarely show themselves. If the water is dead calm you may pick out the odd patch of bubbles but this cannot always be taken as a betrayal of the fish's presence, as in winter there is always a fair amount of decaying weed and leaves on the lake bed giving off gases which can be mistaken for the bubbles of a feeding fish. Small vortexes may also be noticed if the water is calm enough as the fish just tip the surface with their fins, as opposed to the heavy rolling they do in the summer. Generally though, no visual signs are made to assist in their location.

In this situation after a walk around the lake has revealed nothing to go by, I generally opt for areas that I know have been good in the autumn unless there is a really prominent wind signifying that another area might be better. I do not pay as much attention to wind conditions in the winter for I find that unless it is really howling down the lake, and has been for some days, the fish very rarely move on it. The autumn areas I pick are normally ones with gravel and sand bar features, where I fish the deeper gullies as opposed to the bar tops as I would in the summer. These gullies are generally the deepest areas of the lake and can vary from about eight to fifteen feet. I generally go for the deepest water I can find near to known productive areas.

When I have found the area that I intend to fish and have actually set up, I find it pays to be very observant and keep a constant eye on the water looking for any tell-tale signs of fish. This has often led to me moving several times in a day, but at the end of it I have invariably been rewarded with a fish or two for my efforts. I know this sounds a common-sense approach, but you would be surprised at the number of anglers I see just whacking the baits out, diving in the bivvy and failing to notice fish moving at the opposite end of the lake.

Rigs

Once in a swim, we come to the tackle and rigs, which are not materially different to summer gear really. Therefore, I will not dwell here too long. The one rig I find to be marginally better in winter is a rig I call the Buoyant Hook Rig (see diagram) which involves a boiled bait an inch or so up the hook length. The hook is then made buoyant by the use of a small piece of cork or polystyrene. When cast out the weight of the bait anchors the hook. It is, in fact, a similar principle to the pop-up rig where a weight is used to anchor the bait a distance from the bottom, but here the weight is the

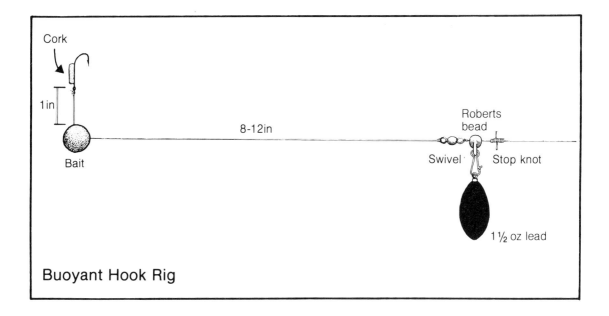

Buoyant Hook Rig

bait and the hook is set a distance from the bottom.

The beauty of this rig is that as the hook is buoyant it is the first thing to enter the fish's mouth should it suck at the bait. I use this in conjunction with a shortish hook length and a heavy fixed lead, which tends to shake the fish from its dormant position and turn what would normally be barely noticeable twitch bites into steady easily hit runs. This rig has already been published in some form in various angling publications, but it was illustrated without the buoyant hook aspect. As a result it was quickly dismissed on the grounds that a high proportion of the fish caught on it were being foul hooked. This is totally unjustifiable and, therefore, should never be used except in conjunction with a buoyant hook. I have fished the rig now for some time and found it to be very effective. With most fish landed on it the hook was neatly embedded some way into the mouth.

As I have already mentioned, in a lot of cases the fish are lying dormant, and even when they have decided to pick up a hook bait and have felt the hook, some fish are still reluctant to stir from their position. They just sit there sucking and blowing in an effort to eject the hook – sometimes for several minutes. Obviously if they cannot shed the hook, they will eventually move sufficiently to register a bite at the indicators. I have witnessed this several times at Homersfield, where the only indication I had was a slight knocking of the rod tip. Originally I put this down to line bites, but it happened regularly enough to make me change my mind. After all, fish that are not moving about much will not cause a series of liners. I then took it that these knocks of the rod tip were fish sucking and blowing at my hook bait and decided to wind down and hit the slightest twitch. I was pleasantly surprised at the solid resistance of a hooked fish on most occasions. Since then if this twitching occurs at any time, summer or winter, I will always strike it and often contact with a fish. I now look back and regret all those missed chances I put down to liners. With this twitcher hitting style I will also endeavour to fish a tight line clipped at the butt and use heavy indicators to register the slightest drop back. Obviously, this is not always possible, especially when fishing small lakes and pits at close range so I always pay particular attention to the rod tips for any signs.

Baits

Whilst fishing a water on a regular basis through the winter, I find that the short feeding spells that occur can become very predictable. This is obviously a great help if the water is local, as a visit to the lake can be timed to coincide with known feeding times and this does away with most of those cold, dark winter nights.

In most cases I have found the most productive time of all the winter waters I fish is between 10 a.m. and about 4 p.m. However, this pattern may change slightly due to weather conditions – which incidentally I have not found to follow what others have written on the subject. The occasional calm overcast and mild days of winter do not appear to fish as well as the cold windier days when water temperatures are falling. My explanation is that on waters that are barren of natural food (generally termed hungry waters) the fish tend to rely mainly on anglers' baits. With the sudden drop in temperature the fish seem to sense a freeze coming and as this means no more food for a while they go on a feeding spree. These same waters obviously fish well immediately after a thaw, as it has been some time since the fish were able to find food and they tend to snatch at most baits cast to them. Some of my quickest winter fishing has been done at

these times and often with the lake still partially frozen.

Bait is a very complex subject at the best of times, but in winter it plays an even bigger part of catching. It is not so much protein content, but the attractor and visual aspect that is so important. A few years ago the general trend was for protein in the summer and carbohydrate in the winter, and that the baits should be of a smaller size than the summer. I do not particularly agree with this, as the fish can still convert and utilise a certain amount of protein even in the coldest conditions, but because of its slowed metabolism it just doesn't require as much to fulfil its nutritional needs. Because of this I use the same protein bait as I do in the summer – a reasonably high milk protein. I do tend to add a little more vitamin and mineral supplement in winter as I feel that as the fish are only eating small quantities of bait, they may, on the hungry waters, become deficient in this as there are no natural alternatives.

Over the past few seasons I have been using a fish-meal in conjunction with milk protein and a certain oil which has been extremely effective. Its viscous nature has meant I have had to use an oil emulsifier to enable it to disperse from the bait. I would have liked to have continued its use into the winter, but unfortunately after several experiments I found that the oil could not be made to release from the bait sufficiently for me to be confident of its attractiveness. However, I did not want to drop the fish-meal as this was also part of the attractor, with its pungent smell and texture. I wanted a liquid attractor as well, something that would release easily from the bait in the cold water and radiate all around it.

After a sort through the bait cupboard, I

Above left   *Snow on the ground, cat ice on the pool and the carp is hooked.*

Above right   *The twenty year old Mark IV bends into a half-circle.*

Right   *John Bailey holds a plump double for a second in the below zero temperatures.*

came up with some highly water-soluble liquid alcohol based flavours, of which one was suited to the fish flavour bait. These flavours are really the only ones to use in water temperatures in the low forties and below, because you can be sure they are doing their job. Even in boiled baits they still give off a good scent. They are obviously better in a paste bait, but due to fairly long-range fishing nowadays and the problem of nuisance, fish pastes are out.

When using a fish-meal bait I find it hard to determine its colour, for even when dyes are used the end result is a brown. I now just leave them their natural colour – a fawny brown. With visibility being a relevant factor I feel confident with this, although some of my friends prefer a lighter colour, such as yellow, in winter when greater depths are being fished. Some people are the complete opposite, preferring greens and blues when fishing deep water in the belief that they are a more visible colour to the fish. I would not like to comment on that theory as I have not tried them to any great extent alongside other colours.

Particle baits can be very successful in winter, although in my case I have always found that boilies seem to attract the bigger fish for some reason. However, in winter a fish is a fish regardless of its size, and I have used several particle baits to great success. I have found chick peas to be more effective than the usual peanuts or tigers in the winter – possibly due to their light colour. Their effectiveness can be increased if, instead of soaking them in water, they are soaked in milk and a heavy amount of flavour and sweetener. I think the milk adds to their attractiveness by giving off a cloud effect when put in the lake. This cloud also helps carry the flavour.

Feeding

The amount of any bait you use in winter is a very debatable point, but I feel you can normally put out more particles than boilies and also cover a wider area, and still feel you have not overdone the baiting. The fish in waters where there is an abundance of natural food are likely to pick up far more particle baits than boilies to achieve the same dietary satisfaction. On one particular water I occasionally fish, particles have out-scored boilies for the past two seasons and this has coincided with a boom in the natural food chain. I think it is a case of the fish being more adapted to feeding on multiple substances, and since this occurrence has come to light I feel it is safe to say that the boilie is the best approach on the hungry water and the particle a good bet on the weedy waters high in natural food substances.

Accuracy in placing free offerings is very important, and can be a problem on many waters where distances in excess of sixty yards are to be fished. Catapults seem to be very ineffective nowadays, due to the increased numbers of waterfowl about. One crack of the Black Widow Sling Shot and the sky is full of gulls and every tufted duck in England is in front of you! If a bait does get past the gull, it will invariably end up supplementing a fat tufty's diet!

Nowadays I use a bait dropper. It is good for distances up to eighty yards and holds about ten to fifteen boilies. It sorts the gulls out and for the time being has fooled the ducks – though I hear in some waters the ducks have cottoned on to this and home in on the splash of the dropper. With accuracy in mind, the dropper I use has the polystyrene cone at the bottom painted fluorescent orange and is highly visible even at eighty yards. After the last cast, it can be left out and used as a marker before you retrieve it.

Another method that seems to be catching on fast is the use of a radio-controlled boat, which can be designed to take out your hook bait and several free offerings. Obviously this is a very accurate way of presenting a bait, but it is also very expensive, with prices around £150 plus for the radio gear alone. There is also the problem of them being banned on some waters, and really, is it very ethical?

For short-range work when the ducks prevent the use of a catapult, various swim feeders can be used. They are an effective way of ensuring that you have a few baits in close proximity to your hook bait and I prefer to use these rather than a PVA stringer. In the cold water the PVA takes a long time to dissolve and this leads to false takes, as the fish attempt to take baits still attached to the stringer.

Another method I have found effective for getting the scent of the attractor around the hook bait is to use an open-ended feeder on the line packed with foam rubber. To this you can add a dilute solution of the attractor every cast, which, when in the water, will seep out radiating all around. Hopefully this will give something for the fish to home in on.

Some angling companions of mine are currently using the match anglers' ground bait bomb. This is a small skeleton frame in the shape of a conventional casting lead, but much larger. It also has a swivel attached to the top. To this, they mould a ground bait carrying their attractor. It is heavy enough to be used as your casting weight, but is limited to close-range work. For long range, you can mould a paste around your casting lead, which is slightly stiffer than the bait and can withstand a fair cast. I have not tried this latter method, although I understand from those who have that it is an excellent way of getting your attractor around the hook bait at extreme range. The only problem I can foresee with this, is that you may get the occasional false take if a fish attempts to pick it up.

The only thing left to say is that winter carp fishing is to be enjoyed and is not an endurance test. If you keep warm and dry, which nowadays is a relatively easy job with all the specialist thermal gear on the market, I feel you will fish more confidently and efficiently than you would if you sat there on the bank shivering with cold, wishing you were at home. Like me, you might put a few fish on the bank, possibly with snow all around you. This is surely the ambition for many a winter carp angler. If there is one outstanding lesson I have learnt, it must surely be that the carp's ideal feeding time in winter does not always coincide with what a lot of books have had to say about it in the past. My advice would finally be to fish on confidently, regardless of any weather conditions that you meet.

Carp Baits

TIM PAISLEY

Naturals, bread, sweetcorn, luncheon meat, specials, protein baits, high nutritional value baits, particles, floaters ... Even for experienced carp men the carp world bait scene is a complex one. To the beginner, the reason for so many alternatives must be a mystery. Why *are* there so many different baits for carp when the choice of most of the species for which the match angler fishes usually lies between maggots and casters? The answer to that is, quite simply, that carp learn by their mistakes to a greater extent than any other fish the majority of us encounter. Productive baits and presentations gradually diminish in effectiveness until they stop catching carp.

Because of this, it is important to understand why and when the various baits and presentations are at their most effective. These vital aspects of carp fishing are not a question of fashion; they are applied to produce the best results in the circumstances that prevail on any given water at any one time and are often greatly influenced by what has gone before on that water.

I will give a simple example of what I mean by that. Sweetcorn is, or was, one of the best carp baits of all time. It has its limitations because it has been fished out on most known carp waters and because it is not an easy bait to fish effectively at long range. The same can be said of luncheon meat in its various forms. Meat was a very popular, and successful, bait during the 1970s and once the carp were really on it, it could be difficult to interest them in anything else. So, be sure that meat and corn have been exhausted on a water before you start complicating the issue and wading into the carp bait undergrowth.

Earlier, I mentioned naturals. They still have an important place in carp fishing. On waters where they have not been hammered (usually only newish carp waters), maggots and casters can be very effective and it is possible to achieve a high degree of preoccupation on them. In addition, most naturals are good stalking baits, and maggots or worms put to carp feeding naturally can bring instant results.

On many carp waters there has been a progression of baits down the years, most changes being dictated by the increasing wariness of the carp through being caught. Once a water is under pressure and the carp are becoming more difficult to catch, the carp man has to be increasingly aware of the bait alternatives open to him. Over the last fifteen years or so this escalating need to keep one step ahead of the carp has resulted in a number of original thinkers coming up with bait principles and baiting situations which have gradually evolved to the current 'ultimate' bait and presentation combination – mini high nutritional value boilies fished in conjunction with

Swan mussels - undoubtedly one of the carp's natural foods.

the bare hook rigs. The rapidly changing bait scene makes it hard to categorise baits satisfactorily so the following brief explanations are rough and ready to say the least.

The three major principles behind the use of a carp bait on a chosen water are those of preoccupation, attraction and nutrition. You use a bait to get a carp to feed strongly enough to enable you to take the fish off guard and catch it. Preoccupy the fish by making a plentiful food source of tiny baits available; tempt the fish to pick up the bait by including an irresistible source of attraction in the bait; lull the fish into a false sense of security by regularly providing it with an alternative food source better than the diet on which it is feeding.

Seeds and particles are usually used as convenient baits for achieving a degree of preoccupation in the carp's feeding. Why do anglers throw in handfuls of maggots? To achieve an element of preoccupation. The more individual food items a fish has taken before it encounters the hook bait, the more likely it is to make a mistake when it does so and get itself hooked. Accepting the importance of preoccupation, the best types of bait with which to achieve it are small ones the carp will eat a great deal of. My own experience with these types of bait are limited but I have found hemp and white dari to be the most successful of the seeds and they are both fairly instant. Of the particles, I feel sure that tiger nuts, which are instant and have an extremely long bait life, together with peanuts which need pre-baiting, are the best on most waters. These are followed by maples and maize, which also require pre-baiting for best results and black eye beans and chick peas, which are instant. Rod Hutchinson was one of the pioneers of particles and seed fishing and he devotes a great deal of space to the subject in his excellent books *The Carp Strikes Back* and *Carp Now and Then.*

The principle of preoccupation is an important one and can be applied to any type of bait, but as this section is about the baits themselves, rather than presentation, I will discuss the main principles behind the use of 'special' carp baits. The principles fall into roughly two categories, those of short-term *attraction*, which represents an immediate appeal to the carp's senses, and longer-term *stimulation*, which results from satisfying the carp's natural instinct for recognising an exceptional source of nutrition. Because attractor baits tend to be of low food value they were originally dubbed 'crap' baits, which is a convenient name to give them here. The longer-term food baits are usually referred to as protein or HNV (high nutritional value) baits. All specials, crap baits or HNVs, start their lives as soft pastes when they have been mixed. Whether they are used as pastes or boiled depends on the angling situation the carp man wishes to create in his swim. The hook is usually buried in a soft paste bait and exposed with a hard boiled bait, the latter form of bait presentation being used to spook carp into running.

Before the current comprehensive range of flavours became available from tackle dealers, the most widely used attractors came from health shops, pet shops and chemists. Amino acids, yeasts, food and drink flavours, pet food tonics and additives, oils and other chemical stimulants have all been used with varying degrees of success. Many of these are still in use but it cannot be denied that the essential oils, flavours, essences and appetite stimulants currently available in tackle shops and from bait dealers have been responsible for a bait revolution. In the first half of the 1980s bare hook rigs and strongly flavoured, sweetened baits temporarily made carp fishing comparatively easy on some waters. Where quick results are required, the bait that acts as the carrier for the attractors can be of low food value, the emphasis being on attracting the carp to pick up the bait in the first place. It is as well to consider this type of fishing to be based on curiosity value baits. When you intend fishing this principle of instant attraction, do not pre-bait. You cannot teach a carp to eat a smell or a combination of smells. Only pre-bait when you are using a bait of reasonable food value which the carp's system (not its mind) will recognise as a food source.

It should be said that our knowledge of the long-term effects of flavours and sweeteners is limited or non-existent. Nutritionists admit that they have no idea how damaging flavours may be in the long term and a recent report issued by the London Food Commission suggested that saccharin may be a carcinogen. Most of the sweeteners being sold as carp bait additives are based on saccharin!

The base ingredients of typical carp baits are soya flour, semolina, ground rice, layers' mash, ground Weetabix and so on. If the ingredients will mix into a paste with eggs, roll into balls and harden on boiling, you have a bait which will do as a carrier for the attractors.

Nutritional value baits are those which are fished on the basis that the carp will recognise the food value of the bait and will learn to include it in its diet. How nutritional must a nutritional bait be? Well, that will depend on the type of water being fished (the quantity and quality of the natural food available) and the quality of the other baits in use on the water. When you fish a nutritional bait, you are trying to get the carp to accept your bait as one of their main sources of nutrition. For that reason availability is almost as important an aspect as nutritional quality and this type of bait should be fed into the water fairly regularly.

It is almost impossible to put together a bait that is not nutritional to some degree, but this type of bait must provide either something the carp needs and is not getting from its diet (high fat baits are usually successful on this basis) or it must take the place of available food sources. I will make an observation I cannot substantiate and suggest that the more 'natural' a water the more nutritional the bait has to be for the carp to become weaned on to it.

What is nutritional in terms of carp and why is such emphasis placed on protein? All nutritional requirements are covered by the following categories of food: protein, carbohydrates, fats, vitamins and minerals. Fish nutrition experts tell us that carp cannot utilise carbohydrate which means that their essential food sources are protein, fats, vitamins and minerals. It is probable that when water temperatures drop below the level of the melting point of the carp's essential fats (six degrees centigrade is a rough guideline) they cannot use them either. This means that protein, which is their natural food source

anyway, is their main, year round nutrient. Again this is an oversimplification, but it is a practical rather than a theoretical one.

Fred Wilton from Kent theorised nutritional value baits nearly twenty years ago and then managed to put them into practice. Perhaps surprisingly in an area that has seen so much change, a great deal of his initial theory forms the basis of most HNV baits in use today. Popular nutritional bait ingredients include the milk proteins – casein, lactalbumin, sodium and calcium caseinate; soya isolate; the fish proteins – whitefish meal, sardine meal, herring meal, anchovy meal; egg albumin; wheat gluten as a binder. All these are reliable and proven HNV ingredients. Add a vitamin mineral mix from a bait dealer or a pet shop and a good fat source (sesame or olive oil), together with an attractor as a label. Essential oils at low level are very often used in conjunction with HNV baits as a label or attractor.

Be clear in your mind that when you intend to use an HNV bait the food value of the bait is all-important and the necessity for high level instant attraction less so. It is all too easy to aim for the best of both worlds and reduce the attractiveness of the food because of the strength of the attractors. Can you eat Vindaloo curries? Most of you will not be able to, and it does seem that too high a level of attraction has the same deterrent effect with carp in the long term.

One final point about HNV baits. High nutritional value does not necessarily mean high protein level. Yes, high level, good quality protein baits are extremely successful, but so are high level good quality fat baits. In addition, always recognise that nutrition does not come from what you put into a bait but from what the carp's system is able to extract from it.

I have tried to separate the three main principles behind the use of carp baits in this section; preoccupation, attraction by smell, and stimulation by nutrition. Earlier, I referred to the 'ultimate' baiting situation where all three principles are united in the use of high attractor HNV mini boilies. But because carp learn by their mistakes, the word 'ultimate' has a very temporary ring to it when applied to carp fishing tactics.

I cannot help feeling that a good food will always be a good food. The carp's nutritional instinct is a genetic one and such instincts are not easily blunted or extinguished. In terms of attraction the situation is less clear. What attracted yesterday will repel tomorrow. But will it attract again the day after or is there a saturation point where all attractors will repel through abuse?

Carp baits are a progression. The stage of progression varies from area to area and water to water and that is part of the beauty of carp fishing. Baits are as simple or as complex as each individual angler wants them to be. Given the option of one bait to take anywhere, I would have to opt

for tiger nuts, and there can be nothing simpler than soaking a few pounds of nuts. They are small enough to induce pre-occupation; nutritional enough to keep the carp coming back for more; they have a long life and can be used for up to three or four seasons on some waters; they are hard, which means that the carp sucks them back to the throat teeth to eat them; they are instant, which means that they must have an attraction value that is not apparent to us. Five points worth considering because they emphasise the fact that while a bait is a food, it is also an angling principle.

I have left that paragraph as it stands from the first edition, but I should add that a number of people are becoming increasingly apprehensive about the long-term effects of tiger nuts. Waters that are heavily baited with tigers during the early part of the season seem to 'produce' poor results as the year wears on, and there is some evidence that abuse of baiting levels with tigers can physically damage the carp, although there is no solid scientific evidence to this effect yet.

Baits: One Man's Progress

LEN BUNN

More than other types of angling, carp fishing this century has gone through several marked stages. Perhaps we can identify the first as running from H.T. Sheringham at the turn of the century to B.B. in the 1950s. It was these two angling writers that sparked off so much interest in carp fishing. They spoke of its beauty, its fascination and its difficulties. They sowed the seeds for the pioneers of the second stage, the giant of which was the late Richard Walker. He and B.B. were friends; they collaborated. They were fellow members of that earliest and greatest specimen group, the Carp Catchers Club. The first movement flowed quite naturally, therefore, into the second.

Walker was uniquely brilliant as an angler in general and as a carp fisher in particular and he gathered around himself friends nearly as exciting. We are into the 1950s now and talking of men like Pete Thomas, Pat Russell and the Taylor brothers. Quite special to both John Bailey and Martyn Page was Maurice Ingham, co-author with Walker of *Drop me a Line*. First published in 1953, no other book gives a better insight into the way that these carping innovators felt their way from problems, to theories, to solutions. They built their own rods and landing nets. They experimented with tackle and baits. They popularised night fishing and camped by the water. They believed dreams could

be caught – and they were! Walker's 44lb carp, Thomas' 28lb fish and Ingham's 24lb fish were all proof of the second stage in the carping revolution.

The 1960s saw a new take-off. The decade was dominated by Jack Hilton and his associates. Carp fishing's charisma was now assured. Carp were still not shorn of their mystery – they never can be – but they were being caught in greater numbers by men of experience. Great research was being carried out and almost impossible waters gradually came to be conquered. Lenny Bunn was one of the great names of this period of carp fishing.

Both John Bailey and Martyn Page were carping in Norfolk by this time, John after serving an apprenticeship in the northwest, and the magical figure of the time was Lenny Bunn. His name was special. His skills, his research, his results were talked of everywhere. He caught Norfolk carp that had never been caught before. For both John and Martyn his contribution to carping was vast: he made the landing of monsters seem a possible goal – more so even than B.B., Walker or Hilton who seemed more remote, less accessible. Lenny Bunn fished our waters – *and he caught*.

Lenny began carp fishing in 1963 and failed totally in his first year. What there was to read, Walker mainly, he did read and during the season of 1964 he set about Taverham Pits. He filled them with floating crust and for one glorious day cracked that most difficult water, with three fish to sixteen pounds. He stayed on there for four years still struggling, still learning, feeling his way. His best season saw seven fish on the bank. The going, then, was difficult.

By the late 1960s he met up with the young Nigel Dennis, who on trout pellets equalled the seven in a season record. Things began to hot up. Together, Lenny and Nigel moved on to faster waters, particularly the Waveney Valley complex and tasted long-range fishing there.

After two years, in the early 1970s, Lenny then fished with Dick Weale and the legendary partnership began. Together they blew open both Waveney and the still feared Taverham Pits. Increasingly, baits dominated Lenny's thinking. At that time baits were the vogue; they were the edge that was believed to put a man ahead.

For a while trout pellet and luncheon meat kept them on top and even that other notorious Norfolk lake, Clearwater, yielded thirteen fish. In 1974 the bait breakthrough for Lenny and Dick happened when they met the protein pioneer, Fred Wilton. That connection was vital. What followed made carp fishing history

A historic shot of one of Lenny's Waveney bags.

Many of the more experienced carp anglers will recognise this shot, it advertised the Black Magic bait.

in no small way.

Lenny and Dick were convinced that Fred's protein theories were of value and they began the serious search for an ultimate bait. They contacted Doctor Pawson at the Lowestoft Fishery Research Centre who was working on the effect of amino acid on sea fish. On his leads, they researched into Japanese literature on fish breeding, they met research chemists and began to develop the amino acid baits that were to make them famous. At first, though, they neither knew how to make them into a bait or even how to use them and they experimented along the guide-lines of the chemists. In the closed season they poured amino acids straight into one of their difficult lakes, not made-up, but neat into the margins. Carp came into the areas and stirred them to a ferment. The two men knew they were on the edge of bait revolution.

The 1976 season came closer and the aminos were mixed into standard bait recipes. Believing carp were wary of bright colours, the baits were made up black: 1976 was to be the year of Black Magic. Lenny and Dick became the talking point of first Norfolk and then of England. In Norfolk alone that year they landed thirty carp over twenty pounds. Taverham, Clearwater, Waveney were all conquered – Waveney 'D' lake even produced five twenty-pound fish in a morning and five smaller fish, whilst no one else recorded a bite. Everyone's faith in the ultimate bait was reinforced. For several years to come, carping effort began to be channelled into bait research.

Particles

In 1977 Lenny moved on to Redmire and on to the second phenomenon that revolutionised the era – the particle bait. Immense work on this had been done by others before Lenny, by Rod Hutchinson and Chris Yates to name but two, and Lenny at first struggled.

His first session was a nightmare. Fishing hemp, he had carp in the swim almost constantly, feeding avidly, digging a hole in the bottom almost, and yet he could not catch. He returned to Norfolk, to find a duplicate water, to work the method out and return with it to Redmire. Again Lenny took Norfolk apart. Again all we ordinary carpers heard the rumours and gasped. In six weeks at Clearwater he hooked twenty-three carp and landed twenty-one, all on particles. His success, almost unbelievable at that time, was the result of overcoming false bites. Simply, his hooks were baited with seeds and cork until an exact balance was created. He returned to Redmire to land a twenty-one pound common.

By now Lenny had risen to the top rung of the carping ladder, helped, he thought then, by his use of and research into better baits. At Redmire he worked a lot on tackle – on hooks, lines, knots and balanced hook rigs. He insisted that all his gear be perfect and with that, used in conjunction with the most acceptable baits, he would catch big fish. He used particle fishing though, for these Redmire fish made him recognise one skill that he had always possessed and until then had not given full credit to – his water craft.

Today, he puts more emphasis on his water knowledge to explain his success than he ever did then, concentrating so much on bait. It was at Redmire that he used all the knowledge of carp and water reading that he had built up so steadily at Taverham, Clearwater, Waveney and the rest.

A realisation of carp catching rules emerged: find the fish; find their feeding times; find the bait. He always spent hour upon hour at his waters, simply watching for cruisers, feeders and all pointers to carp behaviour. He had never put baits out at random, only tight in feeding areas. Margin fishing suited his delicate approach well. He could put all his baits in the area of a saucer, perhaps with a pea shooter, perhaps slid down a drainpipe. Along the margins he could use his mastery of close control, and, above all, read the fish's exact reactions.

Taverham is a case in point. There the carp used a shelf swim when it was not fished. As soon as lines appeared on the shelf, either tight or slack, the carp moved away. Lenny fixed two five-pound lines tight across the shelf and anchored them permanently until the carp saw them as a fitting of the place and would feed with the lines rubbing their very backs. The tied lines were then replaced by tackle and the fish were at last catchable from the area.

Lenny Bunn 'retired' from carping some five years ago to devote his time to bird-watching. Angling has lost one of its giants and we both know that if he ever returned to his rods he would be a day learning the latest development and within a week would be back at the top.

An Interview with Fred Wilton

We end this section with an interview between our artist, Chris Turnbull, and Fred Wilton on the banks of Johnson's Lake in Kent. Fred, we believe, has altered the whole bait concept. More than any man living he has initiated single-handedly a bait revolution and yet there are few men living who really understand what he has done!

Fred's theories have been well documented in the past, notably in *Carp and the Carp Angler,* (Sharman, 1980). To précis his findings, Fred discovered the principle of high nutrient value bait (HNV). The theory is based on a belief that fish can recognise the nutritional value of the foods they are eating and digesting and will instinctively choose HNV in preference to anything else – including natural foods – in the water at the time. Therefore, the higher the nutritional value the more the bait will be preferred and the closer we are to the ultimate bait.

All Fred's baits are based on a very high protein content of which, almost invariably, the leading ingredient is casein. However, much experimentation has taken place around Fred's initial theories and, as will be seen, Fred considers that much of this has digressed, has been misguided and has often produced less efficient baits.

Here, Fred clearly spells out possible future problems and benefits of the bait revolution. Clearly there is still room for development on HNV principles, but where, Fred wonders, could it lead.

C.T. It's been a long time since your HNV bait ideas first hit the angling world. Do you think they have progressed as far as possible?

F.W. There are certainly areas where further progress can be made, but there are problems. Although it is worth pursuing, I wouldn't like to see damaged fish as a result. Personally, if I find a bait which I think is damaging fish, no matter how effective, I stop using it. Theoretically, however, there are lots of areas still open for exploration.

C.T. Do you see this exploration as being new ideas in areas which will take over from the HNV bait, or is the HNV bait the final frontier?

F.W. I do not consider that you can alter the basic way in which fish feed and hence the basic HNV principles still apply. There are certainly ways of manipulating these concepts which could produce more takes. I am unsure, however, whether this would prove to be a wise move. Certainly I have been experimenting over the last two years without actually putting the new baits into lakes, as I am not prepared to take any chances until I am absolutely certain no harm will result. When I do, I will keep it to a small water to evaluate the effects.

C.T. Your original baits were mostly milk protein and after a while many carp anglers shifted to vegetable and animal protein to try to create something different. In many cases this amounted to a drop in the protein content of the bait. Do you think that was a wise move, or do you think they lost out in the end?

F.W. I still only use milk proteins, which are of animal origin anyway. But judging by many of the articles I read and comments I hear nowadays, a good number of anglers are off the main line by now and do not fully understand the concepts involved. For instance, there is no advantage in using vegetable protein as 'vegetable proteins' – they should be used in balance with others. On their own account they serve no good purpose.

C.T. It has been claimed that fish grow well when fed on your baits (i.e. HNVs) and many, for instance, say they are responsible for the tremendous average size of the tench in this water. The whole concept of a quality bait enriching the environment, as well as making the fish bigger, and in many cases, the resulting increased weed growth, is extremely interesting. In turn, of course, damaged fish through losses in the weed and the heavier 'bully' tactics needed to land them is quite worrying. Do you think this is something we will see happening in more and more lakes?

F.W. There isn't much doubt about it. Certainly the weed growth will increase in most lakes. It's almost inevitable that HNV baits will enrich the condition of the lake. Every piece of protein introduced remains in one form or the other; either in the form of fish, fish food, in the bottom mud or in the weed. Hence you are completely altering the lake. A fair percentage of the nutrients taken in by fish are not absorbed – if they were, the growth rate would be phenomenal. However, fish pass some of the nutrients out into the water and you then get a secondary use through bacteria, insects, shrimps, snails, etc. Other fish will share it too. And as the breakdown continues, you will still be left with the fact that proteins all contain nitrogen, and hence, sooner or later, a certain amount will be released in the water, which will in turn assist weed growth. The type and quality still largely depends on the lake itself, but there will be an increase in weed growth once the baits have been used for a long time in any particular water.

It will affect the lake in other ways. For instance, the tonnage of fish that can be supported in the lake will increase. This will not necessarily mean the size, it could mean the numbers of the fish population. Indeed, this could happen in preference to the size increase. Certain weed affords protection for fry and provides better food supplies. Hence more fry may survive, thereby the lake's population increases. The degree to which this may happen depends upon the lake itself. We must wait and see whether the final result on a particular water is bigger fish throughout, or more fish. Carp, of course, will not increase their numbers in lakes where they do not successfully spawn.

C.T. Most carp fisheries will then have received the benefit of increased weight of the carp, with other fish we may see increased populations.

F.W. Indeed, if we look back at 1969 when Savage first wrote articles in the press on sausage, sardine pastes etc. (and these are in many ways versions of these HNV baits), such baits were thrown in for

John Bailey holds a good twenty-pounder taken on an HNV bait.

carp, but being soft-skinned, other fish could cope with them. In addition, the 'pass through' effect still applied. It can be seen, therefore, that this changing of the water's ecology has been going on for some years now.

I am sure carp and tench will keep growing. I don't think there is a limit, just limiting factors set by a particular lake. I can see no reason why we shouldn't see huge carp. They haven't the problems of gravity which stop us growing too big. Lake Cassein shows that huge sizes are possible, and although temperature has some bearing, we are dealing with fish which live a tremendous length of time. For instance, when we first fished Darenth some years ago now, we had fish to 19lb 14oz, and lots of fish. During the following closed season no one seemed interested in Darenth because it wasn't producing 20lb plus fish. I was convinced that it would be the following season as a result of all our baiting, and said so. The next season an enormous amount of 20lb plus fish came out with the best at 27½lb. These fish were estimated at eighteen years old, and put on some 7½lb in a year – that's a one-third increase in body weight in a year!

Proportionally, if you could put that amount of weight on some of the fish around these days, you are talking about some enormous fish. There are, of course,

14 Derrick Amies, the record pike
    holder, wades into Cassein to keep
    a fish from the boulders.

15 Netted at last.

16 Derrick holds his prize under the
    blazing Mediterranean sun.

17   *Ritchie MacDonald holds a 43lb Cassein mirror.*

18 Dave Plummer, the Norwich tackle
    dealer, holds a brilliantly coloured
    French fish.

19   Phil Smith with one of his 40lb plus
     Cassein mirrors.

20 Above   *The clarity of Cassein shows clearly as another big fish is supported before swimming away.*

21 Right   *Son emulates father. Master Amies releases a Cassein twenty.*

22 Above *A torpedo shaped wild carp taken from the Dutch drains.*

23 Below *Lake Michigan at sunset.*

24   *Duncan Kay prepares to weigh a big American fish.*

25 Above *Just one arm of the two hundred acre plus Ormesby Broad.*

26 Below *John Bailey releases a large water common.*

other factors limiting this, such as the lake ecology, peanuts being introduced etc., but certainly the use of proper HNV baits (not some of the rubbish baits often mis-named HNVs, which contain semolina) over a period of time could lead to some truly big carp, tench and bream. It is impossible to go backwards now. This effect on the ecology cannot be stopped, it's interesting, but worrying!

Predators also must receive a boost from the benefits passed on to their prey fish. The secondary effect must ultimately pass to the predators.

Darenth certainly saw a number of big pike turning up in succeeding years. It's interesting, and I admit I sit back now awaiting such results, just watching what will happen. There are likely to be more developments in bait as such and, un-questionably, developing effects which baits themselves have on waters, more than a lot of people realise. I am convinced that given the option of nutritional food, all species including pike, trout and so on will take this in preference to other food. The same basic principles of feeding apply to all fish.

There is also, of course, scope for experimentation in bait size to attempt to deter smaller fish, thereby feeding up only the bigger ones, thereby making them even bigger. This is a basic extension of the selective bait ideas which have been used very effectively at times.

C.T.   Amazing! You have talked about HNV enriching waters. I know you believe some developments have had other less desirable effects. For example, you have been condemning the use of peanuts on waters on the grounds that they damage fish.

F.W.   Peanuts, themselves, damage fish by causing vitamin deficiencies. Despite comments to the contrary, suggesting that fish will not eat something that is bad for them, this is not the case. Peanuts are a highly nutritious food. The trouble is you are offering carp something which nature, evolution, call it what you like, has not prepared them for. You are offering them a type of food that they have never seen before.

A second problem with peanuts is that some of those sold are of the bird food variety. All peanuts in this country are screened for a highly poisonous cancer-producing substance. Any containing it are not allowed to be sold for human con-sumption, but they can be sold as bird food. If you fill a lake with such rejected peanuts, there is every possibility of the fish ending up with liver cancer.

C.T.   So it is not peanuts in general that are the problem – it is those containing the cancer substances.

F.W.   To an extent, however, ordinary peanuts, even ones fit for human consump-tion, eaten by fish in quantity will cause a vitamin deficiency. There is no way really that peanuts are good for fish.

C.T.   In here, at Johnson's, we have seen a bit of a weight loss during the time that peanuts were used in quantity.

F.W.   Yes, this is either due to vitamin deficiency or in some cases to cancers. Some fish are now regaining weight and obviously have not got cancer. The fish with lumps probably have cancers.

C.T.   Is there any way that we can redress the situation once it has been caused?

F.W.   If the fish have cancer, no. But fish weight loss – sometimes in excess of twenty-five per cent of body weight – can be put back on. However the fish may have lost their ultimate potential size and some permanent damage might also have been done.

C.T.   Still, using a good bait and stopping the use of peanuts will help solve the deficiency problem.

F.W.   Certainly peanuts should not be used anywhere. The damage already done is done. Some lakes will have been luckier than others in that the nuts will have been for human consumption. The only way of getting weight back on quickly is by decent feeding – either from natural foods or from introduced baits.

C.T.   Turning to amino acids, these seem to have taken a back seat nowadays.

F.W.   I started using aminos in 1969. At that time I was using glycine as a smell additive more than anything else. Some time later came the article from the Lowestoft Research Establishment as to the reactions of cod and whiting to mixtures of amino acids. They discovered that lugworm gave off a smell made up of six amino acids and that the use of glycine alone would produce seventy-five per cent of these reactions. I was surprised at the time that carp anglers did not question whether Tubifex worms gave off the same smell. Certainly, I promptly gave up using glycine and indeed came to regard the amino acid syndrome as something of a joke, when I realised this. A lot of people were on the wrong track with this aminos thing in the same way that they have fallen for sweeteners since. Once it becomes fashionable and a craze to do something, people will follow blindly without question. A lot of people, for instance, put in extra smells, 'just in case', as an insurance, but this is pointless. If people continue to mix smells and waste smells on short-term 'rubbish' baits, the end situation will be that no smell will react as it should. This is detrimental to everyone.

C.T.   Effectively you are saying that you stopped using aminos because they were natural smells. This suggests that you do not consider a natural smell to be an advantage in a bait as opposed to Esters and so on.

F.W.   I wouldn't say an advantage. As far as I am concerned with smells, if I knew which were more natural to fish I wouldn't use them. If I put a totally alien bait into a lake, the last thing I want to do is put in a smell which the fish confuse with something else. The whole idea is to make a bait which is better than natural food, so it is ridiculous then to put a natural food smell into it – that would just confuse the bait and detract from its identification and effectiveness. It doesn't make sense to me to lower the potential catch rate and hence I cannot understand why people fall for the use of natural amino smells.

Perhaps it is this strange mystic thing which arose about amino acids – there is nothing strange about them though. Every cell of every living thing contains amino acids. A fish bites into a shrimp, breaks a cell and releases aminos. Most of the general food smells, such as those we smell in cooking, tend to come basically from amino acids. There is no great attraction in aminos and they have no use in the HNV bait concept. It is, therefore, back down to the idea of nutritional values. Fish will always pick baits up out of curiosity – that is why particle baits work to the degree they do. But once they have eaten a certain amount of it, if they don't gain much from it they will learn not to eat it in the long term. For instance, if you feed goldfish in a bowl with bread it doesn't take them long to become fed-up with eating it. But trout pellets will be taken with relish for much longer and so on up the line.

Really, I am astounded that over the years there has been so much rubbish written on baits, amino acids being a classic example, and no one has written a word against it. In contrast, when I first wrote on the HNV concepts, I was hauled over the coals for pseudo-scientific nonsense. I am not really concerned what other people think, as fishing is a purely personal thing, where anglers should fish for their own satisfaction against the fish, not other anglers.

C.T. It's all a bit 'brave new world'! When you think about this bait thing, it seems as frightening as it does promising.

F.W. I have now been investigating baits for twenty years and I don't really think I have changed my mind very much about the basic ideas. Certainly, the worries are still there. Many years ago I predicted my discoveries would change fishing dramatically and I am sure you will agree that it has done. I don't think that everything has been for the good. I am not against catching fish, but I cannot see that catching more automatically means more pleasure. If by catching more there is less pleasure from each individual fish, have you really gained anything in the process?

In the mid 1960s half a dozen doubles in a season was excellent going. The pleasure of each fish was phenomenal. I think much of the pleasure of individual fish has now gone, and this is a great loss. However, you cannot turn the clock back. If you combine deadly efficient baits with advanced techniques, you will gradually reach the stage where fish have no sanctuary at all. In the early days, for instance, fish that were at distance were virtually safe. Nowadays, a bolt rig and shock leader, and the bait will be out there! The fish cannot refuse the bait and so will eventually be caught. There is no sanctuary.

This is all a loss not only to the fish, but also to the angler. The mystery is lost and the pleasure is diminished. The happiness that one good fish inspired fifteen or twenty years ago is now spread thinly between great numbers of such fish. The backbiting and unpleasantness which has crept into fishing nowadays suggests that anglers are a good deal less happy than they once were. Much of the sharing of the early days has gone out over the years. Fishing has lost a tremendous amount of comradeship and fun. Youngsters have lost all the pleasure of learning and catching small fish first – they come in with the right rods and tackle, good baits and go straight in at the top with big fish. They have lost all the pleasure of building up to this pinnacle. I myself think it is unfortunate that the apprenticeship period

Duncan Kay, a pioneer in the bait world, holds a near 23lb leather.

seems to have gone for so many young anglers. I can only see this thing deteriorating further as there is more leisure, more pressure and better tackle and baits.

This is not the sort of fishing I want, but it is one of those things in life. Once the ball starts to roll it can never stop. Fishing can be the ultimate relaxation and pleasure, but a gloomy picture of its future is easy to paint. I am not sure how you can change things. Carp fishing is increasingly becoming size-orientated. These baits of mine increase fish size. Therefore the lake becomes more popular and more pressure is put on it. More bait gets in and so the fish get bigger still! It's a circle which I don't think can be broken now.

SMALL WATERS
AND
ESTATE LAKES

BY PRIVATE WATERS

There's peace here and a feeling so sublime
That comes to me from creatures all around;
A scene matured through centuries of time
With wildlife and the wind the only sound.

I look across the lake through misty dawn
Towards the margin-reeds of luscious green,
Which harmonise the beauty while they form
A haven safe for the fish that swim unseen.

So lovely are the trees that flourish here
Soft-mirrored in the water's peaceful calm,
I tremble and I'm glad there's no one near;
So astounded by the vista's thrilling charm.

Then from the water almost two feet clear
A golden fish leaps out with unleashed joy,
Loud twofold thud of massive tail I hear
A sound I've known is carp since just a boy.

And when the spreading water-rings have gone
My mind dwells on the carp that swim so free,
For I have been an angling man so very long
And it will always be the way of life for me.

William H. Whiting
8 February 1986

Eric

JOHN BAILEY

It was October 1985, and Sharon and I were driving home down the track. The gate had been padlocked and as I left the car I saw a note pushed into the link chain. I took it to the headlights and read:

John

Leary strikes! Eric has fallen at thirty-one pounds. Even the Bismarck wasn't invincible. The old man has caught his carp – be happy, the Young Pretender will have his day!
He was caught last week sometime.
No other info.

Roger

The news took some digesting. A whisky helped wash it down. I took the dog for a walk under a rising moon. I was thinking all the time, slightly surprised Eric did not weigh more – I would have put him at thirty-four pounds, but you never can tell quite and his gut could well have been slack. Slightly bitter at first, I was peeved now at blowing my own chances of the big fish in the past. In the end, I had to feel happy for Dan Leary.

Had Eric come out in 1984, I might have felt aggrieved. That was when I put in the work and gave it my all. In 1985 I did not deserve him. Dan did though – for that one year and all the others he had concentrated on that one enormous fish. For, whatever you read in the press, in the books, what-

ever happens at Cassein, a thirty-pound carp is enormous.

I had always wanted Eric, from the moment I first saw him a dozen years ago or more. No! Between 1972 and that fateful October 1985 night thousands of hours of my life had been spent on his two-acre home. Of course, I was rarely alone on the water and many stayed even longer. Yet as far as I know only one, Ken Norton, landed the adult Eric before Dan. That had been in 1976 when Eric weighed 32½lbs.

Eric is legendary still as only a small water fish can be. It is his visibility, his seeming accessibility. Over the years, all his hunters have watched him at rod tip length, sometimes hour upon hour. Then when the sun is high over the crystal water you can see his every fin ray, the colour of his eye, even the unfurling of a barbule as it curls around a pebble three feet below. His colour is vivid yellow below his humped back – peach almost in some lights. For years I have believed him the most beautiful fish I know. He is the wariest. The list of good anglers, great anglers, he has outwitted is long. Dan took years to put him on the bank; and I never even put a bait in his mouth.

Right *Eric weighed 32½lb and lay on Ken Norton's knees like 'a great bronze rowing boat'.*

A small water lets you see all this. Events are not happening at sixty yards or one hundred yards anonymously in deep, dark water. Eric is looking at your bait and you are looking at him. You are not waiting for a 'monkey' to climb or a bleeper to call: you are watching to see the bait engulfed. If he smells a bait you see it, if he tests a bait you know it. And I have been left with the knowledge that I have failed! The nearest I came to catching Eric was on a floater. I wrote the following at the time.

I have taken a penalty in front of a thousand or more people, sent the keeper the wrong way, decided the result of a Lancashire Junior League Championship and I did not bat an eyelid.

Once, I worked as a scaffolder on a job repairing a textile mill chimney, and even when we got to a hundred feet and more I slept well enough at night and risked a pint over lunch. I have taught a hundred children at a time, all of whom would have liked to see me in the grave, and yet I came through. I have had bad times with bank managers and walked away laughing. I have been to the altar and would go there again.

I say all this so that you can see that I can be cool, that I do not panic over nothing, but tonight, I shake. I can hardly hold the pen. It is only fishing that can do this to me, some fishing, for the spectrum of the sport is so broad. It can encompass pleasure to almost unendurable suspense in twenty-four hours or, as today, in just twelve.

This afternoon was bright and breezy from time to time. The session was true pleasure fishing. I was with friends and we were over relatively easy fish and relaxed. There was a take here and a fish there. A good double carp stretched my six-pound

line as thin as roach gut and made the Mitchell backwind like a pedal bike at full crank! A tench came along next and then a good rudd. A super mixed bag began to develop.

Three of us shared a swim, for really, we were there for the conversation and to catch up on old times almost as much as for the fish. There was news since last summer to uncover and jokes to retell, fresh as the day they were born. Afterwards, on the dot of opening time, there was a drink in the local pub, with a packet of crisps, on the lawn. It had been a happy day, three friends, three fish and a tired fighting arm.

I began the drive home. It was still light, but cloud was coming in and the breeze rose slightly to a Force 3, I guessed. Angling values took a lurch. This time it was more than pleasure. The rising wind would be pushing into the fallen tree. The big fish could be pulling in there too, as the dusk settled.

I just smelt the chance, and though it meant a sixty-mile detour, I had the stepped up gear in the back of the van and I hit the accelerator. In the big fish game, you speculate to accumulate, with nothing lost there is nothing gained and finally, what a big fish man has to do, he has got to do!

The light was low when I arrived, lower still under the canopy of the fallen tree and in the shadow of the high bank. The cloud had given a freckling of rain and the wind had driven just enough of the day's debris into the fallen branches to tempt the old carp in. The screech owls started in the wood. There were fewer cars on the road beyond the waste land. The sky went from silver to grey to charcoal and then, out of the coal-black depths, the fish arrived.

One free biscuit went down the cavern that is his mouth. That hippo eyed-in then

'A still July evening at the edge of dusk.'
Eric's Norfolk home.

at the bait. He was an inch away, just a millisecond of thought in his tiny mind. It needed only the merest extension of his lips and the hook would be set. My hand trembled. My heart beat a tom-tom.

Life held nothing else for me then but that great old fish. This was no longer fun or pleasure. It suddenly seemed the most serious thing in the world. The carp swirled at the bait, then boiled and flung spray into my face. The line still hung limp. I swore that I could hear his laughter as he swam back into the open water, away from the betraying tree. The hooked bait still revolved slowly in the eddies he had created and I reeled it in before any of the small carp should make a mistake.

It is 1.00 a.m. as I write. The brief summer cloud has blown over and the night is clear once more, sprinkled with stars. Tomorrow I have two choices: I can have a good evening with friends, perhaps hit a bite or two and enjoy a warm July evening. Or I can go after the dream again, this fish that disturbs all my nights, as he has done these years past. I walk the room, drain the last of the nightcap and pick up the pen once more. Whilst he still swims, I suppose I must go. It is not in me ever to leave him alone.

So now Eric has been caught. At his age I guess he is free-wheeling in the low thirties and I doubt if he will grow a great deal more. I doubt if I, for one, will hurt him again and I hope those others who have permission on his pool will think likewise. There is no need to take him out again. Let him keep his considerable dignity.

The Character and Potential of Small Waters

KEVIN CLIFFORD

There has been a tendency in recent years to equate big waters with big carp. Human nature, being what it is, has developed this further and arrived at the conclusion that the largest waters, with the smallest stocks of carp, yield the biggest fish. This is, of course, a recipe for disaster as well as being nonsense. Past records show that the over-riding majority of big carp caught in this country come from small and relatively small waters. Of the thirty-seven or so captures of carp over forty pounds that I can trace as having been caught in Britain, only four came from waters over about fifteen acres.

There is no doubt whatsoever that even comparatively small waters of three acres and less can grow and maintain very large carp indeed. The most productive water for big carp that Britain has known is Redmire Pool, a fishery of less than three acres. It has produced more different forty-pound carp than any other water in Britain, and the same probably applies to thirty-pound carp also.

There are several reasons why small waters tend to be more productive than large waters. Small waters usually warm up much quicker than large waters. They often have high banks or trees which provide cover from cold winds, and they do not stratify in summer creating an oxygen debt which at worst can kill fish and at best cause discomfort and disrupt normal behaviour. Regardless of what has been discovered in the last twenty years about catching carp in winter, the fact remains that it is a fish which thrives and does most of its growing in the warmer months. Indeed, the truth is that the highest summer water temperatures in Britain only rarely achieve that which allows the carp to fulfil its ultimate potential.

Most of the gravel and sand pits and many of the clay workings are relatively new and were created after the Second World War. Generally, small waters mature at a faster rate than large waters, and so we find with many of these pits dug during the past thirty odd years that the smaller ones have matured quickly. This allowed good growing conditions for introduced fish, whilst the largest pits took much longer to produce a similar productive environment. For example, Leisure Sport's sixteen-acre Yeoveney fishery was only eighteen years old when it produced Peter Springate's amazing brace, weight 38½lb and 36½lb.

Small waters offer other advantages. Location is often much easier, especially in clear water. I would imagine that I have spent somewhere in the region of fifty per cent of my time on the bankside of small waters, looking for and observing carp. This has, without doubt, been well worthwhile and paid rich dividends. Fishing in the knowledge that you have carp in the vicinity of your bait is, to my mind, tremendously important. It inspires confidence. It is too easy in carp fishing to become stereotyped and lackadaisical, especially if doubts exist as to the whereabouts of the fish. Experimentation and determination are assets which tend to be present more often when location has been achieved.

Small waters usually allow a greater variation of methods to be used successfully, often the more intimate techniques such as float fishing, casting to individual fish, particle bait fishing and surface fishing. All too frequently on large waters distance can become the limiting factor and this tends to restrict the techniques that can be employed. Also, smaller waters are almost always more attractive, altogether more conducive to the real essence of carp fishing: 'long lonely vigils spent beside tree-lined misty pools' – a far cry from today's horizon-bashing antics.

The majority of my early carp fishing was confined to small waters, and I don't believe a better apprenticeship could have been devised. Carp, as a species, are capable of making more of a poor environment than other species of fish. Over the years I have come across some mediocre and relatively poor fisheries, yet the size of the carp has turned out to be much better than expected. These 'hungry', overstocked waters are an ideal starting point for the newcomer. Nowadays, it seems more common to find beginners jumping in at the deep end, attempting to catch

Kevin Clifford supports magnificent commons of 27lb and 24lb.

twenty and thirty-pound carp from difficult, hard-fished waters.

It was once the case that carp anglers went through a pattern of at first just wanting to catch a fish, any fish. Then they wanted to catch lots of fish; then the biggest and finally just to enjoy themselves. Nowadays, far too much emphasis is placed on size and numbers of big fish. This, in part, may be due to the way in which Western Society views success, and yet competitiveness is not necessarily bad. In the right context it can, and does, lead to new developments and original thinking.

Certainly, small waters offer distinct advantages when it comes to testing new

baits and techniques. There is little chance in a reasonably stocked small water of carp not coming across a new bait or rig after a few trips. The effectiveness of such baits and rigs will then be determined. On a large water considerable periods can elapse when fish may not be even within casting distance.

For the same reasons, winter carp fishing tends to be more productive on small waters, even when compared to large waters with the same stocking density. I well remember spending many winter weekends on a local, very shallow two-acre lake after carp. Nearly always the carp, consisting of some forty odd fish between eight and eighteen pounds, would be shoaled up in the deepest water, an area about three and a half feet deep at one end of the long, thin lake. Usually a fish or two could be caught even on the coldest day. But now and then, for reasons perhaps only known to the fish, they would be found in the extreme, reedy shallows. On one occasion I found them there on a freezing January afternoon, their backs barely cov-erd, yet with ice slowly forming with the onset of dusk, fish began to feed.

Small waters have taught me far more about the behaviour and character of carp. I remember quite distinctly some years ago standing in the branches of a willow tree, overlooking the shallows of a small weedy lake. Below the tree a friend, Len Arbery, was hidden from view with just the tip of his rod protruding from dense under-growth. A few yards out from the bank his baited hook was surrounded with free offerings. Small groups of carp were slowly moving through the shallows, occasionally up-ending and sucking in

morsels of food. As one of the groups of fish worked along the margin they came across the free offerings and eagerly began to pick them up. In a hushed voice I warned Len below that he should expect a bite at any moment. No sooner had the words left my lips than the carp suddenly spooked and bolted towards the deeper water.

We both found it difficult to believe that the carp had been frightened by the sound of my voice, but further tests as other groups of carp fed under the willow confirmed the earlier incident. There is little doubt that the carp on this particular water have become extremely cautious over the years due to heavy angling pres-sure. It is generally agreed by the anglers who regularly fish there, that no matter how hard they try to be unobtrusive and keep their activity to a minimum, the carp gradually become aware of their presence with the obvious results. This is of course an intrinsic problem with small waters, especially those which have been the focus of considerable angling activity over a number of years.

About ten years ago I spent some time fishing a small, very pretty, tree-enshrouded lake in Yorkshire. Most early mornings during the summer, if the weather was warm, carp would be found feeding on the eastern shallows. During one particular period a friend, Bruno Broughton, and I were catching a lot of fish on float fished maggots. The method, if it could be described as such, was very simple. Maggots would be fired, using a catapult, in the vicinity of feeding carp. Once a fish was seen to take an interest the float tackle would be cast past the fish and carefully eased back into position. Initially some very good catches were made, but it didn't last for long. For although carp

Left *Kevin Clifford with mirrors to 21lb.*

Kevin holds a pristine mid-twenty.

would still feed on the free offerings of maggots, within a short time of the float tackle being cast out the fish would cease feeding and swim away. Obviously something associated with the tackle was frightening the fish.

A change to legered maggot brought a dramatic improvement, suggesting that either the float or the line was the cause of the problem. Some years later, Kevin Maddocks confirmed that he had come across a similar problem during his success-

ful period at Redmire Pool. Fishing a heavy lead with his line fished tight up to a clip, he had seen carp approach his line in mid-water and bolt at the sight of it. He reasoned that the carp had learnt to associate line with danger and from that period he pulled several yards of line from his spool, allowing the slack line to sink to the lake bed. After this he noticed an improvement in his catches.

Small waters allow you to fish in close proximity to the fish and this is the reason why it is possible to learn so much about their behaviour patterns. However, fishing in this way imposes constraints upon bankside activity. Disturbance must be kept to a minimum if success is to be achieved. Hammering umbrella poles and rod rests into the ground does little to instil confidence in the fish! I have noticed even on some large waters, where a reputation has been established that carp can only be caught at long range, that fish often come close to the bank and can be caught there if bankside activity is limited. Long-range fishing is often more to do with the habits of anglers than the habits of fish.

One of the main reasons why those who can cast a little further than the majority are sometimes successful, is that they are putting their bait where the fish are likely to feel more secure. I have always advocated that it is extremely important to fish in places that are not usually fished; where the majority of anglers cannot or will not fish. Carp are just as likely to associate a particular area of a lake with danger, as they are with a particular rig or bait. On small waters, of course, long-range fishing is of no use. But fishing close to, or in, weed beds, under tree branches, amongst snags, or in freshly created swims will bring beneficial results. In fact, trying anything different or unusual is worthwhile.

There is a small, deep clay pit not far from my home. It is heavily stocked with carp which reach just over twenty pounds in size, its well-worn banks are fished by a considerable number of anglers during the course of a season. For the first two or three weeks at the beginning of June the carp fishing is reasonably easy, but soon after that it becomes considerably harder. A couple of years ago someone float fished a boilie, under a bubble float, about two feet below the surface in twelve feet of water! They were very successful and it wasn't long before bubble floats attached to boilies and fished just under the surface were very much in vogue on that particular pond. For a while lots of carp were caught, but finally, as always happens, the fish wised up.

I've heard it said that it is the big, understocked waters that nowadays offer the ultimate challenge. There is without doubt some truth in this, although I've made it clear that big waters are not the sole habitat of big carp. Although the small, heavily fished waters may not be fashionable nowadays with many of the 'big names' in carp fishing, it is on these waters that the real breakthroughs and new developments have taken place. Here the competition to deceive the well-educated carp is often the catalyst to original thought.

Big Fish from Norfolk's Small Waters

GERRY MORRIS

A Thirty From the Graveyard

We love these two tales of big Norfolk carp. There is a lot to be learnt here from a very accomplished angler turning his attention to big carp for the first time and bringing with him a fresh mind and perhaps a new approach. Let us stress the achievement of catching two Norfolk thirties. At the time of writing very few men have ever had even one thirty pounder and perhaps only two or three anglers have achieved this remarkable double. Norfolk as a county has less thirty pounders in it than, for example, Savay alone. There might be just ten in the whole county itself.

PREPARATIONS

In May 1984 I moved back to Norfolk from Dorset, where I had spent two most enjoyable seasons in pursuit of the monstrous barbel that inhabit the Dorset Stour and the Hampshire Avon. In the months preceding the move, my thoughts were increasingly drifting from the capture of big barbel to that of big carp. I had read all I could on the subject and the vision of those huge, beautiful fish fired my enthusiasm more than I can tell. I desperately wanted to experience the thrill of hooking and playing a large carp. I wondered how it must feel to hold a fat bellied carp in my arms.

During the three months of the closed season, I scrimped and saved every penny I could to buy the tackle necessary to start carp fishing. As I did not possess any carp tackle whatsoever it was to prove an expensive business. Two new reels, two new carbon rods, two converted Optonics, a bed chair, a fifty inch brolly, a lightweight bivvy, a sleeping bag, a gas stove, bulk spools of line, spare reel spools and the numerous ingredients required for base mixes – all cost money. I doubt if I would have managed to buy all these items from my salary alone in time for the beginning of the 1984/85 season without the help of my wife, who not only subsidised me heavily, but went without small luxuries for herself. Our nights out became fewer, and despite this she continued to encourage and support me, her enthusiasm for this new challenge almost matching mine.

One of our few nights out was spent in the company of John and Sharon Bailey, in the comfortable surroundings of a North Norfolk pub. Inevitably the conversation turned to big fish and I told John that I intended to start fishing for large carp in the coming season. We discussed several waters in North Norfolk that held big carp, one that John mentioned was a small lake of approximately one and a half acres in size. It contained about twenty-five carp, all of which were doubles, a good proportion of which were over twenty pounds. The water sounded perfect for me, as it was only fifteen miles from my home.

John warned me, however, that it was a very hard water. He told me that over the years many capable carp anglers spending hundreds of hours on the water had failed to even get a run and that an angler was considered very lucky to catch one carp in the season there. Because of this the lake was nicknamed 'The Carp Fisherman's Graveyard'. This did not deter me, in fact it made me all the more determined, as I knew that to catch a carp from there would be a tremendous achievement. My goal was to catch just one twenty pound plus carp from there.

Work began. I made several trips to the water in the closed season, but because that spring was so cold I saw no visual evidence of carp. The water itself was very pretty, oval in shape, with tree-lined banks. Gravel bars intersected the lake, all of them coming within two feet of the surface. The depth of water between the bars averaged between four and six feet. The murky water made visibility poor and I realised that sightings of carp would only be made when they rolled and on hot days when they would cruise near the surface.

Along every bar grew some form of plant life, mostly reeds, but on one bar, the largest in the lake, reeds grew along one half and amphibious bistort (pinkies) grew along the other half. This particular bar ran from one side of the lake to the other. It seemed to be the perfect area for ultra-shy carp to feed on, offering them cover, a plentiful food supply and it would receive less attention from pleasure anglers than other areas in the lake. This was the area I was sure I had the best chance of catching carp from and I intended to fish it whenever possible.

Once I had decided where to fish I was left with the problem of which bait to use. As always when I am unsure or need advice with a fishing problem, I get in touch with a dear friend from my barbel fishing days – Phil White. I explained to him that I wanted to use a boilie that would be fairly unique but still effective, as I was sure most types of bait – good and bad – had been used in the lake without success. We discussed this problem at great length, and Phil eventually came up with an attractive-smelling high protein bait, light enough to sit on the silty bottom without eventually sinking into it and, therefore, out of sight of the carp. He informed me that many anglers fishing soft bottom lakes were using good baits, but that the base mixes were too heavy causing them to sink into the silt. They fished on, blissfully unaware of this, wondering why they weren't getting runs!

The bait he came up with was eighty per cent milk protein base mix which included 3oz of calcium caseinate to make it sink slowly. Phil suggested that I added only 2.5ml of the flavouring to a 10oz mix as he was certain a great many carp anglers were adding too much and consequently ruining a good base mix.

Once I had decided on the bait, I felt relieved. I felt I was ready now to undertake this new challenge.

21 JUNE

I was unable to fish the lake until 21 June, a Thursday, and even then because of work commitments Cheryl and I were unable to get to the water until the afternoon. As we walked around the lake which swarmed with pleasure anglers we passed an angler who had just vacated the swim I wanted to fish. I could not believe my good fortune! Fate had played its part. Now I had to play mine.

I was determined to land a fish if I hooked one and my tackle was carefully chosen to do the job. I set up with two Greys 2¼lb test curve rods, Mitchell 4/10s loaded with 12lb maxima line. The rig was a 1½oz fixed lead with a 2ft Cortland micron 15lb link, dyed brown, a size 6 Au Lion D'or hook, and a 1¾in braided hair. The boilie itself was half an inch in diameter, boiled for four minutes to make it rock hard as a deterrent to a huge population of tench that inhabit the lake.

The left-hand rod I cast forty-five yards out to five feet of water, where the pinkies joined the reeds. I then peeled four feet of line from the spool. I reasoned that by using a slack line, I greatly reduced the risk of causing the carp to bolt, due to seeing or touching the line. The carp were more likely to feed in the baited area if the line was lying on the bottom out of sight.

The right hand rod I cast fifty yards out, onto a bar that ran at right angles to the pinkies. I catapulted ten baits round each hook bait, leaving a gap of one minute between firing out each free offering so as not to spook any carp that might already have been in the swim. Both rods were set up within half an hour, I loaded the bobbins and wondered how long it would be, if ever, before one of them moved up the needle. Men after all had grown old here, John Bailey had told me, waiting even for a run!

It was a hot, sunny afternoon with a cloudless blue sky and a gentle breeze creating the merest ripple on the water.

An hour after setting up, a couple of carp leapt clear of the water, just on the edge of the pinkies, approximately fifteen feet from my baits. Although the fish were not twenty pounders they looked good doubles. My excitement and anticipation increased. The omens were good, surely, as this was the first time I had seen any carp in the lake. Carp continued to leap clear of the water throughout the evening, some big fish well into the twenty pound mark.

This surface activity ceased about 7.30 p.m. and my confidence steadily grew. Now I began to hope the carp would start feeding on my baits below. Fifteen minutes later my Optonic blipped several times in quick succession. The bobbin had moved four inches up the needle of the left-hand rod. It moved another couple of inches quickly and with this I wound down and struck hard. I was disappointed not to feel the weighty thump of a big fish on the end and though I had hooked something I thought it was a tench. The fish was swimming towards me, but as it moved over a bar that ran parallel to the bank ten yards out, it suddenly bored deep, taking me totally by surprise and almost wrenching the rod from my grasp. This was no tench! This could be the dream come true!

A MIGHTY BATTLE

The fish then hammered for the bank trying to reach the submerged roots of a tree to my left. The 2¼lb test curve rod took an ever increasing hoop as the fish neared the trees. She was only feet away from the roots when she decided to change her mind and made her way out into the middle of the lake. I back wound as slowly as I dared, keeping maximum pressure on her. Then it was that she came clear of the water, re-entering as quickly as she left it,

Chris Turnbull. 1981.

water spraying everywhere. She left massive waves in her wake – the body had risen from the graveyard.

Slowly and powerfully she made her way towards the reed beds in front of me and again I applied extreme pressure and managed to turn her. She swam over to my right and tried to reach the reed beds there, but I did not relent the pressure and eventually she turned and dropped in towards me moving over the ten yard bar towards the tree roots again.

She made another determined effort to reach them, but the power of the tackle proved too much for her and she aborted that attempt, swimming out into the middle of the lake. Again she leapt clear of the water as she approached the ten yard bar. It was at this point that I realised what was happening. Because she was swimming so near to the bottom she would be confronted by a four foot high wall as she approached the bar. To get over this, she

would have to ascend almost vertically and would use so much power that she would come clear of the water to enter it on the other side.

On reaching the other side of the bar she made no attempt to gain any snags and just swam in circles as if to regain energy for one more nerve-racking assault. Sure enough she came towards me with desperate power, heading again straight for the tree roots to my left. The third time I knew it was do or die for us both.

Again, I applied pressure until my arm ached but I didn't give her an inch. The rod arched further still, the tip to the water. I could see the line sliced through the surface film only inches away from the submerged roots, a heartbeat away from release. In a last ditch attempt to stop her I took a couple of steps to my right. The line didn't crack. The rod did not shatter. But the most amazing thing of all was that I had managed to turn her. I looked on in disbelief as she moved once more into the lake.

This time I managed to stop her reaching the bar. She was beginning to tire. I pumped her slowly back towards me. She made a few half-hearted attempts to reach snags but within a few minutes I had her moving aimlessly at my feet. The battle was at an end! I remember being totally emotionless as this huge fish was drawn up from the depths of the lake. There was no danger as the landing net was slid underneath her and she just flopped onto it totally exhausted after giving me the hardest and most exhilarating fight of my angling career.

THE FISH

I lifted her onto the bank and hurriedly unravelled the mesh completely covering her tail. Her colossal flanks were totally scaleless. The boilie looked insignificant as it lay inside her mouth and the hump on her back could have been that of a whale.

After the unhooking I placed her in the sling, the scales previously zeroed, and lifted her off the ground. The needle bounced unsteadily as she kicked, but eventually as she settled so did the needle – at 31lb 4oz! I was walking in a dream. I didn't even know there was a fish of that size in the lake and I had caught the fish of a lifetime on this, my first trip. I placed her in the sack and asked Cheryl to check her while I contacted John Bailey to take some photographs. This he did and the fish was returned within one hour of capture. (John says that the dubious quality of these shots is because 'it was sundown and the light was not good, but Gerry is the best – no, the only type of carp angler. He did not want to risk the fish by carrying her to the bank that caught the last of the light, or

even to wait for dark and a flash picture. She had to go back as quickly and as easily as possible').

I managed another trip a few days later and fished the same swim. I had two runs within forty-five minutes landing two immaculate low double common carp. Again, to land two fish in a day was unheard of, let alone in forty-five minutes. I honestly thought I had cracked the 'Graveyard', but it was not to be. These were the last two carp I ever caught from there. Although I fished regularly every week until the end of October putting in hundreds of hours, I blanked with all the rest of the anglers there.

Nonetheless, I enjoyed every trip, chatting for countless hours with newly made friends. All of us wondered why these carp were almost impossible to catch. These conversations and the hundreds of actionless hours spent there made me realise just how fortunate I had been those two fateful days in June.

CONCLUSION

Gerry's last remark on the 'Graveyard' fascinated John Bailey when he came to edit this exciting piece. He himself has fished the place hard in the past – but, like countless others, with no success. Accordingly he phoned Gerry and that night they met to discuss why so small a lake is so desperately difficult and has broken so many hearts.

Gerry agreed that if a man can catch carp at the 'Graveyard' then he can catch them anywhere. Even the introduction of the hair rig made no difference there. It was as though they had seen everything before. Possibly this is an explanation. The carp are old. They were stocked as two year olds in 1962, and had been fished for hard by the early 1970s. From then until now they have had fifteen years of continuous pressure and constant learning. In such a small water they have lived nearly all their adult lives in perpetual anxiety and if not neurotic, they are at least the clearest example of careful fish. Nothing new makes inroads. The carp are resilient to any new bait, colour or flavour. They seem to understand any rig, however subtle. One fish might make an occasional mistake and then the door closes again.

This massive amount of pressure is the telling thing – pressure often from stereotyped anglers who bivvy, day in and night out, clipped up tight with lines crisscrossing the feeding areas like cheese

wires. Gerry likened the carp's situation to that of a man walking in the dark, continually cracking his head on low beams.

Nonetheless, twenty odd big carp have to eat and eat a lot to maintain the bulk the thirty pound fish showed. The 'Graveyard' food stocks are so rich, there is no need for them ever to turn to anglers' baits – not perhaps until they have broken down and become like silt itself. Throughout the summer, the daphnia and bloodworm stocks are so phenomenally high that the fish very likely become totally preoccupied with these tiny foodstuffs. Of course, many have tried caster and maggot prebaiting, but we believe that to be successful you would have to go for even smaller baits than those.

One brainwave after another has failed at the 'Graveyard'. Perhaps it will always be so.

The Big Common

FATE AGAIN

Not more than a twenty-minute drive from my home there is a small privately owned lake, about three-quarters of an acre in extent. I had been told that it held only four or five carp, but the largest of these was said to be a common carp whose weight was in excess of thirty pounds. Obviously I would have given anything to fish the lake, but it was strictly private and for weeks I tried in vain to find out the owner's name and address. Eventually after no success I gave up trying.

Then, as luck would have it, I had the good fortune to nurse an old lady who lived near the lake I so dearly wanted to fish. She told me that she knew the owner, gave me his name and address and

Gerry's dream – the Graveyard thirty.

instructed me to mention her when I asked for permission to fish. I contacted the owner in the closed season and I informed him that I was a nurse who had recently been looking after an old lady he once knew. I seemed to have said the right thing and he gave me permission to fish the lake whenever I pleased. I felt very honoured, as he often refused anglers completely.

FRUSTRATED BEGINNINGS

A month before the season began I decided to pre-bait with a high nutritive value bait. I threw in about 400 baits every other night. They were scattered fairly evenly around the lake to ensure that the carp would get used to seeing them and hopefully pick them up as they patrolled the water. I did not expect them to become preoccupied with the baits, but I did hope they would become part of their daily diet. It seemed a gamble but I did not think I could catch the common by stalking her. What I figured was that as she was considerably larger than the other carp in the lake her dietary intake would be greater than theirs, and because of this I believed that if I only had two or three runs all season, one of them was bound to be from the common.

I finished pre-baiting a few nights before the season started and I had, in fact, put twenty pounds of bait into the lake – approximately 6,000 boilies – in the preceding weeks. I longed for the first night of the season like no other. I had worked hard and could not wait to get on to the lake to reap my rewards. I arrived on the water at 8 p.m. on 15 June. To my horror I saw a couple of cars parked in the meadow and as I hurried up the bank my heart fell to my stomach as I saw two anglers setting up in the swim I wanted to

fish. A further two were setting up at the other end of the lake. I was bitterly disappointed and my only consolation was that they were not carp anglers. I passed them barely able to speak. I noticed that they each had tilly lamps and I knew that I had no chance of catching, so I returned home, feeling despondent. As I was getting married the following week this first night was the only opportunity I had to fish the lake until mid-July.

On my return home from our honeymoon, at the first opportunity I arranged a trip to the lake. Again, as I arrived I spotted a teenage boy fishing. He had three carp rods out and informed me that he came from Essex and that his father knew the landowner, who had given him permission to have a two-week carp fishing holiday, camped on the bankside! I asked him how long he had been fishing there and he told me that during the week he had hooked and lost three large fish.

I could not believe that this was happening to me and I began to wonder if I would ever get to catch the common. Because of the intense 24-hour pressure the lad was putting on the water, I decided not to fish until he left. I had started to become paranoid about the carp in the lake. I prayed that the lad did not hook any more. I went to see him on his last day and he told me he had not had any more runs. Selfishly (I suppose now) I felt very relieved to say the least.

I saw my problems were beginning to disappear, but then I heard through the grapevine that a fishery owner had paid a large sum of money to the landowner for the big common and had removed it. I rang up the fishery owner concerned at once and he reassured me that this was not true and that it was rumour put about by another fishery owner to discredit him.

Satisfied that the common was still in the lake, I arranged to fish the lake for a 24-hour period commencing the following Wednesday morning.

THE SESSION

It was a scorching hot July day, the only one of the summer so far. I arrived on the lake and to my amazement there was no one there. I set up the two Greys carp rods with 8lb line and 1½oz running leads. I used a 12in Dacron link with a 1in hair tied from the eye. The hook bait was the same HNV bait that I had pre-baited with.

I cast the right-hand rod into the centre of the lake approximately ten yards out. The left-hand rod I cast sixty yards to my left also in the middle of the lake, only this hook bait was positioned about four feet away from a sole weed bed. This weed bed was the only real place of cover in the lake for the carp to hide.

Because the lake was so small, I wanted to fish a slack line set up on both rods so that the carp could move freely around the water, but I was in a dilemma. I did not want to fish a slack line set-up and let a carp bolt into the weed bed before I could prevent it. On the other hand, I did not want to fish a tight line and have the carp avoid the area altogether.

I examined the weed bed closer and noticed that it was a fairly soft weed type and that if a carp did bolt into it, I thought I would have a good chance of bullying her out again. So I decided to settle for the slack line on both rods.

I placed thirty baits in a tight area around each hook bait. Shortly after doing this I noticed a large vortex appear at the other end of the lake, obviously caused by a large carp. With great care I quietly made my way down towards it. I crawled on my

hands and knees and as I looked over the bank into the water I saw a large carp moving to and fro just before me. I wished that she would come even closer and I lay in a paralysed state on the bank in fear that I would startle her.

She appeared totally oblivious to my presence, however, and after a few minutes she swam past me only feet away. My heart missed several beats. She was truly a massive fish, covered in golden-bronze scales. This was the fish I so dearly wanted to catch and seeing her had made me all the more determined.

I studied her for several hours, following her up and down the lake in a daze. She obviously saw me but it did not deter her from enjoying the first hot day of the year. I placed about ten Chum Mixer in her path but she just swam under them with apparent disinterest. When she returned I threw out another handful of Chum Mixer but she continued to ignore them. When there were about 150 floaters in the area she stopped and sucked in three of them and then swam away. No matter what I did, I could not get her to take the floaters with confidence, even though I spent most of the day trying.

She continued to cruise under the surface until sunset when she finally submerged out of sight in the area where I had cast my left-hand rod. I sat full of expectation by the rods until midnight, but the bobbins remained stationary. It was a warm night, the sky was clouded over and the wind dropped. The lake itself was like a sheet of glass and the occasional ripple caused by a small rudd was all that disturbed its surface.

Just after midnight I climbed into the sleeping bag. Although very tired I found it difficult to get to sleep, as I was expecting a run from the common any

'He has a golden gleam on his mailed sides and he has the strength of a bull.'

time. I was so close now I felt, as I drifted into a very restless night's sleep. I woke every half an hour or so until first light to check that I had not had a run. Again I dozed until I was woken by the sound of an Optonic at 4.45 a.m. After a couple of seconds the noise ceased, the bobbin on the left-hand rod was at the top of the needle and remained stationary. The rod top was moving backwards and forwards, sending an occasional blip from the Optonic.

I wound down and struck hard. The rod hooped over as I felt solid resistance. The carp had bolted into the weed bed and that

was why the run was so short. Its thrashing about in the weed bed must have caused the rod top's movement. I could still feel the occasional kick through the rod and I was relieved she was still hooked. I kept the pressure on and very slowly I managed to pump her back through the weed bed. After a few anxious moments she came free.

I applied all the pressure I dared to prevent her from getting back and after a couple of attempts I started to gain line and pumped her up the lake towards me. She gave every inch of line begrudgingly, keeping the rod well curved and occasionally taking it to its limits as she suddenly decided to change direction.

As she passed in front of me I lifted her off the bottom of the lake. Her back broke the surface exposing those warrior scales. I had hooked the big common! From then on I could hear my every heartbeat and the sweat started to pour from my forehead. I had put so much effort into catching this carp that when it seemed my dream was nearing its reality I started to fall to pieces. Every time the rod lunged downwards my heart stopped. I could do nothing with the fish and though I tried several times to get her near the net, each occasion she would just bore deeper. The fight progressed. I became increasingly anxious. I cannot deny that I was playing the fish badly and I was sure that if I didn't net her soon the hook was going to pull. I crouched to my knees and put the landing net into the water. It rested on the bottom at an angle of forty-five degrees and the handle lay across my knee. I drew the fish towards the net and when she was just a couple of feet away I lowered the rod. With this new-found slack she bolted straight into the mesh. In a fraction of a second I had lifted the arms out of the water and the fish was mine.

On the bank I simply looked in disbelief. I could not take all this in. She was perfectly proportioned and not a scale was out of place and not a tear was in her fins. She was the most beautiful carp I had ever seen. I placed her in the sack and ran down the bank with sheer delight. I phoned two friends and my wife to witness and photograph her. Not one minded being disturbed at 5.15 a.m. for such a fish. They arrived within the hour. I prepared everything and they all witnessed the zeroing of the scales with the weighsling in place. With a great effort I lifted the fish off the ground in the sling and she pulled the 44lb scales down to 32lb 4oz.

Words just cannot describe the way I felt. Surely this was the achievement of my angling career.

Estate Lakes

CHRIS CURRIE

Their History and Problems

The very nature and antiquity of nearly all English estate lakes throws up a whole set of problems that are not met in such an extreme form on that mainstay of modern carp fishing, the gravel pit. Essentially, the difference rests in the extra years that the estate lake has had to evolve its own charateristic ecology. Briefly, silt deposits are often very deep and as much as the depth of the lake again can be made up of soft, near liquid mud. On top of this, a mature landscape surrounds estate lakes, providing trees that have been depositing their leaves and dead branches onto the lake bed in most cases for upwards of 150 years. Many of the problems encountered on this type of water revolve around these factors.

There are two other characteristics common in estate lakes. Firstly they are almost all made by damming small streams. This results in the depth being at a maximum near the dam or outflow, gradually increasing into heavily silted shallows. Secondly, except where trees have been allowed to block sunlight from the lake bed and where depths exceed ten feet or more, estate lakes can become choked with weed if not tended by regular cuttings.

I always think of carp fishing as beginning on estate lakes. Gravel pits generally are a new phenomenon following in the wake of post-war motorway construction. Most of our estate lakes, although extensively remodelled in the eighteenth and early nineteenth centuries, have much older origins. Many country estates are built up around earlier medieval deer parks. Such was the case of Capability Brown's landscaping of Stoneham Park in the late eighteenth century. In the early fourteenth century the Abbot of Hyde was granted a Royal Licence to create a deer park whose boundaries were not dissimilar to the area worked on by Brown. Research has shown that large fish ponds were commonly found in medieval parks, just as they were in later estates. I am not suggesting that Stoneham Lakes are medieval ponds as there is no conclusive evidence for this, but Brown certainly did not create them all by himself. As proof, I have seen an old account dated 100 years before his improvements which tells of a wall being constructed around one of the 'ponds', plural, in the park.

I mention this example as these lakes made a deep impression on me in the mid 1960s when I started carp fishing. Even with the hair rig and all the modern developments, the carp fishing here is still hard at times. In the 1960s, one good fish a year was all anyone hoped for. Today the record number of fish taken in a season, as far as I know, remains at twenty-six and that includes small fish that were bred in the hot summer of 1976.

Sharon Bailey, proud of her catch, poses before a fine English country house.

Fish Movement and Habits

The first lesson estate lakes teach you is about movement of fish. In summer, a big fish will visit most of the lake in each 24-hour spell. This constant movement burns up energy and accounts for a fact I have long noted: that is, that these fish never put on weight until September. In fact, it is not uncommon for a fish to lose weight between June and August. All sorts of theories have been put forward to account for this. Twenty years on, I am convinced it is caused by continuous movement.

As the heat of the sun begins to intensify around mid-morning, large numbers of carp can be found in the weedy shallows. Some stay until dusk, but many will move out again by mid-afternoon as the heat becomes too much. Carp feed most in the mornings and evenings. During the night a large number of the carp spread out and move around the lake, feeding on food dropped into the margins during the day. As light arrives, they move back to the shallows or thick weed bed where fairly intense feeding will take place in relatively confined areas.

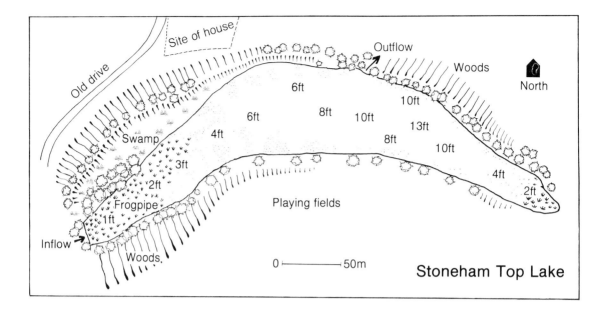

Night fishing on estate waters does not rely on intensive feeding. The carp are browsing and tend to visit every part of the margins. Even heavy baiting will not hold them in the swim, mainly because they sense that margin feeding, even at night, leaves them vulnerable. They take a few morsels and move on, sometimes returning a few hours later.

The carp does not take long to amble around an entire five-acre estate lake. Try going on a very slow walk yourself. How long does it take to slowly walk a mile? At the most, an hour, and in that time a carp could have done a complete circuit of the margins. I feel this is an important point. It showed up time and time again when I used to margin fish. I can remember countless times sitting by my rods after hours of inactivity, looking along the edges for signs of carp moving towards me. Everything would be motionless and I would allow my mind to wander, perhaps for no more than two minutes, then I would lean forward to adjust the indicator. As I leant down, I would spot a carp pushing its way

through the marginal weeds, but it would be too late then. The water would erupt as the fish bolted. Yet remember, two minutes before, there had not been a fish in sight.

Margin carp are very like spooky fish in holes in the weed. Observation of them has taught me that they will enter a cleared area or a hole, circle quite quickly, feed very briefly and then disappear. I make no exaggeration in saying it is like a small boy raiding the larder, who goes in and out as quick as can be, only pausing to pick up his favourite biscuits before being away again. The boy knows he is taking chances, but his greed gets the better of him. So it is with carp in holes in the weed and along the margins. The carp is aware that by being close to the edge it is in danger. That, I believe, is why they are difficult to hold in margin swims.

By margin I *do* mean margin: five yards out is no longer in the margin by my terms. The fish seem to patrol a line at a certain depth. In summer this can be as little as one or two feet of water. In winter this patrol line definitely moves further out. What generally happens is that summer night patrollers feed on the upper shelf, and the winter night patrollers move onto the bottom of that same shelf. Particles are out for this sort of fishing as the carp seldom stay long enough to pick up a hook bait. About half a dozen free samples around each hook bait is enough.

Margin fishing evolved because anglers believed that the carp fed only at night. As we now know that this isn't true it has become possible to catch carp at other times provided we are in the right place. Fish movements on estate lakes are such that mid-morning gives the angler the best

chance of a good catch. This is because it is a time they start moving into concentrated areas for intensive feeding. The margin fish is a browser, moving over large areas but taking in relatively little food. The estate fish seem to have their main meal during about two hours in the morning.

In its natural state, the estate lake, well matured, is a haven of natural food. This leads to intense preoccupation. In the spud and crust days of the mid 1960s, this meant the frustration of watching carp boil and bubble over your humble potato without

'When the mist wreaths across the black mirror of the pool ...'

so much as a twitch on the indicator. The advent of particle baiting techniques in the 1970s led to these fish suddenly becoming catchable and multiple catches were not unknown.

Particles still remain the supreme baits between June and the end of August on estate lakes. All that is required for the use of particles is that the areas of intense feeding are located. At Stoneham it was along the deeper edges of the frog pipe. To make sure of good catches the previous three days would see pre-baiting with a moderate amount of the intended bait. These swims are ambush swims, which carp are known to move through at a time when they are susceptible to preoccupation.

Chris Currie with an estate lake mid-twenty.

At Stoneham the fish would eventually make their way into the more inaccessible weed. As evening came on they would move out again on their way up the lake to patrol the margins. At this time it was often possible to stop fish on their way out if the swim was kept baited. It always helped considerably to get the fish used to finding food on the way out and so if evening sessions were planned I would often pre-bait the intended swim at about 4 p.m. for three days before fishing. Once you have started fishing there is no need to continue pre-baiting, because the bait you use each session is enough to condition the fish to knowing there will be food in your swim.

Not all estate lakes work exactly like Stoneham, but the principle is very much the same on all of them. There are always areas that the fish move between and this

27 Above *Kevin Nash beams down onto his Essex record.*

28 Right *Rod Hutchinson with another of his massive gravel pit carp.*

29 Above   *The second biggest English carp! Ritchie MacDonald holds his 45lb Yateley fish.*

30 Left   *Ritchie MacDonald with a 31½lb Savay common.*

31 Opposite   *Ritchie MacDonald with a 30lb Savay mirror.*

32   *Tim Paisely pauses to admire a superb common.*

33 Above *Tim Paisely justifiably happy with this peach coloured leather.*

34 Below *The bivvied up angler waits in the freezing dawn.*

35 Above *The beauty of a Trent sunset.*

36 Below *The rising sun shines down on Graham Cowderoy's well-deserved winter fish.*

37   *Mist over the gravel pit at dawn.*

38 A chunky big-scaled mirror for Tim
Paisely.

39 Graham Cowderoy shows that he
can catch them in summer too!

movement is almost always predictable. If a route is known then baits can be placed accordingly and fish should be caught. Such schemes can be altered by a number of factors. One of the most important of these is very intensive fishing.

INTENSIVE FISHING

The principal result of intensive fishing is frightened fish. Although their overall behaviour does not change, it introduces variations into the pattern. The same parts of the lake are visited, but catching fish there can often prove difficult. This is so much the case, that it becomes next to impossible to get a proper take in some swims. Over the years this leads to an 'area' reaction: fish will only take baits properly in areas where they feel safe. These areas are not only the inaccessible ones that anglers find it hard to get baits into, but those that are ignored by anglers for other reasons. For example, I had some remarkable successes about eight years ago by fishing a swim which had nothing to commend it other than the fact that the bank was too steep to set up a bed chair. For this reason alone it had been completely ignored by carp anglers for many years.

One of the most prolific waters in Hampshire was the GPO pool (see diagram). It was estimated that there were at least seventy doubles in this lake, which barely makes two acres but is of a very awkward shape. The lake was part of Lord Swaythling's estate, although local historian Edward Roberts has pointed out to me that a lake is mentioned there in the thirteenth century Pipe Rolls of the Bishop of Winchester. It is possibly, therefore, of great age. If you look at the map, you will notice there is a main pool with a number of narrow back channels behind two large

islands. These channels were often gin-clear and fish were very easy to spook. Moreover, tiddler bashers would have to pass by anyone fishing in the channels to get to the main lake. As they were generally noisy and brightly dressed, carp anglers seldom set up permanently in these areas, reserving them for stalking fish when quiet. As the main pool took most of the pressure, the fish quickly became spooky once the season got under way. Most of the pressure was put on just two swims as all the others were heavily weeded and not suitable for long-stay carp fishing. Despite all this, there were so many carp in such a small area that even with the pressure the fish could always be taken from the two 'point' swims.

When I fished the GPO seriously, which was for about two months of short sessions in 1983, I quickly became dissatisfied with the results forthcoming from the hammered swims. I found, and I was not alone in this, that by fishing other swims, no matter how unlikely they looked, fish could be taken. These swims often comprised the smallest of holes amongst fairly thick weed. This weed was of the soft variety, evenly distributed but not so thick as to merit the term solid. It was thick enough to discourage even the float anglers from fishing amongst it, however. I did discover that with a 1½oz weight it was possible to bomb a bait through the strands to the bottom, especially on the edges of lily-pads where the sunlight had not penetrated and where the weed was particularly sparse. This method took some very accurate casting because there is no chance of pulling a bait back after an overcast. The slightest movement of the bait means then that the hook will catch on a weed stem and this will not catch many fish.

In some swims it was possible to get a

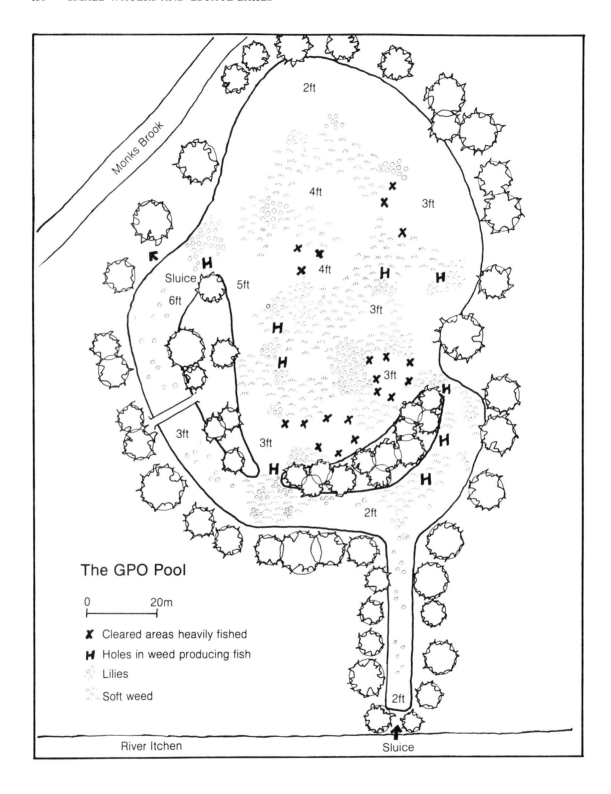

The GPO Pool

0   20m

X Cleared areas heavily fished

H Holes in weed producing fish

Lilies

Soft weed

River Itchen

bait to the bottom using a half-inch hair on a bolt. The weight pulls the hook straight down behind it if the tail is not too long. On a hook length of six to nine inches there is really little need to worry about the hook snagging on weed. Where the holes were too small to enable such tactics to be used, the looped hair was found to be ideal. This rig keeps the hook and bait together but allows for the anti-eject properties of the hair to come into play.

One thing that was very noticeable on this lake was the way in which carp reacted towards baits as a season wore on. After a while, the single hair was no longer enough to catch fish. A series of twitches were discernible on tight line baits that could be quite violent but seldom developed into a full run.

Because of the silt problems I used a buoyant bait that just came to rest on top of the silt. The bomb, I imagine, was well buried. Initially, takes were standard fast runs, but as swims became hammered so a new pattern of behaviour would develop. The carp in the GPO were so numerous for such a small area (although they had grown naturally and the water was very rich on the high alkalinity subsoil) that they could not afford to ignore anglers' food sources. Feeding was therefore ultra-cautious. Free samples were only taken after some deliberation and then only seventy per cent of the time, even the hair rig baits were singled out as dangerous.

The method these carp used to test a bait was to pick it up cautiously on their lips and blow it out again quickly. As I say, about seventy per cent of them would not bolt under any circumstances. Short hairs and looped hairs helped for a while but on normal set-ups bites seldom registered. The way I discovered I was getting bites was to pull the line tight into the clip on the

butt of the rod. If the front clip was used, twitches would occur that would not register on the buzzer so you had to sit and watch the line where it entered the water. This was a strain on the concentration and so the back clip was used.

Because the line was pulled ultra-tight, the slightest twitch at the bait would register a bleep on the antennae indicator. Optonics were not sensitive enough to register a mere tightening of the line. The bleep would alert me that a fish had picked up the bait. It was then necessary to watch the line. If no other movement occurred, the fish had ejected the bait without the hook catching hold. If the hook had caught hold, the fish would stay motionless and blow again, hoping to shed the hook. It would seldom achieve this first time but would keep spitting hard and fast until the hook was removed, usually by the fourth attempt. If the fish spat more than this it was often panicked into bolting. These were the thirty per cent of bites that developed into runs.

The takes where the fish got rid of the hook without moving an inch would be registered by a single bleep on the antennae followed by a continuing tremble where the line entered the water. Sometimes a couple of hard jerks would register on the line, not always registering even on the antennae indicator. None of these indications would register at all on the front clip rig unless you were watching carefully, nor would the line be tight enough for anything to register at all on a standard non-clipped rig.

The great test of this method came from a very confined swim which the fish had to swim through to get into that channel. The bait was placed in a small hole in some lilies at the entrance to the channel on two successive afternoons. It produced six

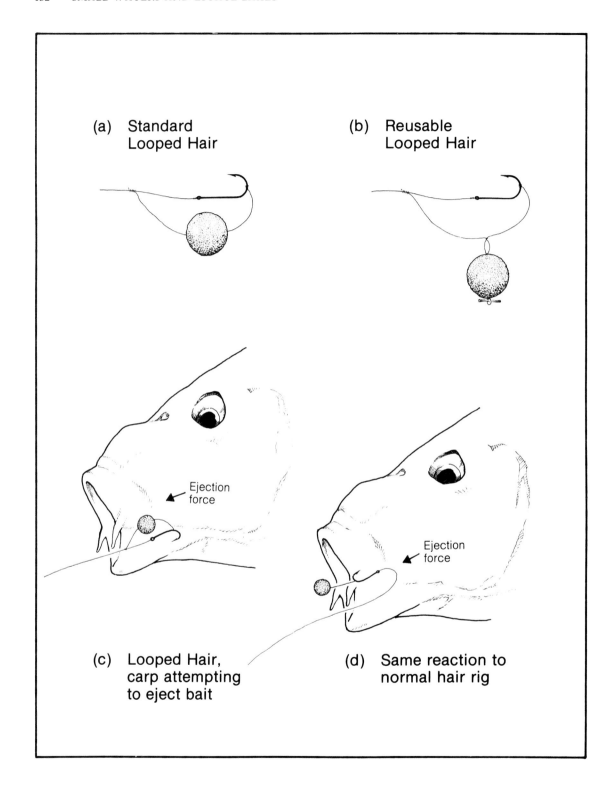

(a) Standard Looped Hair

(b) Reusable Looped Hair

Ejection force

Ejection force

(c) Looped Hair, carp attempting to eject bait

(d) Same reaction to normal hair rig

Back Clip Rig for Indicating Twitching Carp on Hair Rigs

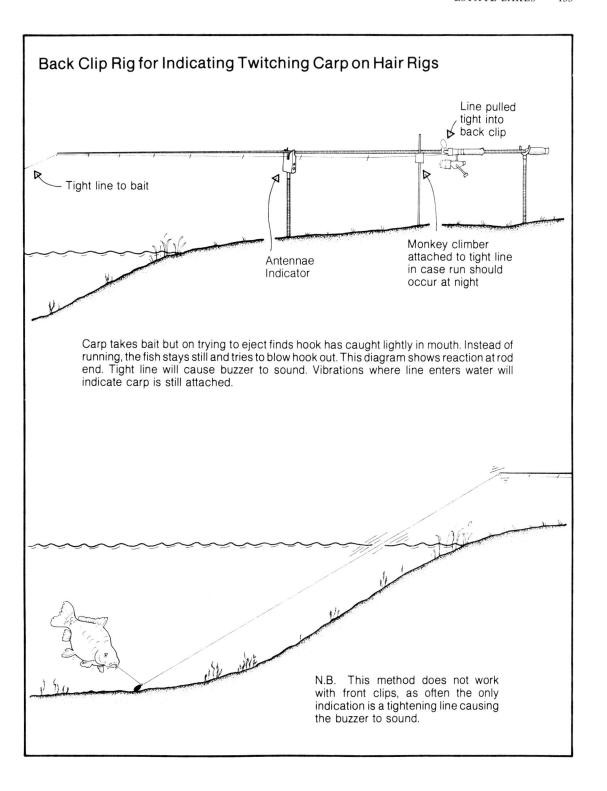

Line pulled tight into back clip

Tight line to bait

Antennae Indicator

Monkey climber attached to tight line in case run should occur at night

Carp takes bait but on trying to eject finds hook has caught lightly in mouth. Instead of running, the fish stays still and tries to blow hook out. This diagram shows reaction at rod end. Tight line will cause buzzer to sound. Vibrations where line enters water will indicate carp is still attached.

N.B. This method does not work with front clips, as often the only indication is a tightening line causing the buzzer to sound.

Chris Currie with a good looking estate lake carp.

convinced a fish was hung up but not moving and the rod was up. I was more than surprised to find a twenty-pound plus fish in my net five minutes later, as the previous lake best was only just over nineteen pounds. Chris Strong of the tench fishers was one of the many witnesses to a fabulous fish that measured 27½ inches.

In all I had a very large number of double figure carp in just two months fishing at that water, with twenty of them coming in a hectic three-day spell. This was not a continuous session either, but a number of short sessions. Of the fish caught, only about a third of them were caught using traditional methods, although even that would have exceeded the catches of all the other anglers using the water at that time. Had I used conventional methods of bite indication, I am certain I would not have caught half of the fish mentioned.

Another facet of the GPO pool was the back channels. In previous years they had been used mainly for stalking fish with floating baits. Because the water here was so clear and shallow, they were often assumed to be devoid of fish if none could be seen. I started to become interested in the back channels when the tactics I have described above started to slacken off, especially when other people were to be found in the swims I had been fishing, even if they were fishing in different places from the same vantage point.

One afternoon, when the main pool was dead, I decided to bait a couple of holes in the weed in one of the channels. The hook baits were placed in with the free offerings, leaving me to retire behind cover to await results. Being behind reeds was most important because the fish were extremely spooky here in the clear water. Even though watching very carefully no

doubles including a twenty-pound fish, the first to come from the water, and not one of the takes moved the indicator at all. All came from continual twitchings on the line. The rigs were standard half-inch hairs or looped hairs, alternated as I was testing one against the other for efficiency. The method was particularly effective because I was fishing a mere five yards out and was able to watch for the minutest signs from my position behind the cover of some bushes.

The twenty-pound fish hit the bait with a fast jerk which made the antennae sound once. The line then bounced three times without causing any further sound on the buzzer. On the third bounce I had become fish were ever spotted, but time and time again the indicator would smash into the butt and away. Curiously the channel carp did not seem to twitch as they did in the main pool and steaming runs were the norm. This was, in some ways, confirmation of my theory that even the most wary fish will behave differently in areas where they do not, for whatever reason, expect to be hooked. Perhaps the most notable thing about the channel carp was their invisibility. Anglers fishing at Redmire had noted this on the shallows there and the same has been the case on many of the estate lakes that I have fished. The moral to be taken from this is never to assume

anything. If fish do not seem to be in evidence, try fishing a couple of hours in complete silence and concealment. The number of times that I have done this and had runs out of the blue is uncountable.

A second point is to never overlook a swim. On hard fished waters, the swims least used are likely to become the most productive at least until the fish catch on. It does not matter how unattractive they may look to us. Most of all *never* ignore a swim because it is uncomfortable. Such pitches have proved winners for me be-

An ambush is prepared at the boat house.

cause most carp anglers these days are so bivvy and comfort orientated they will never fish there.

Baits

My final comments on estate lakes revolve around baits. I am aware that I have plugged the following before, but it is worth repeating. It seems that because natural food plays such an important role in the diet of estate lake fish compared with other waters, to achieve lasting stimulation from carp you must either emulate the mass feeding situation (that is use particle baits) or use baits that provoke a natural response from the fish. Standard artificial flavours, as continually advertised in the angling press these days, are not the best long-term baits.

Contrary to many expectations, estate lakes invariably exist in areas of poorer soil. It would have been illogical for landowners to use the best arable land for setting out parks. Even the very rich were seldom that wasteful. Consequently many estate lakes exist on clay soil. Without this base they would not be able to hold water.

Centuries of deposited leaf-mould on the water also contributes to a phenomenon common on these waters – their acidity. Even when the water comes off chalk, the bottom itself will be acid. I have never been entirely happy with much that has been written about pH. I am not even certain that the lack of long-term success with artificial flavours on these waters has anything to do with the fact that most of these flavours are acidic themselves. To me, whatever the explanation, the thing is a fact.

In the early days, before flavourings were being used by all and sundry, I did have some short-term successes on these baits in the winter, but this was so inconsistent compared with my normal baits that I soon stopped experimenting. Perhaps the more persistent will eventually get it right, but it was not for me. I had three doubles in three hours one winter's day and then spent the rest of the season on that flavour. I did not get another take, not even a twitch. The bait was a milk-based HNV with maple, a flavour very highly rated where it is not being hammered to death. I even tried a couple of drops of amyl acetate, a trick well known to give baits a new lease of life. This was to no avail.

For most of the season, I found particle baits to be best but once the temperature starts falling (even as early as August in some years when the longer nights can cause the temperature to drop considerably) I have found paste baits take over. The most successful ingredients have proved to be various shrimp daphnia and insect meals in a milk and soya protein base. It has been a long time since I have experimented with these baits, because around 1977 I hit on a ready-made feed that contained all the ingredients that I considered best. However, by far the most successful mix in those early days was a combination of shrimp and daphnia meal with calcium caseinate substituted for the casein. I must stress though, that I have never used this mix in boilie form. Other winners were freeze-dried Tubifex worms in an HNV base. The drawback here was that it was very expensive, but it did work. Another good combination that was never followed up was mackerel meal and insect meal in milk and soya.

I tend to cheat these days, because I now add a ready-made animo combination to ensure there are no specifics absent from the final bait that might detract from the result in some circumstances. This is a liquid known as Minamine and it is made from a combination of extracts from liver, spleen and gastric mucosa. My good friend Paul Jackson put me on to it and, from the limited trials I have made it is the answer to the lazy angler's prayer.

Today I find one of the most important factors to consider in baits is buoyancy. I now realise that I must have fished many a time in years gone by with baits hidden in soft silt. This is probably why some of the best particles have proved to be those with flat sides which rest on the bottom without sinking into it. Likewise the addition of light ingredients such as shrimp meal and soya isolate are useful inclusions in boiled baits.

I have not touched much on rigs. In limited space I felt that it was more important to stress other aspects of fishing, such as location. After all, there is not a rig made to catch fish in an empty swim. On estate lakes it always pays to bear that in mind.

Wild Carp

JOHN BAILEY

Ever since Chris Yates' classic book *Casting At The Sun*, we have been aware that the original edition of *Quest* lacked substance on wildie fishing. Holland was included, that is true, but the traditional English fishing that Chris so unerringly brought back into vogue was missing. Of course, wildies are all about tradition – the carp that old Isaak talked about in the seventeenth century were almost surely the long, lean, fully scaled fish that one sees in nineteenth-century prints and that so excited B.B. at Beech Mire in this century. The art of carp culture has moved on greatly in recent years but that does not mean the old strains are in any way devalued. They are not. Like the collections of antique furniture there is a growing band of anglers who only desire old-style fish. Recently stocked carp, like chairs with their wrappings on, hold little appeal for some cultured specialists. Size alone is not important to a man like this: genetic integrity and history are of prime concern. Personally, I greatly enjoy the wildie side of the sport. The fish, the problems they pose and the waters they inhabit are for me quite worth a drop of many pounds in weight. Those men obsessive about 30lb carp will think this precious perhaps – I hope not. In its own way, the 3lb wildie is as much to be admired as the 30lb Italian mirror. For sure, never let a man say the one is better than the other!

I spoke of wildie problems. Probably the first one is to find a wildie water and actually decide what is a genuine wildie. A wildie is, of course, merely a long-established common carp. Its ancestors date back many generations and the selective breeding that gives modern fish their size, depth and overall bulk is entirely absent. These are common carp as natural as you can get – a once stocked fish that has after decades or even centuries reverted as much as possible to the wild. As far as I am aware, there is no positive test to be applied here. Fin rays, scale counts and teeth checks between wildies and commons will all be pretty much the same. It is the looks of the fish that proclaim it to be the wildie. The perfect shape is long and very slim with little shoulder hump and nothing approaching the pot mirror belly. The fins tend to look rather large on such a slender body and the head often dominates the overall look of the fish. Coloration is no real guide as it varies greatly and is generally dependent on the water type the fish inhabits. Gold, however, is less often found than in the typical common. Wildies often display a dusky blue tinge or even deeper gun-barrel grey.

Perhaps the truest test of the wildie is the history of its water. If no stocking has gone on for several generations then one can rest easy. The fish are of the old traditional type and in an ancient lake,

Examples of lost, lovely wildie waters.

Halfway between a wildie and a common – still, a lovely fish.

pond, mere or moat could probably be dated back centuries. Lucky you – you have the genuine article and there are not a great many left. Since the 1950s, a great deal of tinkering has gone on in the carp world. Post 'Clarissa', carp became the growing flavour of the coarse season and clubs stocked increasingly through the 1960s. Many illegal stockings have also gone on until it is comparatively rare at the end of the 1980s to find an untampered stock. Pits, by and large, are too young to contain genuine wildies. The exceptions, of course, are the old marl pits of agricultural areas. These deep, clay-banked, often overgrown waters frequently hold remainders of a wildies stock. The fish are often large. Carp do not spawn prolifically in

such places and what fish exist are not overly competing for food.

Many of the older wildie waters have given way to the spread of civilisation in the south. One has only got to read *Casting At The Sun* to realise that motorways, urban development and land drainage have ended the life of many a wildie strain over the past quarter of a century. Equally, in the more populated areas of England, few waters have escaped notice. The vast majority have been restocked on a regular basis in past years and the wildie stock has either been squeezed out or hybridised past recognition. Any experienced carp fisher can think of examples.

So, perhaps a major problem the dedicated wildie man must conquer is the location of a water. Some old famous names still exist – Beech Mire does I believe – but does Croxby Pond? Areas to search are the farm ponds of rural East Anglia, perhaps the hidden pools of remote Lincolnshire or the lost meres and moats of the Marcher Counties. One of the most productive of modern wildie waters now exists in Wales. I have seen it and it is wonderful. I visited it in October on a golden afternoon when the whole valley was ablaze with autumnal colour. The pool was overgrown and had only three fishing spots – all overlooking the distant river which was sparkling under the setting sun. Despite the lateness of the year, the wildies were well in evidence, bubbling and rolling and occasionally even crashing clear of the water. But I could not catch! I had the odd tremor and once even the float lifted, but that was all.

The local lad next to me had their measure though. Before the early dusk fell he had three out, all unmistakably the genuine article and the largest a very fine 5lb 12oz fish. We packed and he obviously took pride in my interest. We talked long about the lake and, in the end, as we walked to our vehicles, he told me of a lake remoter still in the heart of Wales, almost impossible to find but offering the most magnificent rewards to those that can do so. This, too, is a true wildie lake but the water is very ancient, probably even eleventh century. It is very clear and rich and the wildies are immense, reputedly to 15lb! It sounded the most nerve-tingling wildie water in the country and I decided then and there to make the search once my time allowed. This actually happened at the turn of 1989. I found the lake, with difficulty. Again, it was a wonderful afternoon and the water glowed in the

winter sunlight. Because of the cold, and the sneaking wind, I only saw one fish. It leapt and hung lit a second. Then it crashed back but I knew in that second I had seen a very large wildie indeed.

Obviously, then, remoteness is a key to the continued existence of wildies and travel is going to be likely. I have even heard of a promising water thirty miles north of Perth I mean to check out come spring!

Of course, even when located, the problems are hardly at an end. A wildie is a true carp, let us say the truest of carp, and it possesses all that species' cunning. Also remember that size with wild carp does not equate with age. Even a 3lb fish can be many years old. I guess a double-figure wildie would be immensely ancient. I know of one such fish that is at least forty

Bruno Broughton holds a lovely carp – nearly a wildie but perhaps fractionally too deep set to be the real thing.

years old and has only been caught three times in its last fifteen years, despite quite steady, quite advanced angling pressure on it. Even if the most sophisticated baits and methods have not caught up with these hidden places the carp will certainly have learnt a great deal about anglers, tackle and baits over their years. You will rarely today find wild carp to be mugs.

Wildies are very like common carp in their preference for cover. They will come into the open and sun themselves or bask in the way of mirrors, but this is more rare. Generally you will not find a wild carp far from reeds, weeds, lilies, fallen trees, islands, bicycles, sunken boats and snags of all sorts! Whatever underwater tangle your water possesses, be sure the best of the wildies will be backed right in there and will be loathe to leave. The constant dilemma is the placing of the bait. The heart tells you to get it in close but the head counsels caution. After all, the next problem with the wildie is his speed off the mark. My God, yes, I have had great scraps from mirrors but for sheer sizzling 0–70-in-three-seconds speed the wildie is the turbo of the carp world. A 'mere' five pounder can be a brute to stop over a handful of yards. Why, I remember that good old Norfolk fishermen, Joe Reed, hooking seven wildies in a single afternoon close to an island of weed and fallen tree. Three got into the reeds and three up the branches and one I swear to another continent. Wildies seven. Joe Reed nought. Of course, no one likes losing fish and Joe and I learnt our lesson that day. I am never silly or selfish now but fish where I know I have a good chance on sensible gear.

Gear sensible for a 5lb tench is not quite the same for wildies. It needs to be beefier for, game as tench are, they are not in the wildie class. Compare wildies more with a very aware, much brighter, stillwater barbel and you are close to the mark. A light carp rod and 5–7lb line are about the style. I am generally a Mitchell man but there are those who would never approach a wildie water with anything other than a centre pin. I suppose when in a time warp, it does to go the whole hog!

The question of baits is easy. Anything that catches carp does for wildies. They really will eat anything – especially in the traditional wildie lakes that are shallow, murky and full of nuisance fish competing for food. If one feels a need for high tech. and complication then boilies are of course an answer but not the only one. And I would ask you to think very hard before attacking a wildie water with the terminal rigs now so in vogue. What is right for Savay I would question at Beech Mire. Wildie fishing is not do or die. Keep, I think, a sense of proportion. Try the float. Link leger. Freeline. Try for them on the top or on the drop. To bolt and hair rig these little places for 4lb fish does not seem right to me – for once this approach has been used it is hard to revert back to traditional methods. Think hard before eating the apple of ambition and swallowing the innocence of the wildie! At its best, wildie fishing is a battle of wits in a beautiful place for the gamest fish that swims and self-hooking rigs have little or no place. I hate to make value judgements on any aspect of our great sport but here I am safe. I know every wildie man would agree whole-heartedly.

One of the joys of wildie fishing is in the winter. They cannot be described at all as a summer fish and bite just as freely after the frosts. There are three reasons, I believe, for this. Wildie waters are often poor ones in food content and competing species are frequently numerous. In these circum-

No doubting this: a superb common for Shaun Harrison.

stances wildies have to feed and work year round to live and prosper. Also, wildies never develop the paunch of southern mirrors. They really do have no surplus fat at all to see them through the fasts (if, in fact, mirrors do this themselves). Regular feeding is essential for wildies. Thirdly, the wild carp is very long established in the British climate. He has no recollection of Mediterranean temperatures and he has come to accept as normal the British winter. And the fact that he can survive in Scotland indicates a hardiness rare in normal carp. I do not know how biologically sound this thesis may appear but I am sure that winter fishing is often the cream of the sport. Ice on the water is no deterrent. If you can get a bait in your chances are high. The hardiness of these fish is exceptional. I have known wildie waters freeze solid right to the bottom mud for several weeks. And yet, come March and a thaw when you think all is lost, the float will dip, the rod will arch, the line will sing and you will be a wildie-ing again.

I cannot speak of wildies with too much admiration and love. They deserve all our attention and help. With all the threats the future poses for them, they are our threatened species and we must treat them as carefully as the little chippings of gold that they so truly are.

The Boat House Lake

JOHN BAILEY

I wish that I had been able to read Chris Currie's piece on estate lakes in the days that I tackled the Boat House Lake. Unfortunately I have lost the fishing there and cannot go back. Knowing what I do now, I would murder the place that once caused me so much headache – and come to that, heartache too. I can see how totally the Boat House carp fitted in to the behavioural pattern that Chris describes. Had I understood that then, I think I would have had the key to the water, even without further knowledge of baits or rigs.

The lake was hardly fished and what I was dealing with were carp in as original a state as is possible today. This did not make the carp easy, far from it in fact. Their lack of sophistication was more than outweighed by their nervousness of my presence. No matter how careful I might be, after half an hour or so all carp activity would gradually die down and would eventually cease and I would be left with few clues as to the fish's whereabouts. Location was made more difficult by the general murkiness of the water.

In short, I never came to understand their patrol routes at all. As far as I was concerned, they moved in haphazard ways round the lake and any contact with them I might make seemed always coincidental. Only two areas of the lake did I ever form opinions about. The first was water in the lee of the large island where the carp basked on hot days, from noon until evening shadows. They were unapproachable there. To reach them, I needed to cast eighty yards at least, and the lead required for this always disturbed them on water entry. Furthermore, they were suspicious of floaters and did not seem to feed on the bottom. In all, the island seemed to offer few possibilities.

More promising were the shallows that stretch for an acre or more. Sometimes I saw fish feeding there and once landed a low twenty pounder that fought probably better than any fish I have ever hooked. But, even in the shallows, I never stumbled upon a pattern in their behaviour. They were either there or not and I could find no explanation in either case.

Despite this bewilderment I loved the place. I do sincerely believe that estate lakes are the most beloved waters that any angler can fish. William Whiting set the tone for this section and I can only add that days did exist at the Boat House that seemed to me almost too precious to believe, when the weather really was hot and still, when the pigeons did coo and when the cattle did wade in the shallows and lie in the shade of hedgerows away from the sun. There was a clock that chimed away the hours and the only sound of the twentieth century would be an occasional far-off chain-saw in the park copses. The boat-house that gave the lake its name was Edwardian and was a relic of pre First World War picnic days.

The Boat House held two distinct stocks of carp, vastly differing, both interesting. The majority of the fish were distinct wildies; fully scaled, lean as whippets and barrel-grey in colour – they had been in the water for years. They bred each summer, though their numbers held steady with little apparent increase. Six pounds was a good weight for a Boat House wildie, but they all fought with a frantic power that made me love them. Wildies are tradition itself in so many ways, the real carp of the country; and they are dying even here as the Boat House silts and decays. These wildie lakes are never protected like buildings; a wild carp excites no public sympathy like a bittern or a barnacle goose. In the end the water level will fall to its pectoral roots and another population will be lost forever. I suspect in fifty years wildies will be creatures that only old men remember. The Boat House fish will have gone the way of the maypole, skittles, real ale and built cane!

'Few places are more tranquil than a wood embowered pool on a summer's evening.' The boat house looks on.

The keeper admires John's twenty-pounder from the Boat House Lake.

The minority of the carp were aged mirrors. I say aged though I cannot prove this, their scales seemed to hang on them like the wrinkles of an old woman's face. Their colours were subdued and sometimes they had that slackness around the belly that I associate with well-matured veterans. If anything this venerability only added to their glamour. It made them at one with their historic lake. Their age

bespoke wisdom and an excuse for my failures.

Some carp fishers say that the spirit of a water never affects them and that results are their only business. I am not one of these. If I ever had been, I could not bring myself to mention the Boat House now, and certainly not remember it as fondly as I do.

Round-up

JOHN WILSON

Martyn Page and John Bailey took the opportunity to visit John Wilson in his Norwich tackle shop to talk through the chapters by Kevin Clifford, Gerry Morris and Chris Currie. John is a highly experienced small water carp man who has the added advantage of managing his own fishery and of being a diver. Both these interests give his knowledge a deeper insight into the water types being discussed here.

We began by looking at Kevin Clifford's piece. John reinforced Kevin's reservations about the competitiveness of the modern big water, big carp scene. He adds that this type of fishing is dangerous for the newcomer who does not learn the patience and water craft of those older carp anglers who served their apprenticeship before the long-range/boilie stereotypes of today. To John there is something very sad, pathetic even, about men all hunting the same old, often disfigured big fish on the circuit waters, where nothing but the carp's ultimate size is considered.

Small waters can hold big fish, but often they are off the well-worn track and can give a more intimate type of pleasure. Also, a real insight into the nature of carp can be gained, not just from big fish but from carp of all ranges.

This leads us straight on to John's second point – on small waters the carp can also have an intimate knowledge of you, the angler! People assume that if you are fishing on a tiny water where the quarry can often be seen, putting them on the bank is made easier. Nothing could be further from the truth. One wrong cast, one careless footfall on the gravel, one missed run or one dropped flask and every carp in the pool is aware of the angler's presence and is on its guard.

We talked of water after water where the carp can be spooked by the simple arrival of an angler against the skyline. These are pools that can be very active one second and totally devoid of moving fish after just one careless movement and where those same fish remain unapproachable for the rest of that day.

This observation linked up with a habit of Gerry Morris's that John especially liked. He made reference to Gerry's care in leaving one-minute gaps between firing out each pre-baited boilie. We all admitted that we had never had the patience to do this and yet in the confines of a small water, we saw that to do so could have immense importance. John likened this to the feeding of tame carp on trout pellets. They flock to the splash. Equally, scared carp might just as easily spook from the disturbance of boilies dropping in around them – a noise they have come to associate with danger.

Nothing can be left to chance on a tiny water, not even apparently small details

Above *John Bailey is bent into a small water carp.*

Below *Anxiety! Sidestrain turns the fish from the tree roots.*

Above   *Thinking about the net.*   Below   *The job is nearly done.*

like this one. He made the point that Gerry had immediate and deserved success on the 'Graveyard' but after that the water died on him for the entire season. The first days of the season are certainly the key time to get to grips with ultra-careful small water fish, but even then, they will not tolerate one error or act of carelessness. Immediate success should not be taken too significantly or as a sign a water is permanently 'cracked'!

John was full of praise for the fact that Gerry, in describing the 'Graveyard' swim, mentions the name of the plant growing along the bar there. That plant was amphibious bistort and can only grow in three to four feet of water. Just by seeing that plant, the experienced carp angler has begun to build up a picture of the lake bed. This is where John's diving and fishery management comes in. To a great extent he can read a water's depth and even bottom make-up by the type of surface plants on show. It is this type of complete water knowledge that makes for a thinking, successful carp angler. It is something that only anglers with a thorough apprenticeship behind them are likely to learn.

Moving on to discuss estate lakes, John made the immediate point that we were not really comparing like with like. For example, many estate lakes are over three acres, a size which in our view does not qualify them as small waters. For instance, on three, four and five acre waters an angler can go back to using the standard two rod set-up, which is an immediate disadvantage on a true small water where it is vital to fish really tight.

Left A stirring battle from a very welcome double.

John's first comments centred around the nature of estate lakes and the fish behaviour in them. He focused attention on the shallow silted areas that Chris mentions. These can become de-oxygenated at night as the weed gives off carbon dioxide instead of oxygen. Carp will move through these areas, but they may not feed there or stay around for long periods during low levels of dissolved oxygen. This is backed up by the evidence of eel trappers, John added, whose fyke nets during periods such as the late autumn must be placed accurately if they do not want to haul in a catch of suffocated tench and carp amongst the night's eel takings. The problem lies in thick carpets of falling leaves which, in decay, starve the water of oxygen. They can be caught in the nets whilst moving through an area, but to be retained there can be deadly.

John certainly agrees with the emphasis on safe or inaccessible areas on any lake and for any species. He mentioned a local, heavily fished tench and rudd lake where he had a morning's hectic sport simply by donning chest waders and wading out to an area that had never been fished before. 'Safe' areas can never be ignored – though their success does have a limited life.

Looking at methods, John discussed the problem of the carp wary enough to spit out a bait without bolting or even moving an inch. Whilst Chris tackles the problem by hitting twitches, John suggests that float fishing would be a more accurate method. He would use the same end rigs as Chris describes but under a waggler set bottom end only and with all the line sunk between rod and baits. Fishing like this, John admits, is an effort in concentration, but by holding the rod an instant strike/hand action will put many carp on the bank. These would be deep into weed before a strike could be made on a standard leger/buzzer rig.

Finally, John queries the lengths that Chris goes to in order to make sure his baits remain above the silt. He suggests that as much of the carp's natural food is to all intents and purposes 'hidden' in soft silt, buried hook baits still emit an attraction to patrolling fish. Indeed, he thinks they are less likely to scare a carp by being so hidden, than when unnaturally proud over soft silt, standing out starkly to create immediate visual panic. He compares this situation with Broadland piking, where dead baits sink into bottom silt after an hour or more, but the pike still find them. There, in the silt, is after all where they are looking for their natural food – the eels.

LARGE WATERS
AND A
LOOK OVERSEAS

This, we realise, is a mixed bag of a section, but within it we believe you will find stimulation and great food for thought. The following authors speak of challenge, a pioneering spirit, and above all great carping excitement. We do believe that more and more anglers will travel to find the fish of their dreams and Phil Smith's chapter gives down-to-earth basics, whilst the other chapters concentrate more perhaps on the romantic. A mixture of the two is what carp fishing is all about.

Ormesby Broad: An Evening with John Nunn

JOHN BAILEY

It is a spring evening and I am standing on an arm of Ormesby Broad in Norfolk. The sun has set and turns the still water to placid gold. It was down there a quarter of a mile, just where the mist haze is now, just where the coots grow indistinct in the shadows, that I saw a huge common carp. The month then was June and I was poling along the margins to a tench swim when I chanced on a fish basking in weed. The boat did not scare it at all – why, I nearly grasped it by the tail root before it surged away! It was quite simply an enormous fish and I have never forgotten it to this day.

Tonight I am talking to John Nunn. He has lived on the water's edge these past ten years and I do not think there has been a day in that period that he has failed to go out on the water. He knows about these fabulous fish if anybody does.

J.B.   John, what size of water are we talking about here on Ormesby?
J.N.   This broad is 220 acres and that is just a part of a system which extends over 800 acres. It is so large that it takes me an hour and a half to row from my cottage to the far end of the system – and that's on a good day. I would never attempt it on some of the really windy days. So it is a very large sheet of water indeed. Added to that, most of the system is inaccessible and so we have large tracts of water which never see an angler. Many of the anglers that fish the system are, in fact, very poor oarsmen and as a result the far ends of the broads system are never fished at all. The banks, as I said, are completely inaccessible. There is a margin of reed and sedge, alder and willow, which extends to perhaps 100 metres in parts and this means that there is boat fishing only and given the fact that many of the people are just holiday anglers, they certainly don't venture far from the jetties from which the boats are hired.
J.B.   What we are effectively looking at then, is 800 plus acres that are not subjected to the angling pressure a normal carp lake might expect. If we move away from this extraordinary expanse of water and look at the fish themselves, when were the carp actually stocked into these hundreds of acres?

'When I think of this water, it's always summer.' Ormesby Broad at sunset.

J.N. The old East Suffolk and Norfolk River Authority stocked the system with carp in the early 1960s. At the time a well-known angling writer, Peter Collins, stated in his publication *Fishing in the Norfolk Broads*: 'Since neither shore nor night fishing are possible, the carp might to all intents and purposes just as well have been released in the North Sea.'

J.B. So, these fish that have been in Ormesby Broad for over twenty years now are something of a mystery. Although we don't know exact sizes or numbers when put in, we are, I think, between us pretty sure of the sort of fish we are talking about now.

J.N. Those carp really thrived. In 1969 a mystery killer wiped out most of the bream population. Up until that time, bream had been the major species on the Broad and had accounted for a large part of the food available. With the arrival of this mystery killer and the depletion of the bream stocks, the competition for food was drastically cut and this on a water rich in daphnia. Therefore, it is obvious that those carp really put on a spurt in their growth rates.

J.B. Agreed John, but we are still avoiding the issue. I know it is a difficult question, but how big do you think the carp are that we are talking about?

J.N. I first saw the carp when I was poling along the margins four years ago. Four mirrors and one common. I didn't see them for another two years, but I was left with this memory of some most impressive looking fish. In the closed season of 1984 I chanced upon them at the end of May. For two weeks I saw them every day in the same spot – four mirrors and one common. The four mirrors were approximately the same size as a mirror that I had seen (the one you had caught the previous season). Now I was lucky enough to have seen that mirror the same week as I was observing the Ormesby carp. You told me that your mirror weighed around the thirty-eight to forty pound mark. These mirrors looked exactly comparable. However, the common dwarfed them all. Now, I am well aware that commons sometimes don't have the depth, but this fish certainly had an enormous length and a very impressive fish it was too. They were very close to my boat. I could have touched them with an oar. Each day for fourteen, maybe fifteen days, I watched these fish.

J.B. There are two things that I would like to say at this point. One is to reiterate that the carp not only in Ormesby but in other waters are not necessarily afraid of boats and very often accept boats in their close vicinity. The other thing that I would like to say is something that occurred again and again in the production of this book which is that while in most waters mirrors tend to grow bigger than commons, it does seem that in freak waters, or at least special waters, the fabulous fish, the staggering fish, can very often be commons. My own feeling is that there is always the potential of the record being blasted apart by a common carp, and I would like to think this might be done at Ormesby. I think it would be tremendous to see a carp record broken by an almost natural fish. After all, that common has been in the water now a quarter of a century and I think that this would be a very fitting record.

To move on, you, more than anybody, know the movements of these very mysterious fish on the Broad. Very few people have seen the fish or even guess of their existence. How do you see their movements through the course of a normal summer?

J.N. My observations of the carp have been in one particular area of the Broad. That area is four to five feet deep, hard-bedded with gravel, and has bulrush stems growing along the margins. It has always been at the same time of the year, the closed season, when I have actually observed the big carp. But I have also seen one or two carp in the season in June and through July. Again the shallower areas of the Broad where weed growth is most abundant seem to be the areas favoured by them. An angler was fishing one of the shallow arms of the Broad last year when a carp leapt out in front of him. Again, a weedy area.

There does seem to be some correlation in the movements of the carp with the movement of the bream shoals towards spawning. It's almost as if the carp are attracted by the spawning ritual of the bream and roach, for they spawn in the same area, and the splashing possibly seems to throw them into some sort of excitement over being in this particular area.

However, by the time the season has begun and anglers are out on the water, this is where the problems start for anyone who is seriously considering locating these carp. For I think that once a few days have passed and anglers have splashed their way around the Broad, any fish that might have been in this shallow area have been thoroughly scared. Remember that it is not only anglers who come on the Broad, for we have holiday-makers who come out from Yarmouth – lads who are trying to impress their girlfriends with their rowing ability – and this certainly doesn't help to keep the carp in the shallow areas. By mid-June or late June they have dispersed. Where to? Well, there are plenty of places for them to go to. The margins, as I said, are up to 100 metres in thickness. I have taken my boat through the sedge and I have found pools amongst the sedge. Pools which would make a decent farm pond in certain places and there is no telling which one of these pools they could have got into. But I think certainly if I was a carp it's the sort of place I would make for once the holiday season gets into swing.

J.B. I think, John, you have voiced my feelings on the Ormesby carp. That is, that they do live in a most extraordinary environment. I think that anybody who ever catches a big Ormesby carp will either do it through luck (which would be a very notable event) or more importantly

At least John Bailey can catch the Ormesby tench.

through somehow cracking their lifestyle. Now, it's no secret that one of my greatest carp fishing ambitions is to catch an Ormesby carp. You particularly have fired my enthusiasm for these fish. I have never really come near one as I said at the start of this chapter. I have almost touched one but that was certainly not with one of my hooks! Why have, do you think, these massive Ormesby fish never been caught? Why have they never really been even tackled by anglers?

J.N.   Firstly, there is ignorance of their existence. Not very many people have seen them; I wouldn't think more than half a dozen people. Secondly, there is the fact of boat fishing. Boat fishing is the only access to the water. There is a short stretch up on the road bridge which is available to bank fishers, but this is a very short stretch over-populated with novice anglers, children, holiday anglers etc. Hardly the environment for a serious carp man. The boats are poor to say the least. The rowlocks are ill-fitting and they are noisy. On top of that, the people who hire the boats out on this broad system will only allow the boats out from dawn to dusk so this precludes any ideas of night fishing.

Now, I am in the fortunate position of being able to fish the Broad after dark and yet I have not put a hook into one of these fish. I put my failure down to inability to locate the fish. In the 1984 season I did try for them – anyone would do, I think, who

A fine big water carp for John Watson.

had seen them for fifteen days consecutively. However, by 8 June they had disappeared and my pre-baiting campaign was grinding to a very ominous looking failure. The baits which had been mopped up each day were remaining there and when opening day arrived I was, I am afraid to say, fishing without confidence and I had this feeling that I had lost yet again to the carp that had melted away into the wilderness of water.

J.B.   So, you were defeated again. Have you got any plans for the future to try and tackle these enormous fish? I know that we disagree to some extent over future methods and techniques. I am quite happy

to state that I believe the best chance for these fish is on the top with floating baits. My own belief is that to try boilies or pastes or any bottom bait is to court disaster. I feel that you will be pestered (if that is the right word to use) by the specimen bream and tench in the water. I think that with floating baits you will see the fish, that you will see them accept or reject baits, and that you will know very much more accurately how your approach work is succeeding or failing. Now we have disagreed (if that is not too strong a word) over this approach, have you got any more feelings since the last time we spoke on it?

J.N.   No, I haven't really changed my views. The thousand odd coots that inhabit this piece of water are still here and they are still showing great liking to any floaters that are put out. I feel the problem is getting the carp used to taking the floaters, but the birds just won't give them a chance. So despite the fact that there are plenty of bream and plenty of tench bottom feeding, I still consider the way to do it is to fish on the bottom, possibly with boilies to avoid the bream and tench. The coots show no shyness towards boats, because many of the people who are on Ormesby are people who are out for a row on holiday and they feed the coots, so the coots are possibly tamer than one might expect.

J.B.   I go along with what you say. Yet I must add that for at least five or six years I have had this dream that one could go out at dusk, find the carp, put floaters to them as dark fell and, in the absence of the water-fowl get the fish to take bait on the top and land one this way. Do you still feel there is no mileage in this type of approach?

J.N.   Certainly I think there is mileage in that, because if one were to locate the fish and fish for them after dark with the coots roosting up in the alders, there would certainly be a good opportunity of catching one of these carp – or at least putting a hook in one of them. The problem, of course, is that for most anglers there is no opportunity to fish after dark on this Broad but that is not the major problem. The major problem (for me anyway) is locating them; I have never actually been fishing for those carp knowing that they are in the area in which I am fishing. So we come back to the same old problem of location on such a vast water.

J.B. Whatever you say, the dream still exists. In my wildest moments I have imagined the battle from one of these fish. There are no snags, the water stretches for miles. I have this vision of a fish just going and going and going. You, yourself, must have had the same sort of ideas in the lonely hours that you have fished this Broad.

J.N. Yes, certainly if I was to put a hook into one of these fish I would feel extremely confident of landing it. There are, as you say, no snags, there is a lot of water to play your fish in and, if it does go into the sedges, you have always got a boat to follow it in there. So yes, I would feel confident and I do feel able to fish relatively light line for these fish.

J.B. I think we agree that these strange fish have not spawned tremendously successfully in the twenty years they have been in the water. It does seem to me that they are probably very mature fish, that their future is to some extent in doubt and that if any of these quite magical fish are to come from the Broad, I expect that it will have to be in the 1980s or perhaps early in the 1990s.

J.N. I certainly agree with that. The opportunity will pass by the early 1990s.

Last year I observed a carp about 100 metres from my garden and I thought to myself – this is the chance; I can have a go for it from the garden. At first I went out and had a look to see which area it was frequenting and I put some floaters out. The carp ignored them all. It circled round, completely oblivious of me and my boat, completely oblivious of the floater that happened to be riding on its back and I thought to myself – something's not quite right here. I left her. The next day I went out to the same spot. There she was again.

Immaculate commons catch the rays of the sun as they lie in John Watson's hands.

More floaters. Ignored, once again. And so it went on for two more days until she wasn't there. I rode around the bay, through the reeds, and there sadly she was, belly up, expired. A mirror, I thought between twenty-five and twenty-seven pounds. Her life ended, a happy life certainly, never caught. Twenty-five peaceful years spent in this Broad.

J.B. John, we have wandered in from the water's edge, we've moved into your study that overlooks this lovely stretch of water. I cannot help noticing and admiring this very well-preserved split cane rod. A Richard Walker Mark IV, B. James & Son. I reckon you probably bought it or it was given to you as a gift in the early 1960s. I bet that's got some memories. I am myself very much a traditionalist. I do love fishing with built cane rods. I still use them for the majority of my carp fishing.

J.N. The rod is of particular sentimental value actually. It was built by my brother-in-law who used to work for B. James in the 1960s and he actually has a rod which has never been used. It's a testament to his own craftsmanship and he keeps it in his wardrobe. Mine has been used. It has caught many fish. It has, I suppose, landed more tench than anything else and I fondly remember the feel of my first-ever tench on that rod and it's still something that sticks in my memory – quite different from the glass and carbon rods of today. Certainly something that I still use occasionally just for the fun of it.

J.B. In conclusion, I'm very glad that you said those words. One of the messages of this book is if not to preach tradition, at least not to ignore it. One of the things that I would love to see in the next few years of carp fishing is one of the fish that you have described actually being landed and, if possible, by yourself. Then we wouldn't be talking simply about tradition; I think that we would be talking about a legend.

The Wildies of the Dutch Wilderness

NICO DE BOER

Nico de Boer, the well-known Dutch carp angler, has given us a vivid picture of his carp fishing in Holland. Although he is not talking of big fish, he does describe something very special indeed. Here beats the heart of Low Country carping – miles of dykes, canals and rivers stretching from horizon to horizon in a never-ending criss-cross of waterways. The waters he describes are lost, lonely marshland places, under wide skies broken only by the far scattered windmills.

The fish Nico searches for are the true wild carp, or farm carp, that are the ancestors of all the stock-bred leviathan mirrors. This ancient species amazes him – its power, its beauty and its hereditary cunning. This, then, is the story of a man searching waterland for the genuine carp, the medieval wildie.

The low sun on the lid of the horizon gives the water a golden glow. In the tall grass of the dyke, I lie, taking in the silence. I thread the line through the rings of my carp rod very slowly, nearly lazily, as though I have no appetite for what I am doing. Rather, though, it is a question of slowing down to the pace of this new world. I had hurried home, eaten quickly and raced out here to the wilderness and now I need time to relax, to unwind, to collect my thoughts.

In the far distance, my fishing friend Kees approaches, keeping our meeting to fish for the huge wild carp that live here.

Dutch carp fishing in a single frame!

The dykes of Holland, still home to the true wild carp.

He too is walking slowly, watching the bow-waves of carp moving away, here and there, in the drainage ditches. We greet each other quietly and then go our separate ways.

The slanting sun is a problem and I creep to the water's edge to keep my shadow off the crystal-clear dyke. I pull my tackle behind me and slide everything into action position. I thread a golf ball sized potato on to my line with a baiting needle and gently push my rod over the reeds. I swing the bait out and it settles in three feet of water under a slightly overdepth float.

I lie back against the dyke, enjoying the last warm rays of the sun, watching the dabchicks dive and the warblers hover after the evening flies. Down the dyke, I see Kees grow tense and reach for his rod. For minutes he is taut and then he too settles back like me – another big wildie has moved on.

The sun has quite gone, the wind has blown right away and now the mosquitoes come out over the summertime marsh. I pull up my collar and tug down my hat. I catch a whiff of Kees' evilly strong tobacco, which he uses to clear the air. Then, in the corner of my eye, I see my float drop. The lash of my rod, the whine of the nylon and the screech of the reel break the silence. The water erupts as a torpedo-back breaks the water before me. This is a fish I cannot hold. He is here into weed and there into lilies and in the end it seems as if I have lost him somewhere in the darkness.

This is where Kees shows what a good fishing friend is. Into the water he goes, well over his boots, searching around with the great net. There is a call of triumph and back on the bank we free the fish of its green weed blanket – and the hook. Carp loonies that we are, in the lamp's beam we are still astonished by the beauty of this carp. We are very content, very proud even of what is now a rare achievement anywhere in Europe.

Wildies and Mirrors Compared

Wildies are my sweetest water brothers and yet they are in retreat, even here in Holland, for centuries one of their strong-

The final surge of a Dutch wild carp.

holds. In part, the wide stocking of mirrors has led to crossbreeding and the purity of the true wildie has been tainted. The bigger mirrors feed harder and longer, they are less shy and gradually they overshadow the native race.

Land management too, is squeezing out the true carp of Holland. In the north, dyke management and the conversion of water to land has put the wild fish into retreat. This could be a disaster for they are the only carp species that fit this environment suitably. Their slender shape has evolved from centuries in the shallow water that is now under threat from towns, pollution

A summer evening well spent in Holland.

and encroaching farm land.

Biologically, they are quite different to the mirror carp. They are muscular and even the barbules are stronger, although shorter. They have up to twenty per cent more white blood cells and the sugar content of their blood is sixteen per cent higher. There is less water in their livers and muscles and a higher concentration of fat in all their organs. They have more vitamin E in their eyes and intestines and their backbones are more flexible than the 'axle rods' of their mirror cousins. Their swimbladders are different. Wildies have two bladders that divide the air and inter-act well with their fin patterns. Mirrors here have one large bladder and one smaller one. Equal exchange of air is more difficult and they are more reliant on their fins for swimming and balancing.

In short, all these factors make the wildie the perfect creature for the shallow dykes of Holland. Their bodies help them withstand low oxygen in the summer and severe freeze-ups in the winter. So tenacious to life are they, that wildies can live for forty years in an environment that can only prove hostile to the less resilient mirrors.

Of course, farm bred common carp are stocked and can be confused with real wild carp. There are differences, however. The

A picture of the lone, roving carp angler.

common has a larger head, a more obviously humped back and a less deeply forked tail. They also have a thicker skin that reduces their oxygen intake in the summer.

Water Sense

Come to Holland for the wild carp and forget all the stereotyped ideas of the modern carp scene. Here the most modern baits and presentations have little place – your problem is the extreme clarity and shallowness of these ditches, dykes and canals that fringe the North Sea. Wildie fishing is based not on technical knowledge but on a feeling for the water.

I set off with one rod, a camera and a small shoulder-bag, walking, rowing perhaps, chasing these shadows of fish. My eye is constantly on the wind strength and direction, the sun, the depth of the dyke, any depression on the bed and clusters of water plants. I am a rover, trying bridges, casting to wooden marker posts and sluice gates. Any feature stops me, attracts my potato – cast in hope of the genuine wild carp.

That superb English angler Graham Cowderoy nurses a lovely Dutch mirror.

Postscript

Since 1985 events disturbing to some have taken place in the Dutch carp world. Then, when the book was being put together, the Dutch were just catching up on the English scene. Boilies and a great deal of English gear were being imported but generally their fishing was still in our own early Walker days of the 1950s. The Dutch were catching well . . . but there were plenty of carp.

Of course, England moved from Walker to Hutchinson in thirty years but in Holland the progression appears to have taken three years. The result is a fanatical carp scene to a degree generated by English anglers. Dutch carp have shot from the potato to the very best baits of today and missed out on all the stages between – trout pellets, particles and pastes. It seems impossible to go back squares in the carp game and these formative days have been lost entirely to the Dutch angler. By going straight to the top of the carping ladder, the Dutch boys have

Phil Thompson is a brilliant English angler who has had excellent catches in Holland.

made a rod for their own backs. The process has been unwitting and it is only human nature to fish as well as is possible at the time. Not everybody is happy there and some, it seems to Martyn Page who visits Holland regularly, are turning from the scene.

The accelerated learning process obviously has an effect on the carp. Within three years, the average Dutch carp has had at least a taste of every bait and technique available today. Paranoia has resulted in some places, we are told, and it is difficult to see where the Dutch scene will go if not back to the natural.

Of course, nothing is certain. The Dutch are the most clinically minded, rational people. They understand and think the rigs through. In a year or two, we might find advances made on our exported methods and the teaching process could well be reversed.

Two Weeks at Cassein

PHIL SMITH

Phil Smith is one of the most respected anglers in this country and even if not truly a specialist carp angler, few men know how better to exploit any big fish opportunity. Here he describes two visits to the new European carping Mecca, Lake Cassein near Cannes in France.

Problems and Preparations

Following a friend's successful trip to Cassein, I was talking on the 'phone with Joe Taylor. It soon transpired that we were both interested and our journey evolved. Within a few days the boat was booked, insurances were arranged and other sundry items were being dealt with. We found out later that the date of our week came within the French closed season which runs from 15 April to 15 June. Saved by the bell we found that you could still use one rod in the closed season, although normally three rods can be employed.

The day duly came. We set off, but no words can prepare you for that trip. It is 730 miles down the *autoroute* and with minimal stops this still takes twelve hours travelling at 90 m.p.h. Just think of that! After you have driven for the time of a normal eight-hour working day you would still have 250 miles left to travel. It is a case of seeming light years from home!

Arriving at the lake you will need a permit. This can be obtained from the local cafés along the lakeside at a cost of about £13 for the year. Getting details of the fishing can be difficult with very few people able to speak English, but remember these main restrictions:

1. No night fishing! This is often ignored by English anglers, many of whom find the French enforce a rule vigorously and make raids at 1 a.m. or 2 a.m. all around the lake.
2. No fires! There is a very grave risk of forest fires and the normal practice of cooking on the bankside is not allowed. This is looked upon as a worse offence than night fishing, so do beware.
3. No camping! The fears of fires and night poaching combine to prohibit random camping at the lakeside. However, there are numerous campsites available.

The first and biggest problem the carp angler will have upon arrival is the sheer size of the water. With thirty miles of bank, you can have an awful lot of swims to go at, and choice of starting area is a nightmare. The lake is in the shape of three arms radiating from a central area. One runs roughly west, while the others go north and south. Access to the south is good, with a road following along a major part of its length. Most of the large expanse of the north arm can only be gained by boat, while the west arm is reached by a couple of rough tracks or,

Phil Smith holding a superb Cassein mirror.

better again, by boat.

First Trip to Cassein

Perhaps the best way to proceed from here is to relate my own adventures on the two trips undertaken in 1985. In the last week of May, Joe Taylor and myself in one car and Stuart Martin and Rod Elliot in another set off, and after sailing at 11 p.m. from Dover we arrived in blazing hot sunshine at 2.30 p.m. the following day. We found that English anglers had already been very successful taking fish up to sixty-eight pounds.

With the ease of access we decided to fish the south arm and were soon moving tackle down to one of the many points that feature along the road bank. Shortly after this we were approached by two chaps who proved to belong to the Guard, armed Park Rangers with wide-reaching powers. By sign language they pointed out the rules of one rod only, no stove and no night fishing. Our plan was to fish potato over tinned sweetcorn and with this in mind we had taken over two hundredweight of tinned corn with us and we baited the swim each morning and evening, adding a bucket of peanuts each time to the mix.

The first three days were very patchy. The one rod and no night fishing rules did not help, nor did the crowds of people who were there for the Bank Holiday. Sail boards, paddle boats, swimmers, topless sunbathers, and whole families of picnickers all fight for the bank space. The sandy beachlike swims and the sheer size of the lake make it a very popular daytrip, so be prepared for company.

The first fish came to Stuart on the Tuesday morning and went 31½lb. It gave Stuart the extra pleasure of taking the first

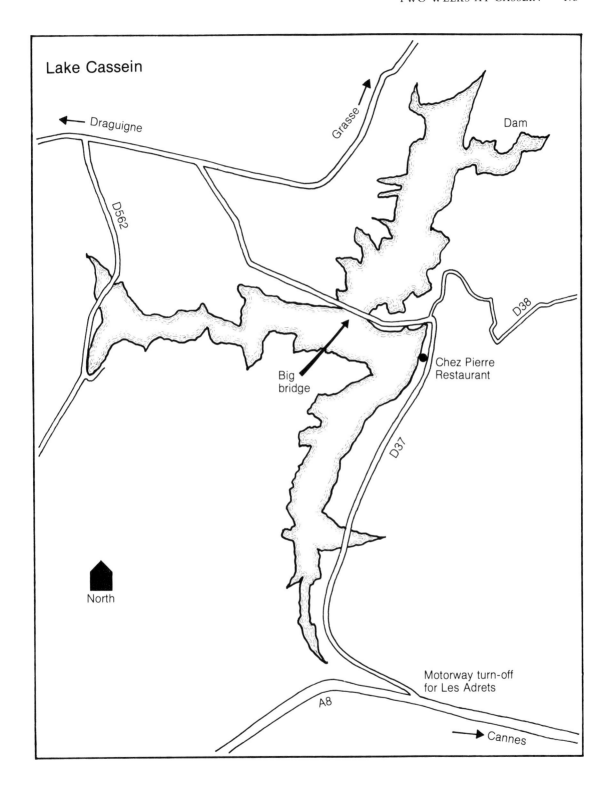

Lake Cassein

Draguigne

Grasse

Dam

D562

D38

Big
bridge

Chez Pierre
Restaurant

D37

North

Motorway turn-off
for Les Adrets

A8

Cannes

of the 'big three' (the 30lb carp, 30lb pike and the 30lb catfish). Tuesday afternoon Joe and I finally opened our account. By now we had changed to HP baits on the hook with three to four hundred baits going into the swim along with the corn. We were, of course, a little disappointed at not having caught yet, but now we had moved swims and at last were seeing fish. You don't see cruisers at Cassein, but they do leap, and leaping fish can always be caught.

Joe had his first take at 2 p.m. Initially the fish was snagged, but Joe walked out to his chest and the fish came free. He was now in trouble as the fish powered off, pulling him with it. He had lost his grip being so far in the water and his only way out was to back-wind whilst walking backwards on to dry land. This done, he was again in control. The fish put up a tremendous fight and, as it was slowly brought towards netting range, the hook pulled out! Doom, gloom and despondency! Three and a half days waiting, only to hook and lose a good fish! It was beginning to look as though a dead robin or two littered our trail to Cassein!

At 3.10 p.m. I had my first run, and run is the word I must use. The line disappeared at an amazing rate and the strike met with a solid resistance. I would gain line, then the fish would take it back. So it went on for twenty minutes as the fish slowly weakened. At long last he slipped into the net and we looked at our first carp from France. Our hope when we set off to Cassein was to catch a 30lb plus fish each, but this fish was something else again. A lot of scrambling around and finally the weight was confirmed by Joe at 41lb. Success!

This was very much a team venture and Joe and I had agreed that after the capture of the first fish we would take alternate turns on the two rods. The system does have some drawbacks but at the end of the day we were quite happy with the outcome. Nothing else happened for us that day, but Rod took a fish of 26lb at 6 p.m.

We got our heads down for the night only to be woken before too long by Rod, who told us their car was a write-off. It appeared they were travelling the hundred yards or so up the road to see us, when they found themselves on the wrong side of the road motoring towards a French car. The result was a head-on collision. Remember that this is very easy to do, so always be well insured and careful.

Rod and Stuart had gone to hospital, leaving the odd bit of tackle in the swim. After a dawn start I gave it an hour and then went down to their swim to collect everything up for them. Arriving back after an hour or so I found Joe had had a hectic spell, losing two fish and landing one of 28lb. It was now my turn to fish and I was soon into another good one.

We took to the boat and after a very good scrap the net went under a fish similar to my forty pounder of the day before. Joe started to row back to shore, but with the net over the side there was a lot of drag. Grabbing the net I lifted it in but all that happened was that the fish rolled out and swam away. Stupidly I had neglected to lift the net frame! I have done many idiotic things in my life but this ranks as number one. Joe just sat there without saying a word. I looked at him thinking that there must be a funny side to it all! It was decided that having not been weighed the fish did not count so when the rod produced yet another run I struck and landed a fish of 29½lb. The next and last run of that morning was Joe's, this fish was snagged and broke the hook length.

This snagging is quite a problem, many of the swims are loaded with sawn-off tree stumps and/or boulders. With this in mind we were using $2\frac{1}{4}$ to $2\frac{1}{2}$lb test curve rods combined with 15lb line. The 2oz leger weights were attached with a weak 4lb paternoster length. A pattern seemed to be emerging. One rod was cast into 25 feet on a drop-off and the other into 12 feet on the side of the bar which ran out from where we were fishing. All but one of the runs had come to the rod in 12 feet of water, so we now drew the other rod closer into the shallow water to fish near it.

Through midday and afternoon we, as usual, lay around melting in the ninety degrees Fahrenheit of blazing sunshine. A couple of points of interest are the tremendous displays of flowers at this time, though by the September trip they were tinder-dry and dead. Another thing we noticed was the lack of wildlife. There were very few birds, no rabbits, squirrels or any of the usual things that can make a day's fishing here in Britain. We did see a few lizards, snakes and very large toads,

however, which were at the very least different!

On the afternoon in question, it was Joe's turn at the rod and the three boilies on a dacron hair rig were taken. Again the speed of the run was incredible and in no time there was a danger of losing all the line on the first run. We made for the boat, the clutch screaming as the fish tore off down the lake. The excitement was short-lived as we found the fish to be jammed solid almost forty yards out. From directly above the snag I heaved, wrapping the line around my arm in order to pull hard enough against the snag. Inch by inch, foot by foot, and yard by yard I got the line back, but there was no indication that there was a fish on the end.

With the slight breeze blowing down the lake, the boat was holding down wind of the snag, so rowing back upwind I pulled again and the line came free. Joe was now back in contact with the fish and what followed was exciting even for me as a spectator. The fish kept deep, and here deep means deep, going down to sixty and

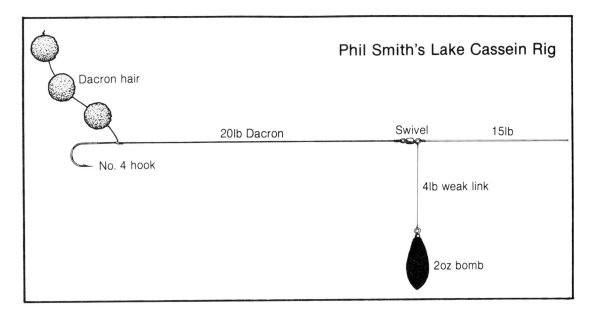

Phil Smith's Lake Cassein Rig

Dacron hair

20lb Dacron

No. 4 hook

Swivel

15lb

4lb weak link

2oz bomb

A boat is essential on Lake Cassein for location, baiting and playing.

even eighty feet. Imagine playing a fish to within fifteen feet of the boat, just out of sight directly beneath, when away she goes again on a powerful run vertically to the deeps! We yo-yoed up and down the lake, a hundred yards here and a hundred yards there, and all this time the fish was resisting heavy pressure put on by Joe.

At last we drifted down the lake and there was still no sign of seeing the fish. After the best part of an hour he finally broke surface and looked big. When he finally slipped into the net, we were almost half a mile away from the original swim. This fish was not going to be tipped back and with great care we made our way to the bank. Quite a crowd had collected now to see the weighing which proved the fish to be 54lb!

Rod and Stuart returned at dusk in a replacement car, neither being seriously injured. After a long talk we got our heads down to prepare for a dawn start. The following morning we all fished the same point and soon Stuart was playing a carp which gave a very poor fight and proved to be very scrawny, weighing 31lb. This was followed by two low 20lb fish to Rod and myself and by Joe taking another pig of a fish that went 32lb.

In the afternoon the lads moved back to their original swim when yet again disaster struck them and in the late evening they came back to tell us that their money, passports and other documents had all been stolen from the car. Joe and Rod went off to try and arrange for some money and to report the loss. While they were gone I had a run and after a very good scrap landed a beautifully proportioned fish that weighed 37lb. The colour was glorious, with the predominance of gold making it truly one of the nicest fish I have ever taken or seen.

Rod and Stuart packed up and we were left with one day to go. Have you noticed how the hours travelling to a venue are longer than the last few hours spent at the

Joe Taylor's astonishing 54lb Cassein fish.

waterside? True to form the next day flashed by, Joe taking a pretty mirror of 24lb which proved to be the last fish of the week.

The following is a list of points to note from that first week on the water:

1.   You must have a boat. Having spent the time, effort and money to fish here you are foolish to lose fish either from their sheer power or more likely on a snag. Boats are available from the waterside cafés. We used Pierre's and the boat cost around £6 a day, well worth it when you land the big fish you would have lost otherwise.

2.   Most English people think that most French people speak English – they don't. Take a French phrase-book at the least.

3.   All food can be obtained at costs similar to England. You may not get exactly what you wanted, but you can live well. There is a large supermarket about four miles away down the south arm. Keep

Another lovely French mirror.

going until you come to a major cross-roads, turn left and you will find the supermarket, camping site and good restaurants a little way along.

4. The *autoroutes* are toll-roads so allow about an extra £50 for the return trip. This is expensive, but the saving of time is an important factor.

5. The right swim for fish can be the wrong swim for leger weights and line, so do not go with less than fifty of these, just in case.

6. After Rod and Stuart's catalogue of disasters, try to remember which side of the road you are driving on! I have gone wrong several times but have got away with it. Keep your documents and cash safe. We were told that several passports get stolen every day at the height of the

season.

7. If possible look to fish where you can see fish. Do not stick in the swim waiting for them to come to you.

We came home vowing to return the following year, but such is the lure of Cassein that we were soon making plans for a return in September. For forty odd years I have stayed in the British Isles without the urge to travel abroad, but now I was going twice in a single year.

The Return to Cassein

For the second trip we used the experience of the first in order to make things easier. We realised we wouldn't need anywhere near the amount of clothes we took, as night temperatures are still quite high. By going on to HP baits completely we could save the tremendous weight of corn we had taken before. By choosing a better sailing time we could make the trip easier by removing the need to travel through the night in England. Leaving Joe's at 8.30 a.m. on the Friday, we had the chance to stop off to look at a favourite tench water and arrive at Dover at 12.30 p.m. in time for the 1.30 p.m. sailing. We stopped three times on the trip down and arrived at the lakeside at 3.30 a.m. We had taken a third angler with us for this trip, a friend from the Isle of Wight – Tony Chaffey.

Going down to Pierre's at 5.30 a.m. we got Tony's permit and arranged for a boat. Shortly afterwards we were back in the swim which produced for us in May. At 7.15 a.m. the sun came over the hill and proceeded to scorch us for the next twelve hours. Along with the sun came the people – a French family, Mum and Dad, Gran, Grandad, several children and their friends all sitting about fifteen feet behind us. At least the topless ladies were back to the left and to the right which did improve the scenery somewhat!

We were fishing HP baits as mentioned, bringing 16,000 for the eight days we would be at the waterside. We baited up around polystyrene markers and then spent the rest of the day watching surf-boarders, paddle boats and swimmers stopping to investigate our white blobs! The more we shouted the more they seemed to gather around!

There was no fish activity until 5 p.m., but then, just as I was saying to Joe that even with the disturbance we could get a take, I had a lightning run. After playing the fish for two or three minutes it became snagged. Going out in the boat, I applied pressure from directly above it and after a few moments it came free. A noticeable characteristic of the fight from the boat is the way in which the carp keep down to the bottom and this fish snagged on me yet again, this time apparently solidly. Twice Joe rowed me around the snagged fish as I pulled with maximum pressure. In the end I felt all was lost and the fish would not come free. I hand-lined for a break and just as I expected the 15lb line to crack, it came free with the fish still attached! Vowing that he would not snag again I really bent in to get him up. On three occasions he took the complete rod under water up to the cork handle and forced me to give line! What power! What a scrap! It cannot be properly described.

Eventually the fish weakened and at long last she lay in the bottom of my net.

With great care we made our way to the shore where possibly forty people had collected. A weight of 44½lb was confirmed. 'Cassein the incredible' had done it for us again!

The Future

As yet I have not fished the north arm so can only make generalisations. It is a very large slice of Cassein and almost the only access is via boat. It has the advantage that once in your chosen swim you will not be troubled by the crowds or other water users because their access is just as difficult. As with the other two arms, there are plenty of features in the form of bays and points with their associated bars out into the lake. I have spoken to English lads who did venture into this relatively unexplored part and who had considerable success.

The newcomer to the water can be hopeful that any swim he chooses will produce carp. Once into fish you can get a forty, fifty or even a sixty-pound fish, as they all pick up the same baits. The recent capture of an enormous catfish opens up another side of Cassein. Pike of fifty pounds, though rare, are caught, as are perch of six pounds, eels of gigantic proportions and many other species which grow to massive size. With a little wider search, you will find other lakes and rivers producing carp to fifty pounds, barbel to twenty pounds, and a French friend tells us of a water-producing zander to over thirty pounds. The mind boggles with the rich waters still waiting to be tapped.

Embalse de Santillana

ALISTAIR NICHOLSON

When you draw together the attractions of scenery and setting, with good weather, friendly 'natives', and some leviathans of the carp world, topped off by the fact that they are all commons, you have a recipe that is hard to beat.

Santillana is set in the foothills of the Sierra de Guadarrama, an imposing mountain range just north of Madrid. The lake is nearly 3,000 feet above sea level, with a truly spectacular castle at Mananares el Real on the shore opposite to where fishing is allowed. In the setting sun, with the castle lit and the mountains rising to 7,000 feet immediately behind, it is the stuff of which fairy-tales are made. As yet another crash heralds the return of a leaping common carp to its watery home, the romance deepens still further.

The lake was formed by the damming of the Rio Manzanares which runs directly south to Madrid. Santillana is now a nature reserve and water supply reservoir. In shape it bears some resemblance to the Isle of Wight, but fortunately it is not as large measuring only five miles broad by two and a half miles across. The map showed an island, but the lake level was sufficiently low to re-form its link with the shore. The shallow water in this area meant it attracted large numbers of feathered birds and their watchers, all strictly controlled by a non-English speaking, gun-toting warden. The graph recorder showed the lake to be one hundred feet deep at the dam end, and without great numbers of fish. Those there were, appeared to be predominantly in the shallow water of up to twenty-five feet deep. This was at the end of the long hot drought of a summer in 1985.

When we arrived at the lake on a late September afternoon, the sight which greeted us was not a happy one. Surrounding the lake was a fence with notices in Spanish – *Prohibio el Paso*. I do not speak Spanish, but intuition said words like that were not good news. The lakeside garage seemed a likely source of information, but it seems you cannot rely on English being spoken, despite what you hear in the U.K. Using sign language, honed to perfection by the end of the week, we discovered there was no fishing without going to Madrid for something. Fortuitously, they told of a lake nearby (Embalse de El Vellon) where the *carpa* could be caught.

Four days on El Vellon provided a surfeit of activity with commons to twenty. Spanish word had it that fish to fifty-eight pounds had been taken, but then we were after 'Bigga Carpa'.

Returning to Santillana we stood on the bridge where the river entered the lake. The water was shallow and slightly coloured, but it could not obscure the activity of fish a short distance away. They were not more than a few pounds, but it was enough to start with. We strolled a mile or so around the perimeter fence and, lo and behold, new additional words appeared on the signs 'Excepta witha the Speciale permissio' – say no more! Next stop was Madrid, as a result of which I now know all about *mañana*.

On going through the gate down to the shore, we were welcomed by a large sandy beach and large rocks. In the sand at our feet we found large scales, a gruesome but effective indication of the lake's inhabitants. The remains, as the nearby skeleton disclosed, were that of a common of perhaps twenty-five pounds.

We set our stall out at that swim and began our exploration of the lake's potential. The evening saw much surface activity as common after common crashed around us; they were no doubt doubles and twenties, but some of the crashes offered the prospect of something rather more. My mind was inevitably drawn back to Cassein and Easter 1985, when fish of forty and more took flying lessons in and around the swim. The comparison was favourable.

Under cover of darkness (no boats allowed) we hastily surveyed the majority of the lake with the graph recorder. Unfortunately the headlight had been dropped and broken at El Vellon, so the night-time visuals were curtailed. Our pitch looked on the face of it well chosen: to our left were the shallows, leading up to the bridge where depths were mainly in

the order of five to fifteen feet, before a pronounced drop-off to twenty-five feet immediately in front of us. It seemed to be similar to river-fed, estate lake features as often found at home, but here they were on a larger scale. Therefore, we thought we need only apply tactics already learnt at home in this situation with information on baits and rigs successful on El Vellon, and, hey presto, we would crack it.

If it was as easy as that, fishing would lose its magic! Forty-eight hours later we had only three runs and two fish to show, but activity over and around the baited area had promised more. We wondered if it had all been worth it as the last full night and day approached. I sat fiddling with the headlight in idle fashion. A severed wire presented itself, the problem was quickly solved with a broken needle and we were back in business.

Once again we took to the boat and headed for the shallows during the calm, at dead of night. At first there was nothing much to be seen as water clarity would not permit the bed to be visible in anything over ten feet. We neared a partly submerged wall about one hundred feet long, extending across the majority of the inlet. There were a lot of partly submerged bushes and small trees with dying branches protruding into the night sky, like macabre skeletons. We edged along the wall in a few feet of water until a gap appeared where it had collapsed. We moved gently through on the electric motor taking care to avoid the branches. I stood in the prow with the headlight aloft and scanning the water. The water deepened off to about ten feet the other side of the wall and we moved gently forward.

The next sight will probably remain fixed in my memory forever, as the 'Arnold Schwarzenegger' of the carp world cruised nonchalantly below the boat. At this point I will have to try and provide some facts, figures and 'guesstimations' to allow you an insight into the vision. A Cassein caught mirror I had at Easter 1985 weighed in at forty-five pounds and measured thirty-five inches (nose to fork of tail). The boat which we were in had a beam of fifty inches. The water was only about ten feet deep and the fish was in mid-water in clear view. As the mighty carp passed slowly beneath the beam of the boat, the fish could be seen quite clearly to be as long as the boat was wide. The shoulders were extremely well developed, and probably eight to nine inches across the back would be a fair estimation. The distortions which water gives to depths did not allow much speculation about the belly of the fish, but I would guess it was not overly large. As we are now in the realms of fantasy, I could not put a reasonable guess as to the weight. At the time, we thought it perhaps fifty pounds, but later learnt that during 1985 the lake threw up a fish weighing more than anything which came from Cassein during the same year.

The gigantic common swam aimlessly around the boat as we both watched and marvelled at a truly 'Bigga Carpa'. We followed the carp for a while until it outswam the boat. Anything further would have been an anticlimax after that and the trip had now fulfilled the hopes and desires we had on leaving England. Nevertheless, we motored on into the shallows where, in one large bay, we encountered several groups of common in about five feet of water. Usually there were up to six fish in a group; we reckoned there were about twenty different fish of which two were small and would have been lucky to make doubles. The jump to the next size up was substantial and I estimated twenty pounds.

Pictures of a locally caught U.K. common of about thirty-five pounds which I have seen since would certainly equate quite well with the majority of the fish we saw. We drank in as much as we could of what lay before us, until it became intoxicating. Time was passing and we just had to give this bay a try.

Morning dawned on us and so did the warden. The fish were in front of us bubbling away and one screaming run had been missed, but the warden intimated it was time to leave. I did not understand the Spanish, but the gun spoke volumes and said things like we were in the out of bounds area, we had not got all the right licences and no boats were allowed. Not wishing to spoil things for another time, we did the decent thing and were on our way home within ten minutes. Well, it was our last day anyway and those mullet in the harbour at Santander were tempting!

The plans for the next trip to Santillana are well advanced, and if all goes well with 'Arnold' and the warden, 1986 could be someone's lucky year at Santillana.

Now that anglers have discovered the delights of foreign parts, I am sure the list of Casseins will grow as it is realised that many places hold carp of fifty pounds plus. Good luck with the tracking down of your fantasies, be they in favourite waters or in new and undiscovered territories. Re-kindle the sort of carp fishing excitement which many have lost over the years by being too parochial. For those who have not felt the power of the big Cassein carp, then, as Ronald Reagan says: you ain't seen nothing yet. The fight from these Spanish commons stretches the frontiers of what are accepted as carp fighting qualities.

The 'Trash' Fish of the States

MARTYN PAGE

Although there are small groups of American anglers who regard carp as a worthwhile quarry, generally they are looked on with contempt and disdain as 'trash' fish.

Martyn Page spent a few weeks in the States in 1985 sampling the delights of the American fishing, meeting up at the same time with Duncan Kay who had been pursuing American carp a thousand miles or so south. Both men witnessed the less enlightened American attitude to these fish, and despaired at the use of snag tactics (carp snagged out on huge treble hooks) and at the fact that most fish caught are not put back.

They gained an insight, however, into why the carp in the States do not enjoy the privileged position of their English and European counterparts. America is a land where fish are plentiful and pressures few. A land where numerous species grow to gigantic proportions. But a land also where tradition has entrenched a 'fish for food' attitude into the sport, and carp are not regarded as the most flavoursome fish by the Americans. Their sporting ability counts for little in the States, for everything there fights hard, grows big and suits the American style of fishing that much better. So it is that they have become the 'trash' fish of the States.

Times are changing, however. Catch and release is spreading and there is a new awareness growing in the States of different methods, different values and styles. Americans are keen to learn and perhaps one day their carp will lose the 'trash' tag.

But what of the potential in this land? Carp seem to abound in many of the lakes and, as Duncan Kay witnessed further south, there is a potential for enormous fish. The fish are all commons, beautiful beasts, uncaught by man (they do not survive more than one capture). Never having seen a boilie they need education to even the basic carp baits used in England nowadays. However, the scope is almost unlimited for our new travelling brand of specialist angler.

There are problems, though. For instance, Martyn and Duncan witnessed beautiful commons leaping all day in Lake Michigan (an inland sea). They were good fish – doubles every one. Catching them would prove an interesting challenge. Martyn motored over the fish in an American fishing boat and picked up the fish on a graph recorder. They were all within five feet of the surface, in water up to forty feet deep. No use legering a boilie on the bottom! Certainly a lot were caught firmly hooked in the mouth on lures, and, as Martyn commented, everything else caught in the States was undoubtedly of predatory disposition.

In conclusion, the States has tremendous potential, especially in the central states such as Dakota. The virgin fish are just waiting for capture, and the country itself contains so many big fish of all species that more of our specialist anglers will travel to reap the undoubted rewards. Expense is perhaps the drawback, but for the ultimate holiday, adventure and experience there can be few lands with greater potential.

Big Waters: Conclusion

There is obviously huge scope both in Britain and abroad for great fish on the very large waters. The challenge is devastating. Apart from Cassein, little work has been done by British anglers on the Continent or in the States and the pioneer has an almost open field.

Rod Hutchinson, talking about foreign potential, made several points, most notably that Cassein is only the tip of the iceberg and that he is sure that equally big fish exist in other more secluded lakes. He also stressed that Cassein monsters are not as plentiful as some might think, and repeat captures of the lunkers are common. This angle has been covered in the press in 1985/86, but it is worth repeating here, even if only to stress the need for care of any fish on the bank.

Rod believes that Portugal, Spain and Yugoslavia all have the potential to better Cassein. What John Bailey saw when he worked in the Mediterranean region leads him to agree with Rod. We believe that Morocco also has secrets to uncover, and German fish are well documented.

Obviously, the temperate climate of southern Europe has a great bearing on the carp's growth rate. Warm winter temperatures can lead a fish to feed nearly every month of the year. A possible drawback, of course, is that warmer water means better spawning and more fear of stunting and overcrowding.

Certainly Europe opens up carping horizons unknown in this country, but it is essential that British anglers behave well once over the Channel. It is no secret that some English fishermen have behaved disgustingly at Cassein. Piles of litter have been left. Tesco sweetcorn tins with a price in pence testify that it is ours. If our explorers and pioneers are to be welcomed and helped by the locals, it is up to all travellers to act as if they were on their local club lakes. Standards must not slip because home is a long way off. If they do, we will all pay in the end.

GRAVEL PITS

Gravel Pit Fisheries

DUNCAN KAY

This is, above all, a realistic chapter. Despite the variety of sections in this book, we believe that the future of carping for the majority of us, lies in the gravel pit fishery. Estate lakes, built for the most part centuries ago, are silting up quickly and sludge pumping is an exercise very few can afford. Already some estate lakes, famous earlier this century, have all but disappeared and are certainly too shrunken and muddied to support big fish any longer.

The country's small waters are always vulnerable to back filling to increase agricultural or building acreage, as the urban sprawl extends out of so many cities and towns into what once was the countryside. While we have talked in depth about rivers too, even here there are numerous dangers. Entire river systems teeter on the edge of destruction from agro-chemical tainting, industrial and sewage pollution, and from abstraction. So whilst there are very big river carp to be had today, it would be unwise to state this will always be the case.

This leaves us with the gravel pit and here the future is brighter. Roads and houses continue to be built, the ground minerals continue to be extracted and so more pits are created. Equally, as carp become more popular, more of these pits are stocked with the species by clubs, syndicates and landowners.

Of all these gravel pit carp fisheries,

Duncan Kay's Mid Northants water is amongst the most famous. Duncan has created a 'carpery' out of nothing, which today both yields very big fish and gives untold pleasure to more than thirty men fortunate to hold tickets there. Here, then, Duncan passes on advice based on his considerable experience to those wishing to build their own fisheries, to those who want to give to angling and not merely reap what others sow.

Winning Control of the Water

The pit has either to be leased or bought. In either case, you have to be certain that the water can be kept almost indefinitely. A lease is always limiting and can only be taken if there is a complete trust between the owner and the operator.

A good carp fishery takes at least eight years to mature. Young stock fish do the bulk of their growing in that time and when they are nine or ten years old the fishing does become truly desirable. This is not the moment that the operator wants to lose his lease. For the time, effort and money to be worthwhile, any lease less than twenty-five years must be rejected.

The Water Itself

An ideal water is neither too big, too small, too deep or too shallow. The old-fashioned

gravel pits dug to eight or ten feet are perfect. Pits today are dug deeper, with less features and, therefore, they offer less interest to the demanding carper. They are fine for big fish at long range, but the all-rounder has less scope.

A perfect size is between three and fifteen acres. Pits between these limits are large enough to retain some mystery and still small enough to stock at a realistic price.

Water Plants and Quality

The ideal carp fishery will have weeds around the sides and not in the middle. If this is not the case, then for the bulk of the hot summers the carp will all congregate way out and fishing will be at remote long range.

Willows are ideal bank-side trees, are best set horizontally, and in ten years grow to maturity and give shade and security to margin fish. Blackthorn bushes can be set in the edges of the lake. Waterlogged banks always hold fish and their cover is especially attractive in the winter.

Lilies are a vital consideration in any lake and again should be set around the margins so that a fish running for cover comes towards the angler, rather than away from him. Lilies grow well next to gravel spits even if not planted directly over them. In their infancy, the roots are vulnerable to attacks from water-fowl and should be guarded by a cage or netting.

Most other weeds grow naturally, though the one to be totally eradicated is Canadian pond weed. This has no place at all in a carp fishery. It can grow to the surface in ten feet of water and has no feed

stocks in it. In fact, the growth rate of carp is visibly slowed down in pits affected with pond weed. In April it is wise to clear this weed, just as it begins to grow once more. Clarosan, made by Ciba Geigy is recommended at ten kilos per acre. It is a powder that kills from the root up, but do not treat more than a quarter or at the most a half of the lake at any one treatment. This could lead to a problem of oxygen deficiency.

When the weed is dead and rotting, it is beneficial to treat the water with lime. This can be trickled in through a feeder stream or left to be drifted and evenly spread by the wind. It is important not to overlime and not to treat every year. A rapid change in the alkalinity of a water can be an irritant to fish. One thing is certain: liming dramatically increases any pit's shrimp population and the carp weights will explode accordingly.

Remember, if in doubt water authorities everywhere carry out free water surveys. Do not risk some of the recent in-vogue treatments to increase a pit's food capacity. Pig slurry, raw manure and sewage can all be very dangerous in summer, especially on waters that do not catch the wind and where oxygen levels are already low.

SWIM CREATION

It is wise to get the hard work of swim creation done early in the fishery's life while the enthusiasm of the members is high, rather than ten years later when young men have grown into householders and fathers!

The modern trend is for very artificial-looking 'bivvy swims'. These can easily spoil the look and atmosphere of any lake. Many pits are steep sided and the common swim type must be a 'notch' cut into the

Left Duncan Kay, fishery manager and famous carp catcher.

Although ugly at first, after careful landscaping a pit will in time look totally natural.

bank. This has to be big enough to fish from comfortably without being too obtrusive aesthetically.

Avoid cutting trees back. This looks unnatural, like a privet hedge. It is better to take small trees out and replace them with bushes.

Yellow iris are excellent as swim cover. The vivid flowers are amongst the first of the lake-side flowers to bloom and they last well into the summer. Reeds, rushes and bulrushes should all be bedded in along with wild flowers, in clumps away from the path or fishing areas. There should not be any carp fishers worth the name who ignore these touches to the lake-side environment.

Stocking

If the pit in question is vastly overstocked with small fish of unwanted species, it is important to net out as many as possible. It pays to be ruthless and sell the fish off to dealers. Do not be amateurish here. Drive a bargain with the fish dealer before the netting takes place; a £50 payment is reasonable to offer a man to turn up with his nets. After that, he should pay money for fish of decent species and size range. Bream over six ounces and roach over four ounces are worth money and most pits can offer valuable surprises as a bonus.

A mixed fishery, rather than a 'carpery', should be any man's aim. Some years are simply bad carp seasons and it is good to have other species to fall back upon. The carp stock can, heaven forbid, die off and

40 Left *John Bailey cradles a quite superb old estate lake mirror.*

41 Below *A stunning catch of foreign commons to Graham Cowderoy and friend.*

42   *John Bailey with a bag of dawn-caught crucians.*

43 Above *The hunky, chunky, adorable crucian in profile.*

44 Below *Four crucians all nudging the 2lb mark.*

45   Fish like these make any amount
of time at the waterside seem worthwhile.

46 Above *A wonderful example of a fully scaled mirror.*

47 Left *Two sensational commons for Graham Cowderoy.*

48 Above *Tricia King looks suitably happy with a very big fish.*

49 Opposite (top) *What a wonderful fish and how lovingly cradled.*

50 Opposite (bottom) *Bruno Broughton happy with a lovely fish.*

51 *It is commons like these that entice*
English anglers to Holland.

A fish farm reared mirror awaits entry into a new pit.

quantity. They could, for example, be very old, tired fish. Carp in the one to eight-pound range from a fish farm are by far the better choice. Their exact ages and backgrounds will be known and they will probably grow quickly to a good catchable size.

Big fish are always an attraction, but good young fish can quickly get to these sizes. For example, I have known four-pound fish double their size in eight weeks and for fish to reach mid/upper twenty pounds in five years. As a glimpse into the future, how about this to whet the carp man's appetite? A pilot scheme in Suffolk is growing carp in warm water to six pounds as yearlings and to twenty pounds as two year olds!

To repeat, it is important to choose proven good growers and, if possible, to deal direct with a fish farm in order to select the best fish and to keep down costs.

Stocking numbers are a controversial matter and density recommendations differ greatly between scientist and angler. In any case, it is hard to lay down rigid guidelines, as so much depends on the fertility of the pit involved: certainly on my own water there is a very high poundage of fish and the carp still grow very quickly. Carp weights alone total between 800 and 900 pounds per acre. As a starter, I suggest that twenty fish per acre should go in, topped up with another twenty two years later. Those first fish will prove to have a very fast growth rate indeed.

There is not a carp angler alive who does not appreciate the fully-scaled common carp and I recommend an equal balance between commons and mirrors. Commons do not grow as big as mirrors on most waters but they make up for this with a superabundance of power and hardiness.

On the subject of removing carp, even a

then the lake would be useless once more for years. Above all, a single species water is unnatural and pike, eels and predators are good for any venue.

A word of warning – carp and tench rarely go well together and the tench are the sufferers. They can become as lean and as yellow as bananas. Also there can be a risk with bream in a pit where, as at Darenth, they are a continual menace to the serious carp angler.

The biggest stocking question hangs over the carp themselves. Big fish over twenty pounds cost well over £100 each and, more significantly, are an unknown tatty fish can be another man's personal best and therefore bring a lot of pleasure. It is also very difficult to net carp that are very much the elusive Houdinis of the fish world. There is also the danger that by removing any carp at all, tench and bream will overbreed to fill in the gaps. In fact, the only time that I would suggest netting carp from the fishery is when they have spawned successfully. Even then, it is wise not to do the netting until the following spring as winter kills can often do the job for you.

The Anglers

Having created the fishery, it can become a club, day ticket, or syndicate water. As the first two options offer very little control, I shall concentrate on the syndicate possibility.

It is important to get the right people who will all pay the right money. Good fishing today cannot be cheap and when rates, rent, fish and water maintenance are all taken into account the realistic price must be between £100 and £200 per year. On a balanced fishery, four to eight members per acre paying this type of money should amply cover costs.

Recruitment is initially a plunge into the unknown. It will prove impossible to make up the list with friends. Certainly some of the members should be general anglers happy to pursue the pike, bream, roach or tench in the water. This relieves the pressure on the carp population and, importantly, it helps create a better, more open spirit in the group.

The anglers that are the curse of the developing fishery are the young, new-style specimen hunters who seem able to fish every day of the summer and who really whack the guts out of new fish.

Ideally, a fishery needs a steady mixture of all angler types who provide a refreshing spread of ambition and character. To let a specimen group in is to court disaster – it can lead to a group within a group. Secrecy, separate factions and jealousy are all the beginning of the end.

Certainly, all the syndicate members must appreciate the importance of caring for their fish. I allow no retention of carp in either keepnets or sacks. A fish can be kept in the landing net while the camera is set up and the scales are zeroed. This means the end of the multiple carp shot so popular in the 1960s and 1970s, but so potentially damaging to the fish. All anglers should be careful not to allow more than five minutes between netting and releasing, especially in the summer when low oxygen makes the carp especially vulnerable.

Caring anglers should pay great concern to their gear. The best example is to put a micromesh floor to the bottom of landing nets. This addition saves drastically on split fins, for remember, if any fin spine is stripped or broken it will never mend. A pea-sized hole punctured into the tissue of the fin will require eight years to mend. Fin rot can be caused by a tear in a conventional net, a disease that leads to the loss of fins.

If all these considerations are taken seriously, not even multiple catches should harm the carp. For example, an eighteen-pound fish in my fishery has been caught over sixty times and not a scale has been dislodged and not a fin has been damaged. Many fish come out between four and six times each year and this has no obvious detrimental effect on their growth rate. To reinforce the point, a well-known two tone fish was caught at six, twelve and nineteen pounds, four times through the twenties and again at thirty-six pounds.

An angler enjoys a man-made carp fishery.

Rules

Committees are dangerous beasts: too much discussion can lead to inaction. It is sometimes better to have a benevolent dictator to lead the syndicate, provided that he is fair to all parties. Nobody wants hassle, moans or political infighting. The single aim of all concerned is a successful, well-run fishery.

There should be one meeting a year and all the members should be encouraged to attend with free sandwiches, cups for best fish and general all-round good spirit. If all members are present then they all know each other and will recognise any poachers on the bank. This is an invaluable aid to bailiffing.

At the meeting new rules can be discussed and amendments can be drawn into them. An element of flexibility is desir-able, but important rules – like fish retention – must be pushed through despite shortsighted opposition.

Guests are important on any water. They should not be charged, unless there are complaints that the manager is getting rich at their cost! Guests lead to good spin-offs. Potential new members are introduced to the water and existing members can form an impression of them as anglers and people. Also, guests generally reciprocate by taking you to their waters which leads to new ideas, new friendships and new experiences. Members should have approximately three guests each season and a water maximum of two guests on a single day and four in a week is

A younger Duncan with a near twenty winter common.

advisable. It is sense to have no guests until August perhaps, when the early season rush has died down.

There are one or two innovations at Mid Northants which have become a legend in the carp world. One is the sensible approach to the booking of swims for the beginning of the season. The weekend before the new season, members can gather at Saturday midnight and peg their swim choice. Their position is then held until the last minute of 16 June. This takes a frenzy out of the opening day and provides another opportunity for members to meet for a drink and a chat.

This emphasis on fun is important at Mid Northants and nothing demonstrates it better than the Opening Night Frolics. Opening day can be a write-off when the long quiet water is bombarded anew by anglers, and so whatever the carp decide, I lay on my own fireworks. Literally! Fire crackers explode around the lake. There is a party, wine and food and perhaps even a stripper or two. I still maintain that the louder the uproar the better the carp respond. Illogical of course, but on a recent opening day, sixteen out of seventeen anglers all caught carp and most were big ones!

Big Pits

RITCHIE MACDONALD

We have interviewed many anglers for this book and for its sister *Pike – The Predator becomes the Prey*. Few anglers though, made the impression that Ritchie did the afternoon we met him in his south London home. It is his commitment that is so powerful, his dedication to big fish is all-surpassing. We came away inspired to tackle waters that we had never dared try before. His confidence and enthusiasm are infectious. He can make you believe that the heights of carp fishing can be scaled – if you work at it and are committed to success. Above all, the man so obviously loves carp, carp fishing, and not least the waterside. He is more than an angler. He ranks as a naturalist who is expert on carp and can read their movements intimately. It is this consummate water craft that we concentrate on in this chapter.

Ritchie himself had only limited amounts to say about baits and rigs. A good protein bait and an effective hair rig, he said, did for nearly all his waters. His time and his thoughts go into reading the pit, tracking the carp and arranging their ambush. Ritchie said that on these vast windswept waters, location of the carp is eighty per cent of the game, so we put him on a large, imaginary pit that he did not know before and asked him where he would start.

Preparation

To succeed on a big pit requires detailed knowledge. You must know the contours of the water like the back of your hand, the food supply like your own larder, and the habits of the occupants better than those of your wife. There are no short cuts to success. You must spend as much time as possible at your chosen water if you are to have a chance of realising your ambitions, and that means starting your homework when other coarse anglers are watching *Grandstand* or sleeping off Sunday lunch.

Start in the closed season, in April or May, or whenever the sun feels warm on your back. Carp acting naturally follow marginal routes, and are only scared out further by the heavy footfalls of an angler or a dog walker. By moving carefully and quietly, back from the water's edge and below the skyline, you should catch your first glimpse of the fish during the early weeks of preparation. This will tell you two important things: the size of your quarry and their feeding areas.

After many years of personal bests I would now find it hard to devote maximum time and effort on a water which did not contain upper thirties, but you must set yourself a realistic target of your own. But make no mistake, once I find a fish I want to catch, nothing is too embarrassing or uncomfortable if it helps me get nearer to

Ritchie MacDonald proves yet again his mastery of pit fishing.

that fish.

Take a pair of binoculars with you on these early outings for they will come in useful, even if they do make you look like a bird-watcher. Use these to look for anything that might attract the attention of carp, such as a tree blown down during a winter gale. Carp are curious creatures and anything unusual will draw them like pins to a magnet.

The usual holding spots must also be located and memorised. Gravel bars, underwater snags, islands, weed beds, and underwater plateaux and shallows are all favourites among most species of fish. Get up a tree or out in a boat to have a good

look at them; and add this invaluable information to the other trump cards you already have up your sleeve.

If you have found a feeding hotspot and can get over it in a boat, don't be content just to peer down from above or plumb the depth. Take your courage in one hand and your snorkel and mask in the other, and get over the side for a closer look at the bottom. As the icy-cold water comes up to your neck, just think of how you'll feel when you are straining to lift up that heavyweight carp for the cameras. I'm sure you'll think it's worthwhile.

What you are looking for on the lake bed is channels between the bars, blood-worm beds, snails, or anything to explain the reason why the carp use this swim. Guesswork isn't enough. To know your quarry intimately you must know what makes it tick, and that includes finding out what goes into the mouth that will one day hold your hook.

In the battle to outwit your quarry, being given a boat is like gaining a secret weapon. You can get close to the fish, often without frightening them, and gain knowledge well out of your reach from the bank. I used to wonder what effect boats had on carp until I fished Redmire Pool. On three separate occasions a trip around the lake in the punt stirred the fish into activity, until they even followed the boat itself, showing no fear. The only things likely to be put off by boats are other anglers, so use them with discretion.

The First Session

The day dawns when you can put all your hard-earned knowledge into practice and reap the rewards of weeks of observation and preparation. Just one more decision has to be made before you can start the first session; the choice of swim. The biggest single deciding factor is wind direction. Carp follow the wind like a salmon seeking out the river of its birth, and if an angler isn't conscious of wind direction he can expect long periods fishing an empty swim.

There is almost always some sort of ripple on a big pit, where trees are often too young to give any shelter, and where a good swell can pick up over scores of acres of water. Almost always I will head for a feature on the side facing into the wind, no matter how strong the gale is blowing. In fact, the stronger the wind the better, for with everything lashed down I'm quite confident with anything up to a Force 9 blowing at me.

Southerlies and northerlies are the best, and the perfect gift is a summer northerly, Force 8, with cloud and sometimes mild rain. The only exception to the 'feel the wind and you've found the fish' theory is on hard-fished waters like Savay. Here, the carp have got wise to people fishing in wind lanes and now stay out of them, forcing anglers to work out which other areas or features would attract them. This water is a clear example of how men can change the natural inclinations of fish.

The longer you stay at a water, the more you will learn about how the weather is affecting the fish and how your baits and tactics are working. But no matter how much gear you have with you or how comfortable you are in a swim, you must move when the conditions tell you to. If the wind looks like changing, you must uproot yourself, night or day, and be on the windward bank with baits out before the fish arrive. They won't be far behind.

Other clues can shorten the time it takes to put a fish on the bank. Steer clear of bays which restrict your view of the lake and possible sightings, unless they are crammed full of fish. Keep your eye on other anglers, preferably without sticking binoculars on them, and talk to them, noting which areas are producing fish and which are not. Scan the surface for sightings of fish, bubbles, flats, fins, swirls, and any clues to the carp's whereabouts.

A fish will normally use a patrol route that only changes with weather conditions until it is frightened off its circuit by anglers. What others do is crucial to the overall pattern of events, and interference can kill an area off and force a rethink of tactics. For this reason I would much rather fish alone. Carp are not difficult to catch, but when you find some which have been caught a few times or frightened off their normal feeding grounds, you have a

*David Judge carefully unhooks a big
Essex fish.*

more difficult problem.

I will usually bait up at the start and then wait for some sign of fish, whether it be bubbles, twitches or a run. Sometimes it takes days, but a lot depends on how hard fished your water is. In my first year at Savay I baited up and stayed put, and I believe that helped me catch what I did. The following year I did the same, but the fish had wised up and kept away from the heavily baited areas, reducing my catches dramatically. In one swim I fished in June, I spent five hours baiting up and not a single fish was caught there until October.

The only guidelines I can give are to look carefully at the weather, the number of fish in the pit and the number of anglers present, and then experiment. Experience will help some of the time, but there is no complete answer. Baiting will always succeed one day and fail on another.

All my baiting up is done with boilies, and if you don't know why, try putting particles fifty or sixty yards out with accuracy and without a boat. Good boilies are no longer the problem that they used to be, thanks to people like Rod Hutchinson, whose protein mix base and liquid flavourings I use. No one need feel inferior about their bait's quality, and if someone is catching more than you, it is probably his water craft which has given him the edge.

If you want big carp, rather than just lots of carp, you will have to be prepared to wait and think while you are waiting, keeping your eyes and ears open without becoming restless. Above all, you must have a good reason for everything you do. If you can see fish somewhere else don't stay put just for comfort's sake, but don't move just for a change of scene or to get out of the wind.

Finally, don't follow the crowd. Sheep follow each other around and they have one of the smallest brains in the animal kingdom. Keep your wits about you and slowly things will start to fall into place.

Turning Words into Action

So that is the theory. Here is an example of how these ideas were put into practice to produce carp from a notoriously difficult big pit, Wraysbury, a 300 acre water in Berkshire. To say Wraysbury is a big lake is like saying that there are a lot of people in China. You could fish a new swim every day for a year and still not see all of the water. The place is massive, and when Peter Springate, Kenny Hodder and I decided to have a go at it in October 1981, we knew we could end up like most of the others who had fished it at that time, wondering if there were any carp in there.

Armed with Pete's rubber dinghy and a lot of lessons learnt from sunny closed season days spent creeping around the banks, I set out down the south side, eyes and ears open. Suddenly a carp crashed out of the water sixty yards from the bank and about a hundred yards from where I was standing. We all looked at each other and without a word headed back to the car to fetch the tackle.

We put our baits out in that area, but nothing happened for the rest of the day. The following evening we had just brewed up some tea when the whole lake went flat and calm, as far as the eye could see. Then out in front of us we saw a line of bubbles. Kenny always has a pair of binoculars hanging around his neck, and peering through these he saw one line of bubbles and then another line and then several others. They had to be from feeding carp.

I rowed Pete's baits out (he can't swim) and at 1 a.m. he had a run – and lost it. But at least we had found feeding fish, and we were even more determined to come back the following weekend and try once again. After baiting the area with the last of our maple-flavoured boilies, we left, returning four days later for another long weekend, having nipped back in between to top up the swim with another five hundred baits, and plumb the depth. It was twenty-five feet, rising steeply to a shallow bar four feet wide and a hundred feet long in five feet of water.

When the day arrived I rowed out three markers to concentrate our bait. The next morning, at 5.30 a.m. off went one of the

Ritchie shows exactly how to hold these lovely fish.

alarms. I cupped my hand over the spool in the usual way and put the hook home into a powerful fish. The carp tried hard to reach some snags, but once I had him over the obstacle of the bar it was just a matter of time before I could draw the beaten fish over my landing net.

With the fish in the net I tried to lift, and found to my surprise that I couldn't. Immediately I thought that this must be a forty, but feeling down the mesh in the dark I found that the net was snagged. I

A hard fighting pit carp thrashes over the
net.

needed help, so I ran across and woke Pete. (I noticed he only had one rod out, and he explained that he had lost two fish and thrown the other rod into the bushes in disgust.) Together we got the fish onto the bank. It was a very long mirror carp which took the scales down to 28lb 4oz.

In all we had nine more chances before the end of the weekend, four of them to me, but only one of them turned into a fish. This was a common of twenty-four pounds which rewarded Pete for all his hard work, but meanwhile I couldn't get another to the net. One took off at an incredible pace, straightening the hook, and others came adrift when they dived into the depths and my line parted on the gravel bar.

All the fish fought like demons, and I believe some of the fish in Wraysbury have never been hooked before. Wraysbury is the biggest and the hardest place I have fished in Britain. Although my personal best at that time was a full ten pounds heavier than the mirror I caught there, I rate that capture as my best angling achievement to date and certainly one of the most satisfying. We spent a lot of time observing the water over several seasons before putting a rod on it, and it was observation, accuracy, determination, patience and luck which helped us succeed.

The Long-range Question

You will notice that gravel pit fishing can involve some long-range work. Let me say at once, I far prefer to fish at fifty to seventy yards. I do not set up for vast distances, because once over seventy yards I find that fishing efficiency begins to drop. I always have a rod set-up with me, however, that can cope with casts of one hundred plus yards if the fish should be showing out there. As I have said, I am never one to miss an opportunity.

Earlier in the chapter, I have made the point that long-range baiting and bait 'dropping' is best done from a boat, but there are cases where to go afloat is not possible and casting a long way is a must. Over one hundred yards, a good twelve or thirteen-foot rod is a necessity, or at least makes the job easier. Some anglers tend to overload their rods, which leads to a struggle situation. I generally use a three-ounce lead, though those with more practice than I get away with two-ounce leads.

I have a feeling that the new Drennan line with the reduced diameters will have a big effect on long-distance work. Up to now, I have generally used a mainline of around six pounds BS, combined with shockleaders of fifteen pounds. Sylcast and Maxima have always been my favourites.

Striking at one hundred yards is not a problem now that the rigs have advanced. I am confident that the fish will be hooked already, which is useful as there is no way you can set a hook by striking at such range. I do slightly modify my rig by using a very short hook length of five to six inches. This makes casting easier and cuts down on tangles.

Playing a fish from such distances can also be a headache. You just have not got the control way out there that you have closer in. Kiting will always be a problem for which there is no real answer. Shallow bars can spell disaster too. Do not pull a fish into the side of a bar, rather give it slack, even by opening the bale arm. This way the carp will find its own way over or around the bar and the fight can begin again. If there is a big snag on the bar then you are lost. Here again, it is a case of knowing your water. It is another essential part of that closed season work I was talking about.

An Essex Forty

KEVIN NASH

Past Encounters

The family of goldfinches flitted through the gnarled branches of the old oak tree, their yellow wing feathers turning from amber to a brilliant white as they captured the rays of the early morning sun. It has always amazed me how near wild birds will come to you when you are twenty feet up a tree. They obviously consider that a human being is not the same threat there, as when he has both feet firmly on terra firma.

Below, in the crystal clear waters of the pool there was no sign of the carp I had come to see. My mind drifted back four years to the time I had first spotted her while sitting up this very tree. She had drifted across the pool, finishing directly beneath me. Even at fifty yards, as I watched her coming I knew that she was something very special. When she came into the Potamogeton I nearly fell out of the tree for my eyes beheld a magnificent mirror carp surely well in excess of thirty pounds! She turned lazily in the sun and I glimpsed her depth: a glorious perfectly shaped solid fish of thirty-three to thirty-eight pounds. After my long search I had found possibly the largest fish in Essex!

The carp of the pool proved a difficult quarry, undoubtedly they had never seen a hair rig and yet every fish was hard won. Slowly, I began to piece the jigsaw to-gether and by October had accounted for fourteen of the pool's carp, the largest at just over twenty pounds. She was a very pretty mirror covered in tiny scales that caught the light and twinkled like stars. Happy times! The carp angler who is fortunate enough to be catching truly wild fish these days is a lucky man indeed.

Then came a special day. I awoke at dawn one October morning, the lake shrouded in such a dense mist that I could not even see Paul who was fishing on a peninsula only twenty yards from me. I felt tense and nervous as if something was going to happen, probably a condition brought on by the muffled eerie world of the heavy mist.

I was brought quickly back to the world of reality when my indicator hit the top of the needle in a millisecond. The buzzer screamed out over the lake. I picked up the rod, tightened down and firmly leaned back. The rod was virtually torn from my grip as an obviously big fish tried for the sanctuary of the sunken trees. It turned and headed out for the snag by the bar.

The rod was taking on a most alarming curve as I tried to turn the fish from the snag. Suddenly it was on the top, thrashing the water to foam in a manner I have never seen a carp do before or since. Even at ten yards in the dense fog I knew it was *Her*. I shook, I screamed for Paul. She had calmed down and was just lying there, wallowing on the surface. I began to use very light side pressure and steer her into the bank; a dangerous process indeed, when a fish has surfaced so far from the bank. She was three yards out when I heard Paul's buzzer sound and then a commotion followed by a tumultuous crash! A yard from the net she opened her enormous mouth – I could see the size 2 hook in the side of her lip and then it just fell out. I lunged forward with the net but could not reach her. Slowly, she sank into the murky depths and was gone. I stood there numb.

I was jarred back to reality when I spotted something out of the corner of my eye. Drifting towards me at the margins was Paul's hat! Where had Paul been during all this commotion? I later found a thoroughly drenched, totally miserable Paul, sitting in his car! He had not awoken at my screams for assistance; but when his own buzzer had sounded, suddenly startled, he had slipped in his precarious swim and had ended up submerged in eight feet of water.

After that, I was jinxed. I caught every fish in the pool bar two (and I had lost both of them) one of which was *Her*. I was determined that this saga was going to end and that in the coming 1985 season I would at last catch her.

Closing In

I snapped out of my trance as I spotted a big fish pushing its way through the tangled mass of Potamogeton. It was not her, but the dark mirror. A very long fish of possibly twenty-eight to thirty pounds,

Kevin Nash displays more evidence as to why he is one of the biggest names in the carp world.

this fish had eluded all attempts at capture being hooked and lost on at least three occasions. I myself lost this fish: when I had her under total control, the brand new line inexplicably parted. We later tested the 12lb line, which broke at 4lb!

The dark mirror made its way to the 'gap' and joined another fish already there, which had seemingly come from nowhere. It was *Her*! Like meeting an old friend, I smiled, happy to see she looked healthy and in as fine condition as when I had last seen her four seasons before. I flicked three minute flat pieces of paste in, she took one and the dark mirror took the other two. Gradually I built up the number of loose offerings until they were both feeding avidly. I was well satisfied.

Bill Lovette and I had been baiting for three weeks with another bait that we were convinced had never been used at the pool. Bill had spotted her for the first time two days previously. She had been agitated and subsequently bolted out of the swim when she came across our bait. After trying seven different baits I had at last found one she liked. The only trouble was I had only 75ml of flavouring left and this flavouring was now unobtainable!

Back up the oak on 15 June 1985, I had fourteen fish including the dark mirror and the fish I was after, all feeding on my bait like it was going out of fashion, which it was as I only had 35ml left! From past experience I had a feeling what would happen next – and I was right.

At midnight on 15 June all the carp went off the feed! These carp knew exactly when the season started, which was not surprising when the peaceful calm of the pool was destroyed by wader-clad match men dumping tackle boxes in every available swim with a resounding crash, illuminating the whole pool with megawatt lamps and tillies.

Two days into the season the fish had settled slightly and had become used to the intrusion as two takes at dawn proved. *She* was still edgy though and seldom showed. So, after the first three days of the season I decided to give the pool a rest for a few days.

As I drove up the motorway at dawn the following Tuesday, I felt unusually confident. A pair of magpies had kindly flown across my path, reassuring my superstitious nature. Also, it was raining and although in my experience rain is one of the worst conditions for catching carp on Essex lakes, there is this one notable exception – the pool. Nearly all my biggest fish had come in the same conditions, fine drizzle, just like this morning.

On arriving at the pool I was disappointed to see a carp angler in the swim where the fish had been showing. I dropped my gear and went for a chat. It turned out George had been at the lake a couple of days without a touch (nothing unusual, for on average only half a dozen carp a year are captured from the pool). I had asked a couple of the local lads to drop some bait in for me the night before. As the swim was occupied, however, they had put the baits in my second choice of swim – an area I knew the big fish patrolled. George mentioned a fish had leapt out over my baited area a couple of times. He said the fish was about eighteen pounds with a very light belly. He was sure the fish was around that weight so I left it at that. All the fish in the pool were very dark, with one exception – the big one, which has a much lighter underneath.

As I tackled up, *She* rolled directly over my baited area, confirming my thoughts: I just knew within a couple of hours I would catch her.

By 7 a.m. my three baits were carefully positioned. Because of the silty nature of the bottom I fished two 'pop-ups' and one neutral buoyancy flat boilie designed to rest on the silt. These were fished over a bed of particles and particle boilies. The base mix for my boilies was supplied by Rod, out of his Catchum range. The flavour was dwindling. I had only 10ml left, or to put it another way 800 baits, to catch the fish of my dreams.

The hours were ticking by, taking my confidence with them. The atmosphere was electric. George kept coming along with cups of tea although I had not met him before that morning. He sensed we were in with the chance of catching *Her*. No conversation needed to pass between us, we were both tense, watching, waiting, sharing the moment when one of us would see his indicator lift towards the butt ring as *She* made off with the bait.

But it did not happen. Morning passed and so did the afternoon. At 5 p.m. I had a slow take which stopped just before I reached the rod. The area I was fishing was alive with tench, so I put it down to that. As dusk fell I disappointedly accepted the fact that I had missed the chance. We had seen no signs of fish since early afternoon. Soon after the rain had stopped the lake had settled down and gone was the electrifying atmosphere of expectation.

Lying on my bed-chair at 10.15 p.m., feeling exhausted and somewhat subdued, the buzzer let out a shrill scream, the indicator was in the butt and line was pouring off the spool at an incredible rate. I put one foot over the edge of my bed-chair into six inches of glutinous clay, picked up the rod, closed the bail and leaned into a fish. Then I sat back down and put my boots on.

By this time the fish was just coming out

Held a second, Kevin's monster returns to the pit.

of the other end of the second bed of Potamogeton. To have travelled so far so quickly it was obviously one of the long lean mirrors of the pool. I wound down hard and heaved with all my might. The prototype blank Alan Brown had given me put on the most alarming curve and George, by now at my side, closed his eyes not bearing to watch as something just had to give. Fortunately it was the fish! Slowly, begrudgingly, I coaxed her back through the two beds of Potamogeton until she was making short deep runs in the clear water directly in front of me. To my horror, she suddenly kited to my right and came in underneath the willow with its dangerous roots. I wound down like mad and the fish rolled into open water again. George caught a glimpse of it and put it at about seventeen pounds; I thought it was more like fifteen pounds, but it was a pitch black night and obviously difficult to tell.

Now, at last, I had everything under control and after a few more minutes guided the fish to George and the waiting net. For the first time, I relaxed and took a deep breath to recover from a somewhat 'hairy' battle. George slid the net over the weed to the bank, opening the mesh and making a statement I will remember for the rest of my life: 'This fish is bigger than you think, my son.' At that moment I knew it was *Her*. I dashed forward, half slipping on the treacherous bank. I opened the mesh myself and immediately saw her immense flank. After four years I had caught her.

The weight to me is incidental. I had achieved my single-minded ambition to catch this fish. On the scales she went 42lb. Deducting eight ounces for the 'Happy Hooker Sling', we settled for 41lb 8oz – a new Essex record. I immediately made for the phone (which although not too great a distance away seemed miles that night) and rang my wife, Carol, to tell her the good news and also to ring Bill. Bill dashed the ten miles to the lake arriving barely after I returned from the phone box. If possible, he was more excited than I was. Bill, George and I stayed together, electrified by the excitement of the occasion. At dawn, Bill cast my baits back out as I was incapable of casting and then left for home.

I am indeed fortunate to have captured such a fish, to have been able to share the capture with two anglers such as Bill and George who were unselfishly, genuinely pleased that I had captured *Her*. They made the occasion one I will remember and cherish for the rest of my life.

RIVERS

We believe this is an important section, because although it is possible that big river fish could be poisoned and therefore die, we feel certain that, barring disaster, rivers offer huge potential.

We include two stories to whet the appetite and follow these with more detail, specifically on the Trent. Here, especially with higher temperatures, is a river capable of producing fish in excess of forty pounds.

City Centre Monster

JOHN BAILEY

I remember a day in Tom Boulton's tackle shop. The news there was quite electric; it was on everybody's lips. A few stopped to talk, though most were buying gear, stocking up on bait, not hanging about, but hurrying down to the River Wensum.

It was the day of the escape, the great escape of fish from the water authority's fish farm north of the city of Norwich. A flood had ripped through the flood plain storage tanks and thousands upon thousands of fish had entered the river. Sport was frenetic. There were roach everywhere along the city reaches and some were a rumoured three pounds! There were bream and tench too, but the highlight was the shoal of carp between two and four-pounds that were fighting like wild things in the fast river flow. There were a few larger carp however, and some of these went upriver to the next mill pool where that afternoon I spotted four fish into double figures. Undoubtedly others the same size followed the flow into the city and spread away down as far as the Wensum's junction with the River Yare.

Eventually things on the river calmed down. Some fish died, others disappeared, perhaps into the dykes and broads of the lower River Yare. Still others settled into the new quarters and, the carp especially, began to grow. The Wensum is a rich river and is slow and deep enough in places to suit carp. At this point in time, Stuart Moir

enters into our story.

In the closed season of 1983, Stuart watched the pool at New Mills Yard, where the river plunges through its last set of sluices before becoming tidal. It was a warm day, the water was clear and what he saw amazed him. As fast as he threw out bait, carp came up to eat it. They were, he remembers, like fish in stew ponds and perhaps reached a dozen pounds.

Once the season began, he fished there and caught carp, not generally big ones but exciting nonetheless and very difficult to land from his swim on the road, high above the foaming mill pool and cordoned off by pointed iron railings. After a while though, the carp drifted away, downriver and into the city amidst warehouses and office blocks and were lost to him.

The following year, 1984, followed the same pattern. In the earliest part of the season he was successful with fish to near double figures until again they left the pool. He deduced that they had come to the fast, oxygenated water to clean after spawning and when that task was done had returned to their normal swims. Either that, or angling pressure was driving them away from a preferred area to hidden beats in the city.

Whatever the reason, in 1985 he knew that to be early on the scene was essential. Once more, before the season started he pre-baited, now with sweetcorn, and he watched the carp accept it eagerly. The fish were much the size of the previous year. There had been some growth, he could see that, but the biggest fish in the pool that he could see, he estimated at fifteen pounds. 'That', Stuart said to himself, 'will do me!' At that time he knew nothing of the monster that was to dwarf this target fish.

Stuart arrived at New Mills early, at break of dawn. The city was quiet. It was that pause in time when everybody sleeps but the angler and his fish. Not even the pigeons were awake. He saw city cats pass

Norwich city centre, New Mills Pool: scene of Stuart Moir's drama.

in his cycle headlight and perhaps a dog amongst alley bins, but otherwise he was alone, the one man with purpose amongst 200,000 slumbering souls.

He put bait into the deep slack to the right of the main sluice and sprinkled more of it into the margin shallows. He set up his oldest rods – breakages were the common result of the hammering the gear took against those iron railings! As light broke, there was no sign of carp in the shallow edge of the eddy and he cast further out into dark water. An eight-pound carp took up his bobbin in minutes. Stuart recast.

If an angler is serious about his fishing and tries hard and intelligently over several years, there might well be a moment in his angling life when he will hook his predestined monster. There is no guarantee of this, but for Stuart this moment was about to dawn.

His bobbin rose to the rod butt. He struck and for fifteen minutes knew all the excitement that any angler can experience. At once he sensed the fish was big, from the way it kept deep and bored upriver into the gushing sluice. This, he was sure, would prove to be that fifteen pounder and he played it like gold, straining his rod out over the railings, desperate to keep the carp from the snags beneath where he stood.

Then came the moment! The fish moved out of deep water over the shallows, now lit by the damp morning light. What Stuart saw, he could hardly believe! In the steadily awakening city the fight took on an almost life or death significance and even though the great carp began to tire, the netting of the monster was becoming a looming nightmare. Stuart kept control. He coaxed the fish around the plume of water from the sluice and led it towards a flight of iron steps that runs from the

One of the biggest river carp ever, the Wensum record.

railings to the water level. An early morning spectator took the net, climbed down to the water to the carp, and at last the fish was Stuart's.

In the weigh net it crashed a set of Avons to the limits. Tom Boulton was called. He found his 56lb spring balance and thought; 'if these don't do the job, don't call me, call Pickfords!' No need! The fish went 31lb exactly: one of the biggest river carp ever caught.

A last question remains. Was the giant an escapee from the fish farm or was it a native Wensum fish? Or could it have been swept into the river from a low-lying pit during a winter flood? Why had Stuart, who knew the pool as well as anyone, never seen the fish before, never even guessed its existence?

Our own feelings – only a hunch – is that there are even bigger carp to be caught from there, in the city shadows.

In Pursuit of a Trent Carp

STEVE TYTHERLEY

Beginnings

The morning of 13 March 1976 saw three anglers standing on the banks of the River Trent, a short distance below the weir at Radcliffe-on-Trent. We were fishing an area of slack water – not quite a bay – and had been catching small fish steadily since dawn. Life was pleasant! The three red-tipped stick floats, Jim's, Paul's and mine, floated sedately on the current. One disappeared and I lifted gently into a fish. The shallow water boiled and something unseen headed for somewhere unknown. My two friends withdrew their tackle and watched with keen interest as I played the fish towards the waiting landing net. It was weighed and admired with the reverence that all carp fishers know. It weighed only 2lb 13oz but was, at that time, the largest carp that any of us had ever caught. It was a good way to end the season and we took ourselves off to the pub both to celebrate and to make plans for the coming season.

Little did I know then that that fish, small as it was by national standards, would form a cloud above my head whose silver lining would be revealed so very sparingly over years of effort.

Before entering upon a description of our carp fishing journey, I suggest that we take a look backwards and set the scene for the present day. The year 1653 saw the publication of Isaac Walton's book *The Compleat Angler* in which he described the carp as being 'the Queen of rivers. A stately, a good and a very subtle fish, that was not at first bred nor hath been long in England, but is now naturalised.' This carp would, of course, have been the fully scaled, so-called wild carp, and it is doubtful if any of those populations have survived to the present day. Walton gave recipes for cooking carp, as does Mrs Beeton, who also informs us 'that the carp's swim bladder could be turned into glue and its gall was turned into a kind of green paint.' When the Victorians said 'waste not, want not' they certainly meant it!

So if we can acknowledge the fact that carp have been swimming in the waters of the Trent and its tributaries for far longer than most people think, we can now leap forward to the situation in the 1950s. September, 1952, saw Richard Walker land his 44lb carp. A fish so large, by English standards, that it caught the public's imagination and was possibly the main reason that so many of the species were placed into the newly-dug gravel pits which line the fields next to the river.

Flood prevention then was not of to-day's high standard and it was a regular occurrence for the Trent to burst its banks and cover the surrounding area, often to a depth of several feet. The waters of the raging river met those of the placid still waters and opened up vast areas of virgin ground upon which the fish could feed. Once the waters started to recede, numbers of carp often found themselves heading towards a new home. Flooding was an almost annual occurrence so the river's carp population was being built up steadily.

The major clean-up campaign of the 1960s helped purge the river and its tributaries of the raw trade and domestic effluent which had once entered it by the millions of gallons from the Black Country. This provided a habitat of reasonable purity and the total population of fish in the Trent showed a dramatic increase.

The head of carp was given a helping hand when a 'tagged fish' competition saw the release of a hundred or so carp at Trent Bridge in Nottingham. As few fish were caught by the close of the competition, interest in them waned and they lived on unmolested. One mile or so above Trent Bridge lies Wilford Power Station and the warm water released from its bowels helped the young carp survive the coming winter and provided a comfortable environment in which to grow the following summer. The hot summers of the mid 1970s saw these fish spawn and provided the bulk of the stock we are trying to catch today.

So you can see that whilst the carp might occur naturally in running water in its native Asia, in this country populations are man-made. They are stocked either directly in the case of tagged fish or indirectly in the case of the flooded gravel pits. Here on the Trent, the power stations

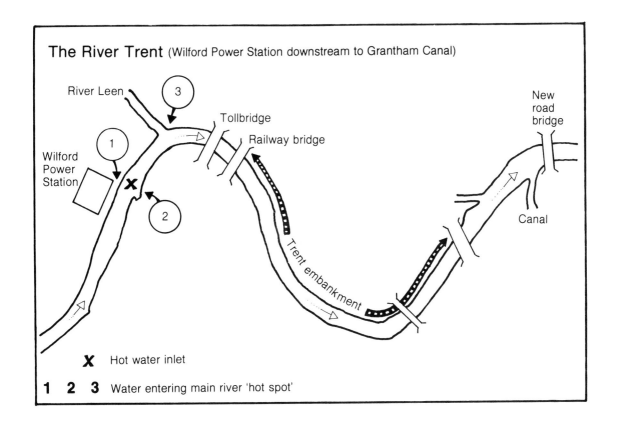

The River Trent (Wilford Power Station downstream to Grantham Canal)

River Leen

3

New road bridge

Tollbridge

Railway bridge

Wilford Power Station

1

X

2

Trent embankment

Canal

X Hot water inlet

1 2 3 Water entering main river 'hot spot'

The boiling water of the Trent weirs.

added that final catalyst in much the same way as they did on the Nene at Peterborough, the setting of the famous electricity cut. The warm water produced helped small fish overwinter and encouraged spawning of more mature fish in the summer months.

In Pursuit

The summer of 1976 saw Paul take two carp of 15oz and two of 2lb 7oz from different areas. This suggested to us that fish were all along the river's length and an evening session at Wilford saw a beautiful fish of 6lb 12oz fall to my rod. Paul went into the river and got soaked trousers whilst landing that fish, so despite having no camera to record the event we both remember the evening vividly! In the Ferry Inn only a short distance away, we celebrated. We knew now that we were starting to fish the right areas and this was highlighted dramatically when a carp of 31lb 12oz was landed from the same stretch during September that year.

The capture of these fish became an obsession to us. Thoughts became entangled as they rushed around my head. Many an evening in the Ferry Inn saw us trying to make coherent sense of all that we were learning. We started by doing what the majority tend to do and began to focus our attention on baits. So far, all of our fish had fallen to float fished maggots or casters, presented on light line and small hooks. The thirty-one pounder however, had taken cheese and fallen to stronger line and a larger hook size. If we fished in that way would we be able to catch several fish or would we have to sit it out for just the one fish? The problem, therefore, was not only of tackle but also of our patience. Fishing the stick float down the near side edge was what we were good at and it caught us fish, often lots of fish. Occasionally one of those fish would be larger than the others and as this situation suited us we stuck with it. The result? The remainder of that season did not see another carp landed by us. We had a lot of thinking to do if we were to succeed.

Metamorphosis 1977

During the closed season my metamorphosis began. The catalyst for all my ideas and those of my friends were old copies of *Angling* and *Coarse Fishermen*. During the 1970s these were the magazines to buy, bringing new ideas and new thoughts to an angling public that was eager to receive them. Furthermore, whilst doing this their contributors – Trevor West, Tony Miles, John Bailey, John Wilson and the rest – also gave the impression that they enjoyed their fishing. So here were a group of writers who caught larger than average fish on a regular basis and through their work tried to encourage the normal angler to do so too. Well, I read and reread all my copies and then I forced what I had read onto my friends.

We were now approaching the new season and 1977 looked like being a good year. The pioneeer spirit of being a specimen hunter instead of just a normal fisher-

man made us light-headed. Paul and I had always worn floppy hats, but now they took on a new meaning!

One thing that had puzzled us during the closed season was the number of carp that we were fishing for, both in given swims or in limited areas. We had noticed that when one carp was hooked, we always had the chance of another, even if the first one was lost. Yet, once you had had two carp from a swim, the area went quiet. Perhaps it is acceptable that the charging around of a hooked fish could scare the other carp from the area, but it also seemed reasonable to presume that the fish were swimming around in pairs. It was suggested that the fishing partner should cast into the productive swim whilst his friend was playing a fish. We never did. All this seemed a bit intense and whilst it might appear naïve, it was and indeed is the outlook that we hold to.

Water speed also began to puzzle us for, with the exception of the Wilford fish, all of our carp had so far come from the faster water – not at all the way you expect carp to behave. Again a change of attitude was required. I decided to fish the fast water below the giant sluice gates at Colwick, Nottingham, at the earliest opportunity.

Specimen Hunting Success

It was overcast on 18 June 1977. The river was up slightly and running quickly. Standing alone on the concrete banks, wondering if I had made the correct decision, I tackled up. The 1lb 7oz breaking strain line had been replaced by 4lb 4oz breaking strain. The size 18 hook had now become a size 10 Goldstrike. A Mitchell 300 and a Bruce & Walker float rod completed the new set-up. Bait was the new wonder 'drug', sweetcorn.

I cast in and scattered a few grains around the float. Half an hour passed without a fish. I increased the numbers of free offerings and the float slipped below the surface. A chub of 1lb 12oz came to the net. This, then, was my biggest chub from the river and the first of the new season. The day appeared to be getting brighter. Fish started to come steadily, first chub and then after a slight lull, the first carp. That morning, four were landed and two were lost, one of those taking me a long way downstream before shedding the hook.

The weighing of the fish took longer than normal and, when completed, showed that I had caught almost twenty-nine pounds of chub and carp. That too was the best weight of fish that I had taken, combined with the most carp that I had ever seen from the river!

I returned again and again. Time, in great quantities, was spent fishing in the shadow of the sluice gates. A tremendous number of fish were contacted, mainly chub, but enough carp were taken to keep my interest going. Even my wife got into the act, having taken a mirror carp of 5lb 5oz one evening in July.

The First Double

Come with me to Wilford, not to the outfall below the power station, this time we shall fish the faster water above. It is autumn and hopefully the carp will have dropped down from the very fast water below the weir some miles upstream. We shall fish an area of steady flow over a gravel bottom and long flowing weed. Fishing at night for those who dislike the dark is no problem, as the bridge crossing the river at this point is a major through-route and is illuminated by large street lamps.

Large carp swim in this fast current, but so far I have lost all the fish I have hooked. They all head across the current to the slower water found under the far bank. We did of course, fish the slower water to begin with, but nothing was caught there. The bottom is not nearly so clean there and I believe this discourages the fish from feeding. However, when talking about fish habits there will always be doubt.

I settle into the swim around 7.30 p.m. I move easily into my routine. Free bait samples are scattered around the swim and more are placed near the hook bait. With baits such as luncheon meat, which I am using tonight, this can be a little haphazard. A meat with a large fat content will be swept out of the swim before you have chance to cast, so I resort to the following method. If you look at the diagram you will see I take a standard baiting needle (as is used in pike fishing) and thread my chunks of meat along its length. I loosen all of the baits except the last one. This will keep the rest in place. I thread the eye of the needle through the swivel on the main line and cast out. Once the tackle is settled into position I strike all the baits off and repeat the process. When I am satisfied that enough bait has been deposited, I bait my hook and send it on its way to join the others on the bed of the river.

That done I settle down into my chair, rod in hand. Tonight is pleasant enough to sit without a coat, and action of some sort or another is expected. The sun slips silently below the horizon to provide an equally enthralling sunrise for fishermen of other lands. Herons appear in silhouette before the glow, on their way to shadowed feeding areas.

Here we go, chub number one is on its way to the waiting net. We have been

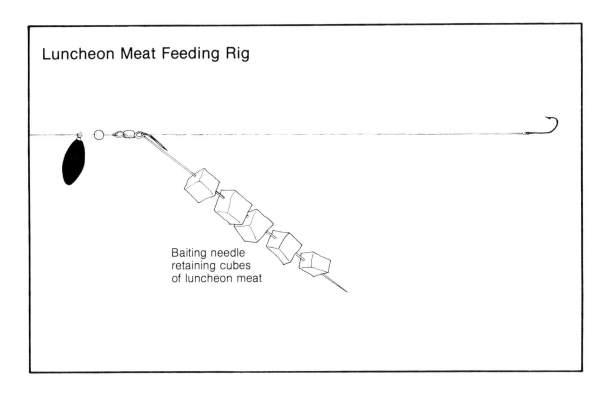

Luncheon Meat Feeding Rig

Baiting needle
retaining cubes
of luncheon meat

fishing for only five minutes and yet this appears to be the norm. Either I start to get bites within minutes of casting in or I sit there for just the occasional fish. Fishing as I do (moving into swims vacated by departing anglers) I come to expect a quick response. Fish will generally already be in the area mopping up loose feed, and other fish will come along after dark to join in this feeding habit.

Most of the bait thrown in during the day will have been of the maggot or caster variety. By the evening carp will have become wary of small baits, though it is at this point that the titbits arrive – my bait! The meat is something totally different and for tonight at least the fish have no cause to be suspicious of it. Nor are they, and an hour after dusk I slip the net under chub after chub.

This feverish bout of activity is replaced by an almost tangible stillness. Voles have ceased to rummage amongst the bank-side vegetation. Even the ducks have stopped their wanderings across the current. How long I sit there, motionless, I hardly know. It seems forever, alone in the half darkness, until the rod bucks in my hands.

Backwinding, I watch the line cut a 'V' across the current, almost to the opposite bank, then moving slightly downstream before slowing at last. Now it is my turn. Keeping a slight curve in the rod, I begin to bring the fish back towards me. I retrieve the line gently, leading the fish upstream and then coaxing it across the current to the water in front of me. The battle takes ten minutes. Then up she comes, the fish is safe, and I am shattered. This is my first double figure carp from the Trent! This lovely fish that represents so much effort now lies before me.

Steve with a sleek Trent double.

The Future

Looking into the future, I see boiled baits making a greater impact on the river. Frozen baits can be bought in tackle shops everywhere, making them available to everyone. This is a trend that I have no complaints about at all, especially as they have a positive effect on the carp's growth rate.

What does worry me, is that in some areas of the river the carp seem to be on the decline. This is brought about by any number of reasons, although it must be said the main one has to be the complete closure of power stations. Some of the remainder are running at reduced capacity and so the river is no longer as warm as it once was. This means that during extremely cold winters or prolonged periods of high flood water brought about by snowfalls, the fat reserves of the carp are being used up and some fish die. Their weakened bodies are unable to withstand the cold or the power of the current.

Yet every cloud has a silver lining and what carp are left have not only spawned but now appear to be bigger. Thirty-pound fish have been taken and if they have not been transferred to enclosed waters, they could very well grow on to be forty pounds in weight. Dick Walker once said that he thought the Trent capable of providing a forty-pound carp to someone. Let us hope that once again he proves to be right. Let us hope further that it is me who catches it – or you, should you decide to join the growing band who find it fascinating to fish for carp in rivers.

Postscript

ARCHIE BRADDOCK

Following Steve's early struggles to come to grips with Trent carp, it would perhaps be interesting to relate my very recent experiences with the fish, built upon years of knowledge of the River Trent and its tributaries. While being a long way from having all the answers, I have spent much time since 1973 fishing the network, including the Dove, the Derwent and the Soar. My total numbers of carp caught are quite impressive, with more doubles than I can remember but not yet a Trent twenty. Still, I have hooked and lost one or two, weighed and photographed them and know the full details of captures of many more, including fish of 28½lb and 31lb, so perhaps I can add a little to the lore of river carp fishing.

Unlike still waters, bait is not a major problem. Sweetcorn, breadflake or maggots have taken the vast majority of the carp that I know of, including nearly all the big fish. Nor are today's complicated rigs needed. Simply, a bait laid on the bottom or even trotted catch the carp.

Your biggest problem is location. Even Lake Cassein becomes a puddle when compared with the total volume of the Trent, and you must believe that these fish do use the river, cruising several miles in a season. The other big problem is nuisance fish, particularly chub.

This leaves two options. You can fish the margins and feed lightly with your chosen bait until a carp cruises by. This is what the majority of river carp catchers do. Sweetcorn is good for this as the chub are not quite as hot for it. Float, swingtip, Optonic – all styles will work – but it can be an awfully slow process if you pick your swim wrongly. I can see the experienced carp man's mind working already, bolt hair rig, the latest 'in' boilie, fishing down the margins with three Optonics and bingo you are in! But no, you will probably do better with one rod and a simple bait if you get the location right.

The second approach and the one I favour is one I have only been using the last two years, but which has brought me more carp than ever before. Briefly, I aim to attract all those chub, bream and anything else into the swims. I want to build up my swim with a heaving mass of fish, digging, rooting, feeding, stirring up the bottom and in general causing an unmissable disturbance in the fish's world. The always inquisitive carp, cruising idly by, has just got to investigate such goings on, which he does! This means you have won more than half the battle, you have attracted your fish.

This is where regularly changing baits can score heavily as you drastically increase the chance of giving the fish something it has never been hooked on. How do you fill your swim with such a mass of feeding fish? By feeding heavily, something the match men found out years ago. Notice how many big Trent carp are recorded as caught by such means. What I have done is to scale up the tackle and try and improve on the baits.

You will need a quivertip rod that will, on occasions, be called to cast a filled swimfeeder of four ounces or more. Yes, such rods do exist, it is a matter of sorting out which one suits you best. I make my own feeders from aluminium vacuum cleaner tubes. Commercial models tend to break up rapidly under the hammering that repeated casting gives them.

I fish a fixed paternoster rig with a one-foot feeder link and a hook link of about four feet, all joined at a swivel. I fill a feeder with a holding food. This can be a particle, like hemp, or tares, or anything to carpet the bottom to keep the fish in the swim. The open end of the feeder is plugged with a mixture of ground bait, bran and attractor. The bait can be a simple paste containing the same attractor.

To give an example, ground hemp is added to the ground bait mix and hemp essence flavour is added to the water used to dampen the ground bait. Finally, ground hemp and hemp flavour is mixed into a simple bread paste and you have cracked it! Your carp follows an appetising trail of hemp-smelling bread particles upstream until it finds an area heaving with feeding fish who are busily mopping up a bed of particles. Then it spies a lump of that special paste ...

As I said, a change of baits can often work wonders, while still feeding the flavour of the day. I have used exactly the above approach very successfully many times, but anybody can see that the scope is endless. Just one example, try using the new mini boilies as both holding food and bait – and your own choice of flavour, the bait, the filler and the ground bait? You will undoubtedly catch more and bigger chub and bream than before, but your chances of carp are also increased dramatically. Whichever way you look at it, river carp fishing can be fabulous.

My Thames Record Carp

JOHN CADD

The Medley is one of the most famous stretches of the River Thames. It runs through Port Meadow, a piece of common land on the outskirts of Oxford, and is the scene of many historic events that date back to the Domesday Book. For as long as I can remember, 100 foot aspen trees have stood as sentinels along the tow path, as if guarding the jewels of great fish that lie in their tranquil shade. I have fished the Medley all my life, but it was only in the late 1960s when the Thames night fishing ban was lifted that I realised the Medley's full fishing potential. Groups of us young budding specimen hunters would spend many summer nights there.

One of my favourite swims was known affectionately as the Sandy Banks because of its striking resemblance to a sandy beach. I have always fished from the tow path side of this spot and cast some twenty-five yards to where masses of underwater cabbages almost stretch to the surface. They were edged by tall bulrushes stretching fifty yards on the Port Meadow banks. All this made for a grand backdrop to a picturesque swim which was a secluded haven for most species.

The famed shoals of Medley's large Thames bream were what I used to specialise in those long ago days. I have caught many hundred pound plus catches from Sandy Banks, from deep down in the seven-foot swim. It was on one of these first night fishing sorties in the late 1960s that I realised there were some unseen monsters lurking in and around the cabbages. At least once in every four trips to the swim, one of our fishing group would be broken by a very large fish. One chap was even broken on 7lb BS line.

At last the night came when I actually hooked and landed one of the swim's big fish. This turned out to be a barbel of 8lb 12oz. 'That's it,' we thought. 'The tackle smashers must be barbel!' This theory was short-lived because two weeks later three of us were broken, each on 5lb line, on the same night. Furthermore, what appeared to be massive fish, far bigger than any barbel, would leap in the water in a farewell, far off in the darkness.

Season after season I would fish the same stretch of the Thames, haunting many swims, still coming back to Sandy Banks and still with the same results. Still I took massive bags of big Thames bream and still those slow, ponderous runs resulted in lost tackle. It called for a rethink on my part, a constant fishing assault was needed. I stayed nearly two weeks in the swim in the August of 1974, catching many bream, roach and chub, but I did not even hook or lose a big fish. It was as if the tackle smashers had taken two weeks off as well!

The first week of September came and the usual Friday night stint was planned. The evening was really mild, with the slight hint of a breeze. It had rained heavily in the week and the river was running slightly faster than normal. I had tackled up my ten-foot swim feeder rod, which even had the old-fashioned brass ferrules. My reel was a trusty old Mitchel 300 that I still have to this day, loaded with 4lb BS line. My end tackle consisted of an open-ended swim feeder, stopped eighteen inches from a No. 8 eyed Sundridge specimen hook. I mixed my breadcrumb ground bait for the feeder a little on the stiff side and my throwing ground bait heavier still because of the river's extra push. In those days I always started my fishing sessions by throwing in six large balls of ground bait before casting out with my ground bait feeder.

I commenced fishing at 6.30 p.m. using small pieces of breadflake on the hook. By 7.30 p.m. I had caught two nice roach of 1½lb each. Catching two roach like this was nearly always the prelude to catching many bream. This had been the pattern for me for many years and this night was to be no different. The first bream came at 9.30 p.m. at about four pounds. This fish was followed at approximately hourly intervals by six others roughly the same weight. Then a distant clock chimed 3 a.m. and as if by magic the bream stopped feeding.

For an hour I waited without so much as a tremble on the rod end. Cast followed cast, putting more swim feedered bait into the swim. Ten minutes later I hooked another fish, this time a very rare Thames tench of 3½lb. It was almost 4.30 a.m. now, still dark with just a glimmer of light on the horizon preluding the dawn, when I had a half-inch pull round on the rod tip. I struck firmly and the 'thing' was on. I had no idea what it was except that it was very, very big. Unlike the other big fish my friends and I had lost in that swim, this one

powered off downriver instead of making for the safety of the cabbages opposite. It took 100 yards of line in a single rush, getting perilously close to the backing. The monster ended up diagonally across the river, beaching itself on a mud bank.

It lay there for fifteen minutes until I took matters into my own hands. I waded downstream, getting a bootful in the process, until I was approximately at right angles to the fish. I just prayed and pulled as hard as I dared on 4lb BS line. Luckily for me, the 'thing' slithered off into deep water, moving away downstream again ending up near the Medley Sailing Club.

I then had the difficult task of working the fish almost 200 yards upstream to where I had left my landing net. In all, it must have taken forty minutes. I netted the fish first time as it rolled in the shallows, then drew it towards me. It was only then I realised just what I had caught. I staggered up the bank in the half-light with the huge leather still in my landing net. Laying it carefully down on the grass, I unhooked it, and then placed in in my other larger keepnet, not putting it with the other fish I had caught previously. I honestly knelt down and said a prayer when the fish was safely in the keepnet. I had caught plenty of big fish before but nothing like this. I did no more fishing that night.

Later on that morning the fish was weighed and then photographed in front of at least thirty people, many of them anglers who had given up their morning's fishing to witness the carp. It was weighed in a hessian sack on a brass Salter 40lb spring balance. When the sack weight was taken off this made the true weight of the fish 31lb. The great carp was released soon after the weighing ceremony none the worse for its ordeal. It swam strongly away, never, I believe, to be seen again.

Canals

It was pointed out in the first edition that many of the southern and central canals at least hold large heads of often big carp. We were told that matchmen found them first in many instances and that specialists sometimes moved in later – though this of course has not always been the case. J.B.'s own first beginnings in the carp world were themselves on a canal. In 1961 he heard the Peak Forest Canal held them. He fished Marple Locks, the bottom one by the sunken barge, with bread baits all summer holiday. He blanked. He began 1962 there and this time actually saw a fish. Thank God Roman relieved him and gave him a carp or we do not know if he would have stuck it out! Mind you, he was only just into double figures himself and hardly an expert!

Richard Bendall's piece is important for it does not simply show technique but also the optimism required and the mental approach to waters not always the most lovely.

Canal Fishing

RICHARD BENDALL

Introduction

To bolster my ideas on canal carp fishing I have drawn upon the experience of Mr Norman Jarvis of Fleet, Hampshire, who has fished the Basingstoke canal for most of his life. Norman is the 'old man' in the piece. I did not know his name at the time and hope he is not offended by the reference.

In general, canals have holding areas which attract carp. Some of these are large enough to fish as you would a lake. Others are small, and here the carp may have different habits to elsewhere. These are the type I am writing of here. I call them 'safe houses'; it is from these that the carp patrol the canal during feeding times. Fishing the 'safe houses' should produce fish; perhaps the larger carp monopolise food sources in these areas, and do not rove for food with their smaller brethren. What appeals to me, though, is lying in wait for the mobile carp.

Norman and I agree that some of the best places for surprising roving carp are around bridges, which often coincide with 'safe houses', such as barge turn-rounds or a widening of the canal. As these small holding areas can be isolated, with stretches of featureless canal running away from them, and the water is often very clear, the carp will not venture out until evening, returning early in the morning.

Norman has followed the early morning rovers back to their 'safe houses' and, as I have found, feels he can near enough set his watch by them, given that conditions are normal for that time of year. If it were not for time constraints I would have had a few more fish than those described in the piece below by identifying what time the fish were passing through.

I was lucky to hit on an evening when the temperature rose rapidly, altering the normal time of the carps' evening feeding jaunt. It might even be possible to prepare several swims along the route, moving on to them as time and catches dictate. Norman insists that bread and lobworms are as good a bait as any. I tend to use whatever is left over from fishing elsewhere.

The carp working these routes are often not used to being fished for outside of their 'safe houses', and will hoover up well nigh anything. Rigs too can be kept simple. Access to the bank opposite the tow-path which is generally quieter will enable you to place baits precisely in otherwise unfishable swims.

Light in the Dark

Imagine a canal, a footbridge, a road and a barge turn-round pool. The water is clear, the weed profuse and lush. Roaring traffic rumbles past for a large part of the day.

A shot of Richard's canal – a far cry from the secluded pools of legend.

Street lamps burn till the early hours. The pedestrian bridge is a meeting-place for the local youth. Occasionally the detritus of glue sniffing sessions can be found on the footpath beneath the foot-bridge. Illiterate graffiti on the bridge is crude. The hideous trauma of a daylight rape can hang heavy for those that know of its occurrence.

It's a million miles from the quiet country pools I tend to frequent, yet there are carp here, the same species that inhabits the estate lakes. It felt different though. Nevertheless, I was inevitably drawn by the chance of a carp, not by the same deep vibrations that touch the core of my being elsewhere but still tangible and undeniable.

Peering down from the foot-bridge I can see large clumps of weed and the occasional string of bubbles. I remain for a while, pondering the whereabouts and size of the fish. An old man who fishes for the carp whenever he cares informs my mother (whose garden runs down to the canal) of his progress. Recently he has taken an eight pounder from the spot I am looking into. Bread flake laid on hard is his preferred method.

'Why don't they use bread?' he asks of the younger carpers. 'They never seem to catch much on those boilies.' It is September and chilly. 'The carp will be holed up further along the canal in a deeper section' is the old man's word. Maybe, I think. I want a fish from the turn-round though, or better still from the garden.

Starting with liver paste in the turn-round, I find the curse of curses is present – a soft green weed that blankets the bottom

(Canadian pondweed I think). The bait just vanishes in it. The next morning I try a pop-up. Huge eruptions of bubbles near the bait has my hand straying to the rod anticipating a run, but no. The story is the same for the next two mornings. I have been trying evenings in the garden, also to no avail, yet all the bait is gone each morning. The carp are passing through too late for me. I'm here on a family holiday, so an all-night session is out. All is not lost. During the morning I see a common travelling at mid-water from under the pedestrian bridge. I am too slow to present a bait. They're here, though. From the bridge I see a small common push up through the weed to turn below the surface and plunge back down.

The family spends the day at The Hawk Conservancy. We spot Miss Marple from the TV. The Hawk Conservancy is thrilling, Miss Marple slightly less so. Arriving home as another shower is stopping, I can see the cloud cover thickening. The evening temperature rises. This is it. Chickpeas go by the edge of the weed raft less than a yard from the bank onto a clear patch of bottom. Liver paste is introduced some way to the left. The baits, on hook-out bolt rigs, are dropped in. Due to a blemish on the line and impending darkness, the hook length on the paste rod ends up at three inches long.

As I'm fishing close in, the water being some two to three feet deep, I sit well back on a piece of hessian to keep a low profile. The rods are laid on the ground with only an inch or so of the tips protruding over the water. Silver paper bobbins are set on a yard of loose line. The cars whizz by, their headlights flashing across my face. Up on the bridge the adolescents grope each other and boast loudly of conquests real or imagined, drinking and shoplifting. The

usual things? Soon it is as dark as it will get before the street lamps go out. The kids drift away. By quarter to nine the traffic has slowed. Things are beginning to feel more 'carpy'. I concentrate on the water. I must get a take. Rustles and squeaks as you would get anywhere emerge. The air is damp.

I pass the time imagining the bobbin being dragged towards the rod. I run through the strike, low and to the left to avoid overhanging branches, then push the rod out to get above the fish in the deeper water. There is no room for manoeuvre to the right. A quiet splash and a semi-circle of ripples move out from the bank next to the raft – carp over the chick-peas. Shaking with anticipation, the take is awaited.

Five minutes, half an hour – who can tell at times like these? Then a short rustle from the bobbin, a pause, a blur of silver and I'm in. The rod keels over, the carp races to the left, snagging the other rod. Crouching, I open the bail arm on the second rod. I've turned the fish and, as planned, the rod is above it in the deeper water. The fish goes crazy. Eventually it comes up though and, with some difficulty, is netted. The hook is removed and the prize carried to the patio. Pat comes out to photograph an 8lb-odd common.

Deciding to have another go, I set to sorting out the mess between the rods. First the successful rod. Holding the hook in one hand I pull some slack line in. I receive a sharp stab in the thumb. Muttering under my breath I irritably pull in more line. The line bomb must have slipped pulling the line tight.

Minutes later the rod is cleared and laid to one side. Now to the other. Several loops of line near the rod tip have interwoven to form a knot. As the last loop falls out there is a tug. I'm puzzled for a second,

Richard poses with his canal common.

then it clicks and I wind down to another fish. As the first carp had swum across this rod, another must have been in the process of taking. It comes across from the far banks reeds with only a few heavy thumps and, as so often happens with mirrors, lies sedately on the top for netting. Ten pounds and one ounce – a canal double. Watching a returned fish swim off is something I enjoy immensely. Then I sit back to relax and enjoy what is now a treasured memory.

The night and the stars are the same as anywhere, the feeling of well-being is just as intense as at Williambury or Horse pond. Here, though, a sick mind assaulted an innocent person, disaffected youth sought chemical release, an insane amount of traffic hurtles by and I found a few moments of intense happiness. What a paradox.

Then I had an odd thought. Somewhere I had read that in the Great War during lulls between bombardments, skylarks could be heard singing as they rose heavenwards. I feel a distant connection of sorts and silently vow to look for light even in the darkest of places. It may be a melodramatic sentiment, but it's something I'll try not to forget.

Epilogue: An Afternoon with Rod Hutchinson

Sharon and I left Rod Hutchinson's home at dusk and took the low-lying road towards Louth. During the day we had talked on every aspect of fishing – for neither Rod nor I are single-minded about carp – and Rod had told me of a good roach water close by. I could not resist a detour. We parked on a bridge over a small drain that ran straight towards the gathering dusk and watched. The breeze of the day had died, the rain was a light drizzle, the temperature was mild and, as I hoped, roach were on the move. I saw some wonderful fish – just as Rod had prophesied. Some were near two pounds – fifty plus pounds smaller than the fish he has been used to catching this year, but still appreciated and valued highly.

There was something like a breath of wind over my shoulder and no more than four yards away a barn owl ghosted up the drain. His creamy feathers glowed in the last of the daylight. Old saucer eyes watched me, coal-black, inquisitive, and then he was gone into the mist and dead sedge. As Rod knows, an angler sees magic all around – if he has the sense to recognise it.

The drive was a slow one. It was a bank holiday and we picked up the coastal traffic from Skegness. I had time and more

for thought, to relive the mood of the day. My mind went ever back to the evening before, in our tiny country local. The publican had been describing a farmer. He ended with a simple term: the farmer was 'a big man'. There is a lot in that short phrase: knowledge, respect, experience, dignity, a man to be listened to. Rod is a 'big man', perhaps *the* big man of carp fishing.

I had gone north to interview Rod on techniques. I did not do that in the end for, simply, I do not think they are of paramount importance to him any more. For that day, at least, it was the state of the carp fishing art that concerned him. In Rod's chequered career, he was once a scaffolder. Some jobs he turned down, because although the money was good the 'crack' was not. Another phrase this, which speaks volumes. The 'crack' is the quality of life around the job. It involves the workmates, the food, the beer, the nightlife, the whole spirit of the venture. It is the 'crack' that Rod looks for in his carping.

Cassein he adored for its big fish, but also for the French way of life: for the sun, the food, the wine and the entire experience. Cassein was for him more than a fishing expedition, it was a sensational

'Wallis Wizard in hand and reel on back
and yet another calm and lovely world
waiting to be enjoyed.'

holiday.

The one thing Rod is not is intense. He likes short varied sessions. He hates secrecy and backbiting. Fishing is a release, to be enjoyed. It is about catching a fish, not beating the man next to you. Fishing to Rod is that part of life where a man can keep a sense of proportion and where he should never lose it. Rod has never fished to be the 'Number One'. (I thought back to another genuine 'big man' of the carp world – Chris Yates. When a reel manufacturer described him as the country's leading carp angler, Chris wrote a letter to the press disclaiming the advertisement.)

This is part of Rod's 'bigness', because although I believe no other man has caught more huge carp than he, his life is still rich in other pleasures. For years he adored soccer and still plays. Weight-lifting keeps his fitness now and he has been known to enjoy a night in the Lincolnshire pubs! While he loves carp – his life does not need them like some destabilising drug.

This book is littered with the pictures of immense fish. Thirties, forties and fifties are more common than doubles and twenties, but this should not be seen as the norm in carp fishing. Remember in Steve Tytherley's chapter the excitement that two and three pound fish generated? This is how carp fishing should be. Any carp is a great carp and big fish are very often the easiest to catch after all.

Rod mentioned a trip to Cassein. It was phenomenally successful. He put the net under fifties, forties and thirties and drove home a happy man. He was even happier on the road north when he saw the gale that was blowing. He drove straight to a local lake where he knew fish would be stacked against an island. He had seven fish in an hour and a half. None was big by Cassein standards, but to him they represented the feat of the year!

Bigger is not better – never think that; and if you pitch things too high, however are you going to accept the inevitable failures? There are thousands of fresh doubles to catch. There are untold challenges to sample. There is a whole kaleidoscope of beautiful waters waiting, so get out there and enjoy them all!

These were the big man's last words to me. They will do for us all now.

Authors and Contributors

Martyn Page

In recent years it would be true to say that I am better known for my involvement with the P.A.C., as Treasurer and, for a time, Secretary. More recent projects have included my co-authorship of *Pike – The Predator becomes the Prey*, with John Bailey, and a move into the tackle trade itself, having lately acquired a retail shop at Wroxham, plus taking part in a tackle design and wholesale operation known as Marvic.

My angling career dates back many years and as such, always showing an interest in larger sized fish, I have caught numbers of twenty-pound plus pike, double figure barbel, seven-pound tench and so on. As you will have gathered from this book, my interest in carp has predominately centred on the excitement of catching fish on the surface and I have caught substantial numbers of carp in this way. In the summer of 1985 I broadened my horizons further with a visit to the States in pursuit of muskies, giant salmon and the many other exotic species that abound there. I foresee my angling pursuing this path, looking increasingly to the more unusual quests and the excitement generated by new challenges.

I have also become involved in the management of two fisheries, one of which is now producing twenty-pound plus carp. I have found that this aspect of my waterside pursuits is not only rewarding but most definitely educational, which in turn inevitably leads to more fish on the bank.

I have many thoughts, like John Bailey, on the future of angling, some of which are covered elsewhere. My main concern is that anglers, although beginning to, are not uniting fast enough to form bodies to protect our own and our children's future fishing.

John Bailey

I caught my first carp in 1962 at the Roman Lakes at Marple, Cheshire and followed that with fish from the Peak Forest Canal, Disley Dam and Capesthorne Hall. Since the late 1960s I have been carping in Norfolk, with just a three year university break after the species in the London area. For more than twenty years therefore, carp have been a part of my life and along with roach they have become my most cherished species. I will always carp fish. I see no end to their attraction and mystery and, for me at least, there are so many challenges left. A big river carp is a dream as are the Continental monsters. At the other end of the spectrum, I long for a double figure 'wildie' here at home on a split cane rod!

This is part of carp's beauty for me – big or small every single specimen has its attractions and desirability. A double is nice and a twenty is a fine beast, but any carp is a wonder whatever its size.

Richard Bendall

Richard's angling is often solitary – he only has one regular fishing companion. He is careful to limit his time on the banks as there is a dormant seed of obsession within him that he does not care to germinate. Richard limits himself to one weekday evening with half a weekend day during the summer and during the winter. His ambition is to have the chance to fish Redmire, and ultimately to do so without a bait on the hook.

Nico de Boer

Nico is thirty-nine and married with two children. Although virtually all our contributors are established authors of books or articles, Nico is perhaps our most prominent, having written ten books on angling himself and contributed to thirty-one others. In addition Nico is Managing Director of a publishing and printing company and Editor of the leading Dutch angling magazine *Sportvissers Journal*. Indeed he has been involved in writing on angling for some twenty-five years and in the publishing world for the last twenty.

Nico is as happy fishing for blue fin tuna as roach, and stresses that such variety maintains his enthusiasm. However, he is most at home fishing in Holland for his great love, carp, or with fly rod in hand after trout or sea trout.

Tom Boulton

Tom, a Norwich tackle dealer, is best known as a leading match man with Essex County. His record in local, national and international matches is an enviable one. Tom also produces a weekly radio show for Radio Norfolk in which he displays his wide knowledge of all areas of the sport and also a deeply caring attitude towards its conservation and future.

Archie Braddock

Archie, a well-known contributor to the angling press, has been fishing for thirty-five years. He was always a carp fanatic and made his name famous with the species early in his career.

As the River Trent improved in quality, he returned to it in the 1970s in pursuit of barbel and then carp. In particular, he has worked on the swim feeder method there which, he says, has improved his Trent carp catches fourfold.

Len Bunn

Len was one of the great names of the 1960s and 1970s when his exploits in Norfolk and at Redmire had a great effect on the carping scene. He rose to national fame over the marketing of the first super bait 'Black Magic' which proved highly successful on many waters. Len gave up angling a few years ago in favour of ornithology – a move we see very much as our loss.

John Cadd

John has a remarkable amount of big fish to his name, especially from his native river the Thames. Apart from his huge carp, he has taken tremendous roach, pike, carp and barbel from the river and its tributaries. However, it is wrong to see John simply as an obsessive big fish man. With his piece he sent this poem, his tribute to the Thames:

The Thames and I, we are at one
Large fish I seek when work is done
With baited hook a fish to catch
A record fish to better or match

The King of rivers do I fish
Or is this just my fond-held wish

It's a grand river, big and bold
True Old Father Thames is getting old
But not I think too old to know
It's got many more big fish to show.

Kevin Clifford

Kevin is thirty-nine, married with one young child and is self-employed. Although he is perhaps best known for his carp fishing exploits, particularly at Redmire Pool, he has always fished for other species. Kevin has an impressive list of big fish, all the more so because he lives in an area of the country which is not particularly renowned for producing specimens, and has never been involved in 'saturation tactics'. His largest fish include chub to 6lb 12oz, barbel to 9lb 5oz, numerous large rudd to 2lb 9oz, perch to 2lb 15oz, four tench over 9lb, the best at 9lb 10oz, several double figure bream to 12lb 1oz, 35 carp over 20lb, the best at 40lb 8oz, more than 100 roach over 2lb, the largest at 2lb 13oz, crucian carp to 2lb 14oz, grayling to 2lb 8oz, and pike to 30lb 8oz. He is particularly proud that he has caught carp and pike both over 30lb, an achievement which only a few anglers can claim.

Kevin has tried to put something back into the sport which has provided him with so much enjoyment. He has been a delegate member of his local Hull and District Angling Association for sixteen years, and is now the Vice President and Fisheries Officer. He is also a member, and ex-Secretary, of the East Yorkshire Fisheries Consultative Association of the Yorkshire Water Authority. He has always been an enthusiastic member of several specialist angling groups, including the National Association of Specialist Anglers, the British Carp Study Group and the Pike Anglers' Club. He is also a keen supporter of the Anglers' Co-operative Association and would like to see the day when membership is mandatory.

Kevin has never really set himself targets or ambitions to achieve, but rather he has taken advantage of opportunities as they have come along. He would, however, like to catch a few catfish, a large zander and eel, and a big lough pike. When he retires, he dreams of buying a well-equipped motorised caravan and travelling with his family, fishing here and there, as and when the fancy takes him.

Graham Cowderoy

Graham has carp fished for over twenty years – and indeed, living in Kent made it inevitable that as an angler he would move on to the species. His first double came from Brooklands Lake at Dartford and from there he moved to Horten Kirby, Sutton and Darenth. He soon teamed up with local anglers and enjoyed several productive seasons with numbers of fish in excess of twenty pounds.

As the pressure on the Kent carp scene mounted, Graham began his pilgrimage up the A12 to Norfolk, where he has been very successful. Despite the pressures of his A2 specialist flavour supplies business, he still makes trips to Homersfield Lake in Suffolk, where he achieved an old ambition of catching a common carp of over twenty pounds.

Graham finds it sad to see the growing numbers of youngsters coming into the sport as instant carp anglers. He feels that they would be better off with those few years of general fishing that serve as an angling apprenticeship. He says that it is important to learn the fundamental skills before moving on to the specialist species.

Chris Currie

Chris has been carp fishing since 1966. In that time he has broken innumerable local records and, up until the time of writing, holds the Hampshire record for the species. He was a long-serving member of the South Hants Specimen Group, being its leader from 1976 to 1984, when it was one of the largest and best known groups in the country.

He currently works as an archaeologist and is researching for an M.Phil./Ph.D. thesis on the history and archaeology of medieval fish culture. He is the author of a number of academic articles on the subject. As a leading member of the Save the Avon Campaign he is actively involved in conservation and the countryside and has dealt many a blow to those he considers the enemies of angling.

Chris feels that the angling press represents the sport in a very poor light and is very concerned for the fate of angling as we know it if this does not change. Although he feels the current carp scene to be both vital and lively, he prefers to fish alone. His fishing these days is restricted to waters that are not generally popular with other carp anglers, regardless of the size of the fish. Nevertheless, he is secretly hoping to stumble on a previously uncaught monster in a lonely unfished lake. His greatest ambition is to catch a twenty-pound wild carp, a fish that he knows from his historical researches is very possible.

Duncan Kay

Duncan has been fishing since the age of seven and was a rod builder even before that! He served a thorough angling apprenticeship catching roach, perch, tench and even sea fish on the way to his first double. This he believes is the correct progression for any youngster.

One of his earliest successes was a twenty-pound fish from the infamous Billing Aquadrome – the first fish out for four years. From there he moved to Cuttle Mill and on to Hemingford Waterways. This water was a fifty-mile round trip and by 1972 Duncan wanted a more local water. This led him to develop the Mid Northants Fishery on his doorstep.

Duncan has long been a member of the British Carp Study Group and is famous for his thriving bait business, but he remains an all-round angler whose interest is in anything that swims.

Rod Hutchinson

Rod is one of the most respected anglers of today, both in Britain and abroad, with a tremendous tally of big fish captures. He is a pioneer, establishing amongst other things particle bait fishing as a valuable side of carp angling. Still into bait, he now markets the highly successful Catchum brand of carp flavours and bases.

Rod is also one of the most genuine writers on the scene today and his excellent book *The Carp Strikes Back* is a modern classic. He is a man who loves his fishing and the whole environment and who will act passionately to preserve both.

Ritchie MacDonald

Ritchie, captor of an English 45½lb carp, is one of the most successful big fish anglers in the country and yet he is reticent about his fish and modest about his achievement. To look through his collection of colour slides, however, is a mind-blowing experience!

He longs to see the day when every angler behaves sensibly, with true sportsmanship towards each other and the carp themselves. He has been carp fishing for twenty-two years and values the steady learning that has led to his standing today.

Stuart Moir

Stuart, seventeen, has been fishing for six years. He soon moved into match fishing but found this held little interest for him and he began to look at big fish. He caught some good Norfolk tench and big roach from the River Wensum in his home city of Norwich before looking at carp. As far as any ambition goes, he says he has already achieved it. The Wensum record is his dream fulfilled.

Gerry Morris

Gerry's first loves were roach and barbel and he has had great success with both species before moving on to carp fishing. Now he is one of the very few men to take two Norfolk thirties. He is very concerned with the present public view of angling. He does not think we are yet seen as the caring environmentalists which in fact we are.

Kevin Nash

Kevin is one of the few anglers to have caught a forty-pound plus carp in England, an admirable achievement in itself. But this fish is backed by numbers of big carp and years of experience. Kevin, however, is best known for his fishing tackle business which caters for the specialist angler and in particular the carp fisher. Indeed, there can hardly be a carp man in the country who doesn't have at least one piece of 'Happy Hooker' equipment in his possession.

Berni Neave

Berni has been one of Norfolk's most respected specialist anglers for over fifteen years. He made his name early on for excellent tench catches but over the years has landed superb rudd, roach, chub and perch. An all-round carp angler, Berni has concentrated even more on crucian and is an acknowledged expert.

Alistair Nicholson

Alistair is a catholic angler, rather than a carp angler specifically. During 1985 he was attracted to carp fishing again having last fished for them in the 1960s in any concerted way. He has been drawn back to them only because of the chance to relive the sheer enchantment they gave in those long gone hedonistic days. The chance to fish for 'monsters' of the deep in new and uncharted territory both at home and abroad afforded no ambivalence as the 'bug' once more gained ascendancy. Long may it remain, for these are the early days of a new era where all the old enthusiasm is heightened and old age will hold fond memories of what has been.

John Nunn

John, a teacher, has lived the past ten years on the side of Ormesby Broad, Norfolk, where he runs a guest house for anglers. Certainly, no one is better suited to pass on advice, for John is truly an all-round angler, well known for barbel, roach, pike and tench. He is very much at one with the life of the Ormesby Group and nowhere is he more at peace than out on its waters.

Tim Paisley

Tim is one of the best known carp anglers of today and has played a leading part in the success of that flourishing group, the Carp Society. He is a catcher of big fish, but combines this with a real concern for their welfare. In this, he is a model for every young angler. Tim also appreciates deeply the beauty of English carp waters and is a sensitive carp fisher, not a compiler of big fish for their weight alone.

Phil Smith

After twenty years of fishing for specimen fish, Phil has reached a point where improving a personal best for different species becomes more and more difficult. Phil's personal bests include eels to 6lb 11oz, zander at 14lb, roach at 2lb 11oz and rudd at 3lb 6oz. In 1985 Phil had a very pleasing capture, a roach × rudd hybrid at 4lb. Phil's favourite pursuit, however, is for tench and bream and he has accounted for numerous 8lb plus tench, the best at 9lb 1oz along with twenty-two double figure bream from five different waters. Indeed, his greatest ambition for future seasons is to capture a 16lb plus bream to better his current best of 14lb 15oz.

Phil cannot seriously see himself fishing for carp for any prolonged period in England, having been spoilt by Lake Cassein with its reliable weather and truly enormous carp. Phil's main message for the 'up and coming' angler is the fact that big fish can be just as easy as their smaller brothers, by using a good method on the right water, with a little luck thrown in.

Chris Turnbull

Chris is an excellent angling artist and specialist fisherman. The list of his personal bests grows each year despite the limiting effects of his work commitments. Today, he is very concerned about the future of fishing and fisheries.

He is a member of the Anglers' Consultative Committee in Norfolk. He works tirelessly for the P.A.C., N.A.S.A. and has been a fount of ideas for the River Wensum Action Group, founded in 1986.

Steve Tytherley

Steve, thirty-four has been married for eleven years and has one daughter. He works for a Nottingham company of hardwood timber merchants as a salesman. He acknowledges the help and support given to him by other anglers and in particular Paul Walker. Steve has been a member of the N.A.S.A. Committee for quite a few years but stepped down during 1985 to concentrate on an Open University Degree course. Steve believes that all anglers should become involved in angling politics, even if they then give them up because they don't like them.

Having concentrated on carp these last few years he is now going back to the all-round approach, enjoyment being his prime consideration. He is an optimist about angling's future and believes that we will all start pulling together, setting aside those barriers that have been erected over the years. Whilst what he has written in this book is based on fishing the River Trent, he knows that the information given has resulted in fish being caught from other rivers with a reasonable carp population.

William Whiting

Bill is a much loved and respected carp man who combines a score of big fish with a true feeling and sensitivity towards the natural life of his waters. Always open, always ready to give advice to those who ask, Bill is the epitome of the generous angler and friend.

John Wilson

Having fished for most of his life, John has caught impressive numbers of big fish of most species in England, plus many more exotic specimens around the world. John is not only a well-known Norwich tackle dealer but also one of the country's leading angling writers and photographers. He enjoys catching carp most by more traditional means and foresees more and more anglers returning to aesthetically pleasing methods, such as floats for carp. Perhaps this in turn will lead to the search for bigger and bigger monsters becoming less intense, a sort of backlash on current attitudes.

Always an active conservationist, John owns and manages his own carp fishery, which has been developed to allow members to enjoy quality fishing in pleasing surroundings. The lake has been thoughtfully stocked with a good variety of different carp types. Currently he is working on a book covering fishery management and the creation of good fisheries which is scheduled for completion in about three years.

Fred Wilton

Fred's theories on bait blew the carp world apart so totally that it has still not settled down fully. Of course, as an innovator, Fred took a lot of criticism in the early days of his discoveries but he remains the most genuine of anglers, totally open with words of advice. His gravest concern today is for the future of the species he loves so much.

Chris Yates

As captor of the biggest carp in England, Chris will always have a place in the record books. More than that, he will always have a very special place in the affections of those lucky enough to know him. He has a sensitive outlook to the sport in which natural beauty, companionship and the method of the capture are as important as the fish themselves.

A photographer, and author of the splendid book *Casting at the Sun*, Chris is now turning his attention more to rivers, and to barbel.